D0746994

DAVID WOOD
FOOD·BOOK

DAVID WOOD with Karen Barnaby,
Daphna Rabinovitch, Darlene MacDavid,
and Krystyna Schmidt

WHITECAP BOOKS LTD.
Vancouver & Toronto

ON THE COVER   David Wood in his store on Yonge St. in Toronto

Copyright © 1988   David Wood

First published 1988 by Whitecap Books (Toronto) Ltd.
Second printing, August 1989
77 Mowat Avenue, Suite 403, Toronto M6K 3E3

All rights reserved. No part of this publication may be reproduced,
stored in a retrieval system, or transmitted in any form
or by any means, electronic, mechanical, photocopying, recording
or otherwise, without prior written permission from the publisher.

Production Management by Paula Chabanais & Associates
Designed for Paula Chabanais & Associates by Jean Lightfoot Peters
Cover Photography by Peter Paterson
Edited by Beverley Beetham Endersby
Printed and bound in Canada by D.W.Friesen & Sons Ltd.,
Altona, Manitoba

ISBN 0-921396-04-X

Canadian Cataloguing in Publication Data

Wood, David, 1944 May 7-
  The David Wood food book

Includes index.
ISBN 0-921396-04-X

1. Cookery.   2. Food.   I. Title.

TX715.W66 1988   641.5   C88-094180-4

CONTENTS

INTRODUCTION

We share something of ourselves in the food that we serve to our families and friends. Sharing, and the spirit of generosity that infuses it, can take many forms; it just happens that food is the one with which I feel most comfortable – it comes naturally to me, but that doesn't mean it comes easily. Putting yourself on the line, which is a part of any kind of sharing, is never particularly easy; but, with practice, I have become more accomplished with my form of it, and in that way it has become a little less daunting.

This book is about what good food means to me and to the people with whom I work at the David Wood Food Shop. And, since food cannot be judged to be good or bad in a vacuum but, rather, must be measured in context – of the people who are eating it, the pleasure that it brings them, the place in which it is being served, or the season or occasion or the thousand other lesser variables that apply – in this book we want to share with you what we have learned about bringing all the facets of good food into harmony. If this book can make the experience less daunting and more pleasurable for you, we will have accomplished all that we hoped for.

Good Food

I have always tried to resist the tendency to classify our shop as a "fine" or, worse, "gourmet" food shop. I don't think there is any difference between fine, gourmet, and plain good food. Good food is identifiable by what it lacks more than by what it has: it lacks preservatives, artificial flavourings, and chemicals; it has natural flavour, freshness, and honesty, and its only additives are the loving care and respect with which it has been prepared. There is certainly nothing élitist or intimidating about those qualities.

Style

Many people think that what is really meant by good food is the flair or style with which it is prepared and cooked and, in North America, that seems to say "French". Actually "style" is a matter of personal taste and has nothing to do with whether food is "good" or not. There are still people who are convinced that food prepared in the French "style" is by definition good, but a French dinner comprising an inappropriate menu and inferior ingredients poorly prepared can be as bad as a similar disaster in any "style".

There are very few cooking styles that I do not like. In any other part of life, such catholic taste would be impossible to tolerate. However, one of the great characteristics of food is that it does not require you to practise favouritism –

you can change your loyalties each time you change your menu. I have always thought that one of food's most conspicuous pleasures is that it gives you at least one chance each day to mirror your mood, your company, and your surroundings. And every day it offers you the opportunity to erase any previous mistakes and start afresh with a clean slate.

At the shop we have four principles that guide our cooking and that, taken together, define our individual style. First, we try to choose a menu that is appropriate to the mood and setting of the event. Second, we select the best-quality ingredients we can find, then cook them in a way that preserves as much as possible their individual character. Finally, we present the food naturally, with an eye to colour and texture. Through these four stages, we try to take pleasure in what we do without falling victim to the seriousness that sometimes surrounds food and its presentation and usually ignores its purpose – joyous consumption.

APPROPRIATENESS

Food should reflect the mood of the occasion at which it is to be served. You would no more think of serving Lobster Thermidor in Puff Pastry at a five-year-old's birthday party than you would hot dogs at a formal dinner party.

The first thing to think about when planning your menu is the setting. Although you might think there isn't much to consider when you are serving in the same dining room you have been using for the last twenty years, you could think of that room as a new setting each time you use it insofar as each meal you serve in it is unique and special. Even the most familiar venue will have a new "feel" each time you use it. As for the unfamiliar – the dinner on the terrace, on the deck at the cottage, or, best of all, on holiday in some foreign and exotic place – those settings, too, should influence your choice of what to serve. Each place affects each of us differently and so you can never be criticized for having made a mistake. Accept the challenge of translating the feeling of each setting you use into a harmonious interaction of taste, texture, and colour. It is just that harmony that salutes you as a giver of great dinner parties.

The nature of the party will also influence your choice of foods, as will the people you have chosen to invite. We have learned not to serve chicken wings at business cocktail parties as executives do not consider sticky fingers suited to corporate image. The longer I live the more I am convinced that finding your path in life is a process of elimination; choosing a menu is no different. If you find that you have no ideas, start with something, anything, no matter how unlikely it seems. Then ask yourself why it is not right. Would scrambled eggs be a good choice for an intimate dinner? Yes, in some ways: they convey comfort, a feeling you will wish to evoke, but they are also perhaps too intimate, suggesting, as they do, breakfast. Also, they may perhaps be a bit too informal. Now, by listing the negatives and the pluses, you have determined that you want something comfortable and friendly; fairly intimate, but not too informal; and impressive rather than humdrum. What about seafood (faintly suggestive, and therefore intimate) in a creamy sauce (comfortable), perhaps in puff pastry (impressive)? By the process of elimination you will be able to come up with the perfect choice.

INGREDIENTS

It is a truism that what you get out is only as good as what you put in, so, at the shop, we try to start with the best ingredients. "The best" does not mean, as some people seem to think, using the best cut for every dish. Using filet of beef in a Boeuf Bourgignon is not only a waste of money, but is also the sure route to an inferior-tasting stew with an inappropriate texture. "The best" means the best quality that is right for the dish.

The less an ingredient will be transformed during cooking, the more important it becomes that it is the best quality. If you are preparing a plain boiled egg for your breakfast, it should be fresh and, preferably, from a free-range hen; however, if you are adding an egg to a number of other ingredients, it becomes a means rather than an end – an egg from a battery chicken will thicken a sauce or lighten a batter as well as any other. Similarly, the success of a simple grilled fish rests entirely on its being fresh and perfect to begin with. The success of fish served with a green peppercorn and cream sauce will depend on its having a perfect texture, and that is a matter of proper cooking.

COOKING

Our aim is to bring out the natural flavour of first-rate ingredients. You will find the book peppered with pleas to abstain from overcooking. If a sauce accompanies the main ingredient, it will usually be formed of a reduction of the juices of that ingredient or will be a commingling of herbs, spices, and vegetables that have a natural affinity with the main item. And, the sauce should sit under what it is to enhance and not smother it.

We try to maintain the original qualities of what it is we are cooking. For tender cuts of meat, fish, and chicken, that means cooking it as lightly and as simply as possible. For vegetables, it means undercooking – not to the extent that they taste like raw vegetables with a nodding acquaintance with heat, but to retain their unique texture, colour, and shape.

On the whole, our cooking methods are not revolutionary, but rather careful, simple, and natural. Flavour is important, but it too must be natural. For that reason we avoid prepared bases and mixes, preferring to start from scratch to ensure that only the best goes in to produce the best.

PRESENTATION

We like to respect the natural, as well, in our presentation of food, adding a judicious hint of drama. We try to make best use of the natural colours and textures of the food to create complements and contrasts with impact on the eye as well as the palate. Garnishes should offset but not substitute for the impression the food itself makes. For this reason we have resisted the prevalent temptation to use flowers on dinner plates or gratuitous exotic fruits or unrelated herb bouquets. Food presentation is an art. If you were born with the talent you will have no trouble; the rest of us simply need practice.

❦

HOW IT ALL GOT STARTED

My upbringing was gastronomically unexceptional. We lived in the west of Scotland, where the goodness of food was a measure of the quantity of sugar in it. There were periodic low points in my culinary education, which coincided with being sent away to boarding school in England, and it was not until my mother moved to a London flat a stone's throw from Harrod's Food Hall that our food appreciation hit its stride. In terms of food merchandising, no one puts it together better than the Big H.

I often get asked when it was I decided I wanted to open a food shop. The truth is that it never crossed my mind until that old process of elimination I talked about earlier was applied to career choice.

My first job was in Mexico. I was living alone and soon tired of eating alone in restaurants. That led me to learn to cook, a not altogether peaceful pursuit, but one that gradually became more a matter of enjoyment than of tantrums. Later, I became a photographer's assistant in London, and made it my business to scout out the best and most interesting restaurants on location shoots in France, Italy, and Spain. That broadened my interest in food.

My first job in Canada was with Pollution Probe. After a couple of very enjoyable years there, a friend and I decided to put our money where our mouths were and we started up a business to sell solar-energy systems, specifically, heating for swimming pools. Deals, agreements, and multinational shareholders spiralled at a dizzying rate and I went home nights successful and frustrated and mystified. Soon it was time for me to leave and go on to something I understood and could succeed at on my own terms.

Opening a food shop is where the process of elimination came in. There are not many food operations you can start up with limited capital – a restaurant or café, a fast-food franchise, or a small grocery store, none of which appealed to me. In the early 1980s there were only a handful of specialty food stores in Toronto, but the business was growing in the United States. It seemed a fair bet that the demand for take-out prepared food would increase at a comparable rate in Canada.

I took the business plan I developed to a few friends, including two who had asked me to cook for the audiences of a series of films they were showing, one night a week for six weeks. That gave me a chance to show what I could do, and for people who might have an interest in the venture. The opportunity paid off and I was able to interest people in buying shares, people who responded to my idea on a personal level and were as convinced as I was that the venture could only be a success. I was in business.

Hard work did not terrify me then, but I have a new respect for it now. I imagine that starting up any small business is a matter of gruelling hours, hard labour, and roiling anxiety. I spent most of my time running around the kitchen like the proverbial headless chicken with the equanimity of a tormented bear. To their eternal credit, none of the people who worked with me was discourteous enough to question my choice of career. When I finally did hang up my chef's whites for a year and a half, it was my idea. By then even I could see that I had someone better qualified than I to be a chef and, frankly, I was never more relieved in my life.

Despite all the trials and tribulations of our first four years, we are still here, working a bit less and enjoying it more. Many people in the food business have a love-hate relationship with it – we hate and complain about the hours, the scale of operation that turns food into "product", the public-performance aspect of the business, and the constant vigilance required to keep up the standards, but at the same time, these are the things that we love. Even the complaining is ambivalent, since we know it would be louder and more serious if we were in any other kind of business. There are few opportunities in business to garner such appreciation from your clients or to be creative on a daily basis. In this less-than-perfect world – even though I would usually much rather be a customer of mine than a shareholder – food is a pretty good way to make a living.

THE CAST OF CHARACTERS

A friend recently told me about a cartoon that appeared in a magazine a few years ago. In it, a beaver and a deer are standing at the edge of the forest, looking out at the Hoover Dam towering above them. "No," the beaver is saying to the deer, "actually I didn't build it, but it's based on an idea of mine."

I would feel much the same way about this book except for the fact that the idea for it came from someone else – Nick Rundall, of Whitecap Books. As far as the actual work is concerned, the beaver and I are in the same boat. Much as I would like to say that I did it all, without any help, fear of justifiable reprisals compels me to say that others helped out here and there. Without that help, there would not be quite so many recipes in this book, and most of them would have cream sauces.

I am equally compelled for many reasons to point out that the lion's share of the work, on the book as well as in the stores, has been and continues to be done by others. If you have ever had occasion to work with talented people, you will understand what I mean when I say that it can be very hard on the ego – and mine is fragile at the best of times. All seemed to go smoothly when my co-workers were less talented than I, but that situation did not last long, which is why the business *did* last. Now, I find myself forever having to give credit to others – and it doesn't come naturally.

Just for the record, the people who wrote this book are: Krystyna Schmidt, the catering manager and my strong support from even before the early days, when the store was a twinkle in our eyes (it has since relocated to the wrinkles around them); Karen Barnaby, our chef, who has an extraordinary feeling for food and the extraordinary good sense to say that it coincides with mine; Daphna Rabinovitch, our pastry chef, who can produce a tart that will transport you right back to Europe; and Darlene MacDavid, our catering chef, who is something of an ally in the cream-sauce protection society.

There are lots of other people at the shop (our accountant would say too many others) and I won't mention them here, having dispensed enough credit here already, but if you want to find out who they are, drop into the shop any day – they'll be the ones doing the work.

Apart from these few relatively insignificant contributions, I did it all myself.

MENUS

SIT-DOWN DINNER

Sit-down dinners are nerve-wracking affairs, even when they go smoothly. We can offer no advice about what you can do to help your nerves – drink doesn't seem to be the answer – but there is one thing you can do, which the Boy Scouts do all the time to make things go smoothly: Be Prepared.

Putting on a dinner party is a major undertaking – a day watching our catering department's preparations for such an event will be persuasive if you are not already convinced of the truth of that statement. Of course, you can hire a caterer (more on this later), which means that someone else will do the work and leave you with even more time for worry. But, sometimes it's better to have something to do to fill the worrying time.

Being prepared means a number of things: first, it means sitting down with your appointment book and finding a day for the dinner party that gives you enough time to devote to it – few things are worse than trying to juggle competing pressures. Second, it means making a guest list and issuing the invitations – we will leave that stage up to you.

Now the menu: There are a few things to bear in mind when choosing what you are going to serve. The food should set the style for the evening – formal food will create a formal occasion, but there are a number of food-style options: impressive (as in "Wow! How did you get the apple to stay in its mouth?"); elegant but understated (when it's elegant and overstated it becomes impressive), when you don't want the food to outshine either the wine or the conversation; friendly, when most of all you want to make people feel comfortable and at home at your table. Some styles, such as casual and fun, are better-suited to a different format, for example, a buffet; others are better left alone altogether (those such as favourite boarding-school recipes, and the like).

Do not be put off by the thought of having to decide the style of a dish; if it doesn't strike you as being, say, particularly formal or trendy, the chances are your guests won't think so either (most people's friends have quite similar tastes). If you are worried about guests you don't know very well (the dreaded boss and spouse), follow the Japanese custom and err on the side of caution (the boss would lose face if you were to serve something more impressive or expensive than would normally be served at his or her home). In this country such caution does not necessarily mean serving something inexpensive; simple elegance is always a safe choice.

It is important to balance the menu, but the most important element in that balance is not culinary style but ease of last-minute execution. (If you have a *deus ex cuchina* you may skip this section.) It is possible to include one course that requires some last-minute fiddling and still enjoy the party, but if you try to include more than one, your guests will be as likely to tip you as they leave, as thank you. Spending a lot of time in the kitchen is not a lot of fun for you; but, remember, it's no fun for your guests either. Your dinner party will be far more successful if you spend less time with the food and more time with your guests.

Once you have got the menu organized the next hurdle is buying everything you will need for the occasion. As far as I am concerned, this stage is the worst part of the whole affair, and was a major motivating factor in my opening up my own shop. Our suppliers deliver; yours almost certainly won't. You will have to trail around the city, tracking down ingredients. I never do it, but it is smart to telephone around first if you are looking for something unusual – or even if you are not: the most mundane ingredients have a tendency to become rare the moment they appear on your shopping list.

It is hard to overdo advance preparation; anything that can be done ahead should be. Most of our recipes are marked to show you how much early preparation you can safely do. Do it all, even the day before, if possible. Get all the ingredients ready for any dishes that require last-minute cooking. Even if you can't cook them ahead, at least you can prepare the ingredients – wash lettuce, cut vegetables, trim and tie meat, separate eggs. You absolutely cannot be too organized. It's a good idea to prepare a timetable for yourself, showing when you plan to seat your guests at the table, and how long before that you should do the various things that need to be done: turn on the oven, put the main course in, take it out to set in a warm place before it is carved, put the vegetables in and take them out, warm the plates and the bread, and attend to all the other details that are easy to forget during last-minute preparation.

When To Pour the Wine

Pour the wine before you serve the food. Before each course make sure that all the guests have their glasses topped up, or pour a new wine if you are serving more than one. Then go ahead and serve the next course.

FIRST COURSES

COLD

Veal carpaccio, p. 35
Bocconcini with red and yellow tomatoes, p. 40
Prosciutto and melon
Smoked salmon mousse with watercress mayonnaise, p. 39
Shrimps, scallops, and squid in a creamy tarragon dressing, pp. 34-35
Smoked salmon
Mussels on the half-shell with coriander and tomato sauce, p. 33

WARM

Warm beef tenderloin with crisp-fried onions
and shaved Parmesan, p. 111
Goat cheese baked in parchment on a zucchini lattice, p. 42
Shrimp wrapped in Chinese cabbage with beurre blanc, p. 43

PASTA

Black fettucine with shrimps and a lemon champagne sauce, p. 48
Buckwheat linguini with a putanesca sauce, pp. 50-51
Tagliatelli with fresh salmon, crème fraîche, and chives, p. 54
Fettucine with asparagus, prosciutto, Gorgonzola, and cream, p. 49
Tortellini with cream and spicy sausage, p. 52

SOUPS

Lobster and black bean soup with coriander pesto, pp. 20-21
Shallot and wild mushroom soup, pp. 18-19
Tomato and fennel soup, p. 19
Beet consommé, p. 22
Potato, leek, and Stilton soup, p. 21
Gazpacho, p. 23

SALADS

Arugula salad with warm Gorgonzola and walnut toasts, p. 39
Warm goat cheese salad with olive toasts, p. 41
Spinach salad with sweet and sour onions and
Camembert fritters, p. 38
Watercress salad with chicken livers, bacon, and
honey mustard dressing, p. 44

MAIN COURSES

FISH AND SEAFOOD

Salmon in parchment, p. 77
Fresh salmon with hot tartare sauce, p. 78
Seared salmon in dolce-forte sauce, p. 75
Oven-poached salmon with beurre blanc, p. 79
Sea bass with mussels, p. 84
Fresh tuna with eggplant caviar, p. 81
Halibut with muscat grapes in mustard, p. 75

Meat and Poultry

Lamb loin with figs baked in port, p. 118
Leg of lamb stuffed with provolone, spinach, and
sundried tomatoes, pp. 118-19
Lamb tenderloins and spinach in puff pastry, p. 114
Rack of lamb with tzatziki and garlic chives, p. 115
Veal with wild mushrooms in puff pastry, pp. 120-21
Veal tenderloin with tarragon cream sauce, p. 122
Loin of veal with mustard and sage, p. 123
Beef Wellington, pp. 110
Cashew-breaded pork on mustard sherry greens, pp. 130-31
Pesto-stuffed chicken breasts, pp. 90-91
Chicken in phyllo with orange-ginger sauce, pp. 92-93
Chicken with porcini mushrooms, p. 91
Duck with radish cakes and beet and apple purée, pp. 103-04
Duck with ginger and black bean sauce, pp. 102-03

Vegetables

Belgian endive braised with prosciutto and cream, p. 144
Sweet potato and Gorgonzola purée, p. 146
Baked red onions with balsamic vinegar and sage, p. 145
Broccoli with garlic, anchovies, and hot peppers, p. 145

DESSERT

Apple crêpes with cider beurre blanc, pp. 151-52
Apple feuillettées with caramel sauce, pp. 152-53
Apricot and cognac parfait, p. 186
Fresh strawberries with champagne sabayon, p. 160
Chocolate marquise, p. 194
Pears in pastry with caramel sauce, pp. 162-63
Pears with mascarpone, p. 159
Rum amaretti parfait, p. 187
Chocolate mousse, p. 166
Summer pudding, pp. 160-61
Tiramisu, p. 163
Frozen lemon tangerine soufflé, p. 201
Chocolate and burnt almond ice cream, p. 180
Espresso chocolate rum truffle ice cream, p. 181

Fig ice cream, p. 183
Strawberry rhubarb tart, p. 174
Brandy and ginger peach tart, p. 171

ELEGANT DINNER
(VERGING ON THE IMPRESSIVE)

Gougère puffs with Stilton and prosciutto, p. 29
Marinated shrimp with fennel, p. 28

Smoked salmon mousse with watercress mayonnaise, p. 39

Beet consommé, p. 22

Lamb loin with figs baked in port, p. 118
French green beans with fresh thyme
Minted baby carrots

Arugula salad with warm Gorgonzola and
walnut toasts, p. 39

Frozen lemon tangerine soufflé, p. 201

FORMAL BUFFET DINNER

Formal buffets are for big occasions: engagement parties, anniversaries, graduations, winning Lotto 6/49.... They are a lot to undertake on your own (this may be the time to hire a caterer), but they can be done, particularly if the party is not too big: 30 is getting close to the limit of what I would undertake on my own, 50 to 60, if you have people to help. Beyond that number you are in catering country.

A few words about working with a caterer: The most important consideration in hiring a caterer is whether you feel you can work with him or her. The caterer's job is to translate your idea of a good party into a reality. To bring that about you have to be able to establish a rapport with your caterer, so that you can make clear just what your idea of a good party is. From talking to you and seeing where you plan to hold the party, a good caterer will be able to pick up your style and, with your help, deliver a party in that style, just as if you had done it all yourself. A caterer is doing a good job if he or she makes you look like a great host. If you don't have a good feeling about the person, go somewhere else. A party where you and the caterer are at odds is doomed from the start.

A large formal buffet is expensive to put on, when you consider all the different elements involved. Consider rentals: they are a convenient solution, if not an absolutely essential one, since few people have enough dishes, cutlery, and glasses for 30 guests. When you rent, you don't have to wash up, and nowadays attractive items are available, as is a wide choice of coloured tablecloths and napkins. But, this service is expensive – if there is one item on the total bill for your formal buffet that will give you heart failure, it will be the rentals. Then there is the liquor, which certainly isn't cheap…and the flowers, which can be pricey…and then, the question of whether you will need staff…

For a small party you may be quite happy to do without waiters; for a larger party you probably cannot avoid hiring some. If you are using professional staff, please make sure that you hire a sufficient number to do the job properly and look after your guests as well as you would yourself. Better to buy a less expensive wine or choose a simpler menu than to skimp on staff. Too few and you will kick yourself afterwards, but probably not until after you have kicked your caterer.

For a formal buffet dinner, seating is important. It will not be enough to provide a sufficiency of tables and chairs; you should also give some thought to how you are going to let people know where they are to sit. Obviously, one way is to number the tables and post a seating plan, but this method is really only appropriate for large, very formal events. For smaller parties (but large enough that you shouldn't trust the seating arrangements to memory), make up a master seating plan, listing the guests' names alphabetically with the table numbers beside them. Enlist the help of a few friends (or waiters) and when each guest comes in, find his or her name on the list and have a friend or waiter show the guest to the designated seat.

There is another method for arranging seating that we have seen work well. Have two hats with place numbers (i.e., table number and seat number) in them, one with all the even-numbered seats and the other with all the odd; have the women choose from one hat and the men from the other. You get a random seating arrangement with tremendous potential.

Now, to the food for a large buffet dinner: Our advice is to serve a first course only if you have enough tables and chairs to seat everyone comfortably; if your guests are going to be perching on whatever they can find (cushions, stairs, etc.), a first course will make things unnecessarily complicated. (In this case, it might be a good idea to serve a more substantial hors-d'oeuvre, so that the guests don't feel short-changed.)

If you are serving a first course, it generally works best to have it set out on the tables before the guests come in – and this means choosing something cold. The guests will only have to make two trips to the buffet table – for the main course and for dessert – which is quite enough lining-up for most people. In this case, the wine should be poured *after* the guests have been seated.

For a small party (30 or so) you can choose to serve just one main-course dish. For a larger crowd you should have two or even three – partly to take care of unknown likes and dislikes, and partly to give some grandeur to your buffet offering. But bear in mind that when you provide more than one main dish, most people will take some of each thing offered – less than full serving of each, but more than half a serving – and if you have planned your quantities on the basis of one full serving per person you will experience a peculiarly nasty sinking feeling as you watch the number of servings decline at a faster rate than the number of unfed guests. Count on at least one and a half servings per guest if you have more than one main dish. (A caterer would station a waiter to serve the main dishes – and anything else where quantities might be a problem.)

For reasons that I do not quite understand, it does not seem to be particularly important that the main dishes you choose go well together, just so long as they do not disagree violently. It is more important that they offer different tastes and textures. If one of your choices is a hot casserole, say, chicken in a cream and lemon sauce, the other should be cold and without a sauce, perhaps poached salmon or filet of beef.

If you have a hot entrée, it's a good idea to have two or three salads, particularly if you don't have a hot vegetable. Bear in mind two things when choosing: the colours, shapes, and textures should vary as much as possible and the dressings should be different (if one is a vinaigrette – which seems inevitable – one other should have a creamy dressing and the third, straight olive oil or something using a different vinegar, such as balsamic).

If you are inviting more than 50 people you should think seriously about two buffet set-ups; for more than 70 it's essential.

HORS-D'OEUVRE
(KEEP IT LIGHT IF YOU'RE SERVING A FIRST COURSE;
OTHERWISE, GO TO TOWN)

Crab dip with blue corn chips, p. 28
Guacamole and salsa with corn chips, p. 26
Karen's pâté, pp. 40-41
Smoked salmon mousse, p. 30
Beef or chicken satay, p. 26
Escargots with Roquefort in puff pastry, p. 31
Bacon-wrapped filet with Bearnaise mayonnaise, p. 27
Marinated shrimp with fennel, p. 28
Gougère puffs with Stilton and prosciutto, p. 29
Hearts of palm with prosciutto, p. 27

FIRST COURSE
(ON THE TABLES)

Smoked salmon mousse with watercress mayonnaise, p. 39
Smoked salmon
Veal (or beef) carpaccio, p. 35
Bocconcini with red and yellow tomatoes, p. 40
Prosciutto and melon
Shrimps, scallops, and squid in a creamy
tarragon dressing, pp. 34-35
Seafood salad, p. 86
Gazpacho, p. 23

COLD MAIN DISHES

Cold poached salmon with dill mayonnaise, p. 79
Vitello tonnato, p. 119
Cold breast of chicken with red pepper salsa, p. 97
Oriental chicken salad, pp. 100-01
Thai beef salad, p. 112
Singapore shrimp noodle salad, p. 57

HOT MAIN DISHES

Salmon en croute, pp. 80-81
Salmon coulibiac, pp. 82-83
Warm beef tenderloin with crisp-fried onions and
shaved Parmesan, p. 111
Beef Wellington, p. 110
Veal with wild mushrooms in puff pastry, pp. 120-21
Lamb tenderloins with spinach in puff pastry, pp. 114-15
Chicken in phyllo with orange-ginger sauce, pp. 92-93
Casserole of chicken with lemon and tarragon, p. 101

HOT VEGETABLES AND COLD SALADS

Scalloped potatoes, p. 147
Sweet potato and Gorgonzola purée, p. 146
Belgian endive braised with prosciutto and cream, p. 144

Mediterranean salad, p. 139
Fennel, orange, and caper salad, p. 137
Tabouleh with pinenuts, p. 142

French green bean and carrot salad, p. 137
Snow pea and red pepper salad, p. 136
Bocconcini with red and yellow tomatoes, p. 40

DESSERTS

Caramelized apple cheesecake, pp. 190-91
Chocolate bundt cake with fresh berries, p. 189
Opera cake, pp. 198-99
Strawberry rhubarb tart, p. 174
Mango tart, p. 172
Chocolate marquise, p. 194
Chocolate sour cream cake with chocolate buttercream, pp. 192-93
Chocolate truffle tart with raspberries, p. 169
Chocolate mousse, p. 166
Lemon mousse with raspberry purée, p. 156
Crème caramel, p. 155
Pavlova, p. 158
Summer pudding, pp. 160-61
Tiramisu, p. 163
Hazelnut meringue torte, pp. 194-95
Chocolate brandy truffles, p. 167
Biscotti di Prato, p. 217

INFORMAL BUFFET DINNER

These are occasions when the Queen is NOT coming to dinner – maybe a family reunion or a group of friends you haven't seen for a while. The focus is not on the food, but that doesn't mean that it shouldn't be good, only that it should not steal your time or your attention away from your guests.

Any of the items suggested for the more formal buffet dinner (see pages 7-9) would be fine for this evening. What we have suggested here are some less-formal dishes that create a more casual and friendly atmosphere.

Again, the things that are important to remember when planning an informal buffet dinner are generally the same as those that apply to a more formal occasion (you might want to read the introduction to that section again). The dishes we suggest here are ones where most of the work can be done ahead.

You probably won't want to serve a first course; it creates extra work, which will be apparent to your guests and will detract from the informal feel of the evening. Far better to serve a variety of hors-d'oeuvre before, so that people get a good chance to talk to each other. Once they are well on their way you can slip into the kitchen and do whatever is necessary, and with luck they won't notice you've gone until you announce with a flourish that dinner is served.

HORS-D'OEUVRE

Gougère puff with Stilton and prosciutto, p. 29
(one large gougère, cut into sections and passed around hot,
would be impressive; all your other hors-d'oeuvre could then be cold and no
one would think any the worse of it)
Crab dip with blue corn chips, p. 28
Guacamole and salsa with corn chips, p. 26
Karen's pâté, pp. 40-41
Smoked salmon mousse, p. 30

MAIN COURSES

Hot

Pesto-stuffed chicken breasts, pp. 90-91
Chicken and ham pie with biscuit topping, pp. 96-97
Chicken pot pie, pp. 98-99
Oxtail braised with Amarone, p. 113
Osso bucco, p. 126
Tourtière, p. 129
Veal shoulder with warm new potato salad, p. 121
Veal and black bean chili, p. 124
Vegetable lasagna with butternut squash, p. 52

Cold

Vitello tonnato, p. 119
Oriental chicken salad, pp. 100-01
Singapore shrimp noodle salad, p. 57

Hot Vegetables and Cold Salads

Scalloped potatoes, p. 147
Sweet potato and Gorgonzola purée, p. 146
Belgian endive braised with prosciutto and cream, p. 144

Mediterranean salad, p. 139
Fennel, orange, and caper salad, p. 137

Tabouleh with pinenuts, p. 142
French green bean and carrot salad, p. 137
Snow pea and red pepper salad, p. 136
Bocconcini with red and yellow tomatoes, p. 40

DESSERTS

(see also suggestions under "Formal Buffet Dinner", pp. 8-9)
Carrot cake, p. 190
Lemon roulade, pp. 196-97
Warm berry compote with orange custard, p. 157
Italian chocolate hazelnut gelato, p. 182
Peach blueberry pie with streusel topping, p. 173
Apple cranberry tart with ice cream, pp. 167-68
Fresh fruit, with a selection of:
Chocolate chunk cookies, p. 218
Lemon squares, pp. 218-19
Nanaimo bars, p. 220
Oatmeal raisin cookies, p. 219

LUNCH OR LUNCH BUFFET

The recipes that we have chosen for lunch are light, fresh-looking, and often served cold. You do not have to restrict yourself to these dishes; you can certainly serve any of the recipes suggested for a dinner buffet at lunch time, if you feel that they would be more suitable for the occasion you have in mind. You could also use the suggested lunch recipes for an evening buffet, particularly in the summer, when (I am told) people like to eat lighter food (I will eat anything at any time of year, so I am not a good judge of such matters).

If you want to serve a first course at lunch, keep it light, even in the winter. However, except for quite formal occasions, people do not expect a first course, so you can leave it out with confidence. The same is true of any hors-d'oeuvre; it somehow seems like too much, unless there is an unusually long time between yours guests' arrival and the serving of lunch.

FIRST COURSE
(FOR FORMAL LUNCHES)

Bocconcini with red and yellow tomatoes, p. 40
Veal carpaccio, p. 35
Gazpacho, p. 23

Warm goat cheese salad with olive toasts, p. 41
Arugula salad with warm Gorgonzola and walnut toasts, p. 39
Artichokes stuffed with herbs and Parmesan, p. 37

MAIN COURSE
(FOR A LARGE PARTY CHOOSE TWO OR MORE DISHES)

FISH AND SEAFOOD

Crab cakes with jalapeño tartare sauce, p. 85
Salmon in parchment, p. 77
Cold poached salmon with dill mayonnaise, p. 79
Fresh tuna with eggplant caviar, p. 81
Seafood salad, p. 86
Singapore shrimp noodle salad, p. 57
Thai squid salad, p. 87
Shrimps, scallops, and squid in a creamy tarragon dressing, pp. 34-35

MEAT AND CHICKEN

Warm beef tenderloin with crisp-fried onions and
shaved Parmesan, p. 111
Flank steak with red wine aioli, p. 108
Vitello tonnato, p. 119
Cold breast of chicken with red pepper salsa, p. 97
Oriental chicken salad, pp. 100-01
Thai beef salad, p. 112

SALADS

Bocconcini with red and yellow tomatoes, p. 40
Fusilli with tomato buttermilk dressing, p. 55
Eggplant salad, p. 136
Diet salad, p. 135
Fennel, orange, and caper salad, p. 137
Mediterranean salad, p. 139
Tabouleh with pinenuts, p. 142
Tomato, artichoke, and feta salad, p. 143

DESSERTS

Lemon mousse with raspberry purée, p. 156
Lemon roulade, pp. 196-97
Pears with mascarpone, p. 159
Summer pudding, pp. 160-61

Fruit sorbet or ice cream with a selection of cookies
Brandy and ginger peach tart, p. 171
Aunt Dorothy's cheesecake, p. 193
Crème caramel, p. 155
Strawberry rhubarb tart, p. 174
Pavlova, p. 158

Barbecue

While I was struggling with my purist conscience about whether to buy a gas barbecue, I was told the story about the sky diver whose parachute failed to open. As he was hurtling towards the earth he was surprised to see someone rocketing up towards him: "Know anything about parachutes?" he yelled. "No," the answer came back. "You know anything about gas barbecues?"

I am glad to say that I was not deterred from what I am now convinced is the only sensible course for someone who likes to eat barbecued food (not, you notice, someone who likes to rub sticks together or utter incantations over barely smouldering lumps of kerosene-soaked charcoal, an admirable calling, I'm sure, but not for the hungry).

Cooking on a barbecue is a very good solution to summer entertaining. With two barbecues (one borrowed) you can produce dinner for 20 to 30 people much more easily than you could from your kitchen. When we cater large parties in the summer, we almost always use a barbecue to cook the food. Most people would much rather have even a simple kebab straight off the grill than something far more exotic reheated in a warming oven.

Most things are easy to cook on the barbecue, but fish sometimes gives a problem by sticking. You can almost always overcome this if you let the grill get really hot and, then, just before you are ready to put it on the grill, dry the fish well, dredge it with flour, and dip lightly in oil. If the coals are hot enough, a light crispy coating will form and the fish should not stick.

Vegetables can also be done on the grill, but it helps to partially cook them first; this can be done by putting them on a baking sheet with a little water, covering it with foil, and baking them in the oven for 5 to 10 minutes at 350° F.

PRE-BARBECUE NIBBLES

Taramasalata, p. 25
Guacamole and salsa with corn chips, p. 26
Bruschetta, p. 31
Marinated shrimp with fennel, p. 28

Crab dip with blue corn chips, p. 28
Mussels on the half-shell with coriander and tomato sauce, p. 33

ON THE BARBECUE

FISH AND SEAFOOD

Halibut with muscat grapes in mustard, p. 75
Seared salmon in dolce-forte sauce, p. 75
Fresh tuna with eggplant caviar, p. 81
Whole red snapper baked in banana leaves, p. 76
Shrimp wrapped in prosciutto, p. 87

MEAT AND POULTRY

Lemon mustard chicken, p. 98
Thai barbecue chicken, p. 89
Kebabs (beef, lamb, pork, or chicken) with lime mustard or
Thai marinades
Thai beef salad, p. 112
Marinated lamb with lime, mustard, and basil butter, p. 116
Leg of lamb stuffed with provolone, spinach, and sundried tomatoes, pp. 118-19
Rack of lamb with tzatziki and garlic chives, p. 115

VEGETABLES

Grilled chayote with mint and balsamic vinegar, p. 138
Fried eggplant with gremolata, p. 140

SALADS

Diet salad, p. 135
Caesar salad, p. 134
Tabouleh with pinenuts, p. 142
Broccoli with garlic, anchovies, and hot peppers, p. 145

DESSERTS

Pavlova, p. 158
Summer pudding, pp. 160-61
Tiramisu, p. 163
Mango tart, p. 172
Strawberry rhubarb tart, p. 174

WARM AND COZY FOOD FOR FRIENDS

Warm and cozy food creates the kind of mood that soup companies try to evoke in their ads – warm, nourishing, comforting, and familiar. When you serve this kind of food to your friends you are sharing something that is personal and quite intimate. You invite them into the world in which you first got to know these dishes and you let them share the memory of the surroundings where they acquired for you their associations of comfort and warmth of friendship. Even if not everyone joins in your love of a particular dish, it will be clear what it means to you, and that you are sharing something important. Not everyone may like the taste, but the sentiment cannot help but be valued.

When you cook for your close friends and family, they will not mind joining you in the kitchen while you do the finishing touches. Warm and cozy food is the kind that smells so good while it is cooking that it is hard to keep people out of the kitchen anyway. Some of these dishes need this kind of attention; but, generally speaking, this is food that requires long, slow simmering to bring all the flavours together and to give the proper tenderness time to develop. Where a recipe does call for a long cooking time, make sure that the temperature of the stove or oven is turned well down and that the cooking is gentle – better it should take a little longer to cook than it should fall apart from rough treatment.

Everyone has a personal collection of familiar, warm and cozy recipes, and we are certainly not suggesting that you abandon them. But, you might want to expand your repertoire with some of ours – some of them old favourites, and some new variations. I think that you will like them – they work well for us.

Crab cakes with jalapeño mayonnaise, p. 85
Fresh salmon with hot tartare sauce, p. 78

Osso bucco, p. 126
Pot roast of beef with saffron noodles, pp. 108-09
Oxtail braised with Amarone, p. 113
Canelloni with sweetbreads and mushrooms, p. 128
Veal kidneys with rosemary and balsamic vinegar, p. 125
Veal shoulder with warm new potato salad, p. 121
Chicken with porcini mushrooms, p. 91
Chicken and ham pie with biscuit topping, pp. 96-97
Chicken pot pie, pp. 98-99
Chicken fat rice, p. 95
Vegetable lasagne with butternut squash, p. 52

Bitter greens with hot pancetta dressing, p. 143
Tabouleh with pinenuts, p. 142
Belgian endive braised with prosciutto and cream, p. 144
Scalloped potatoes, p. 147
Sweet potato and Gorgonzola purée, p. 146
Winter vegetable casserole, p. 146

Crème brûlée with candied orange, p. 154
Warm berry compote with orange custard, p. 157
Rhubarb peach cobbler, pp. 176-77
Orange steamed pudding with orange hard sauce, p. 175
Pears in pastry with caramel sauce, pp. 162-63
Fresh strawberries with champagne sabayon, p. 160

SOUPS

Not so very long ago, dinner in French households invariably started with *la soupe* or *le potage*: it was not dinner without it. It was the same story over much of Europe. Even in Scotland, when I was growing up, we had soup at dinner every single night, without fail. Nowadays we are too sophisticated for that, it seems; we regard soup as too humble a beginning for all but the simplest of family dinners, and I am as guilty of this as anyone. In our search for new and different first courses, we seldom stop to consider how good a choice soup can be.

Soup has all the right associations in the hearts and minds of your guests. It is warm and friendly, homemade and full of goodness – who would not want to serve food that conveyed these feelings? It is true that soup can be informal – even humble, if that is what you wish – but it can just as easily be exotic, sophisticated, elegant, or classic. In this section you will find soup recipes that fit into all of these categories, including some that can be a meal on their own. As a starter or main course, there is nothing better when you need a little comfort.

CHICKEN SOUP WITH COCONUT AND LIME

Make this unusual soup if you are planning a South-East Asian dinner.

Serves 10.

6 cups	**Chicken Stock** (see page 226)
4 cans	**coconut milk**, 14 oz each
4 stalks	**lemon grass** (see page 114)
10 slices	**galingale** (see below)
6 strips	**lime rind**
4	**chicken legs** OR **breasts**
2 Tbs	**Thai fish sauce** ("Squid Brand") (see page 114)
2 tsp	**salt**
½ cup	**lime juice**
1 cup	**finely chopped red pepper**
1 cup	**finely sliced green onion**
½ cup	**chopped fresh coriander**
¼–½ tsp	**hot pepper flakes**

1.   Trim the lemon grass and cut each stalk into 2″ pieces. Place the stock, coconut milk, lemon grass, galingale, lime rind, and chicken pieces in a large pot. Bring to a boil, then reduce heat to a simmer and cook for 1 hour.

2.   Remove the chicken and allow to cool. Strain the soup and discard the herbs. Discard the chicken skin and bones; chop the meat into ½″ cubes. *(May be done ahead to this point.)*

3.   Return the soup to the pot, add the chicken meat, fish sauce, salt, and lime juice. Bring to a boil and add the chopped red pepper, green onion, coriander, and hot pepper flakes – the spicier you like it, the more you can add.

> **GALINGALE**
> Pronounced "gell'engle". A ginger-like root, but hotter and more fragrant. Available dried or fresh in Vietnamese and Chinese stores.

SHALLOT AND WILD MUSHROOM SOUP

Serves 8.

1 oz	**dried morels** (see page 83)
1 oz	**dried porcini mushrooms**
½ cup	**butter** (see page 23)
1 cup	**finely chopped shallots**
1 lb	**fresh mushrooms**, thinly sliced
6 Tbs	**flour**
6 cups	**Chicken Stock** (see page 226)
¼ cup	**sherry**
	salt and **pepper**
1 cup	**Crème Fraîche** (see page 226)

1.   Put the dried mushrooms into separate small bowls. Pour about 1 cup of boiling water into each and leave to stand for 1 hour.

2.   Remove the mushrooms and squeeze as much water as possible back into the bowls. Strain the liquid through a paper coffee filter or doubled cheesecloth; reserve.

3.   Cut the morels in half; remove any very hard parts from the porcini. Put them all in a bowl of water and rub them between your hands to remove any residual sand. Remove from the water, drain, and chop them coarsely.

4. Melt the butter in a large heavy pot; put in the shallots and sauté over medium heat until translucent. Add the sliced fresh mushrooms and cook until they have released their juice and it has evaporated. Add the flour and stir for 2 minutes. Whisk in the chicken stock and reserved mushroom soaking juices.

5. Bring to a boil, stirring steadily. Add the wild mushrooms, reduce the heat, and simmer for 1 hour, stirring occasionally. Add salt and pepper if necessary. *(May be done up to 2 days ahead to this point.)*

6. Reheat the soup, stir in the sherry and crème fraîche, making sure that the soup is hot before serving.

TOMATO AND FENNEL SOUP

Serves 8.

2 28 oz cans	**Italian crushed tomatoes**
4 cups	**Chicken Stock** (see page 226)
½ cup	**butter** (see page 23)
1 cup	**finely sliced white onion**
½ cup	**finely sliced carrot**
½ cup	**finely sliced celery**
6 Tbs	**flour**
1 sprig	**fresh rosemary** OR
1 tsp	**dried**
	salt and **pepper**
2 Tbs	**finely chopped dill**
2 Tbs	**finely chopped parsley**
2 Tbs	**finely sliced basil leaves**
1 cup	**finely chopped fresh fennel**

1. Combine the crushed tomatoes with the chicken stock in a saucepan and bring to a boil; set aside on the back of the stove.

2. Melt the butter in a large, heavy pot; put in the onion, carrot, and celery and cook over medium heat until the vegetables are slightly softened. Add the flour and stir for a few moments; then pour in the hot stock and tomato mixture. Increase the heat and bring to a boil, stirring constantly. At the boil, add the rosemary, reduce the heat to a simmer, and cook for 1 hour, stirring occasionally.

3. Pour the soup through a large sieve, pushing through as much of the vegetable juices as you can. Return it to the pot, add salt and pepper, put in the dill, parsley, and finely chopped fennel. Simmer for 5 minutes more and serve.

LOBSTER AND BLACK BEAN SOUP WITH CORIANDER PESTO

Serves 8.

1 cup	**dried black beans**
2	**1½ to 2 lb lobsters**
1 cup	**finely chopped onion**
¼ cup	**finely chopped celery**
¼ cup	**finely chopped carrot**
2 tsp	**finely chopped garlic**
2 Tbs	**extra virgin olive oil** (see page 133)
1½ tsp	**ground cumin**
1 tsp	**ground coriander**
½ tsp	**hot pepper flakes**
½ cup	**canned tomatoes**, drained and seeded
½ tsp	**dried oregano**
2 strips	**orange peel**

FOR THE CORIANDER PESTO

2 cups	**fresh coriander leaves**, well packed
2 tsp	**finely chopped garlic**
½ cup	**extra virgin olive oil**
¼ tsp	**salt**
2 Tbs	**slivered almonds**, toasted (see page 185)
1 cup	**Crème Fraîche** (see page 226)

1. *Soak the black beans overnight in a large pot of water.*

2. The next day, drain the beans and rinse them. Return them to the pot, cover with fresh water, and bring to a boil. Reduce the heat to a simmer and cook for 2 to 3 hours until they are tender (the cooking time depends on the age of the beans). Add more water as needed to keep them covered. When they are ready, scoop out 6 cups of the bean cooking liquid and reserve. Drain the beans and set aside.

3. Cook the lobsters: Bring a large pot of salted water to a boil. Add the lobsters, cover the pot, and cook for 8 minutes. Remove and allow to cool. Save 2 cups of the cooking liquid.

4. Split the lobsters and remove the claws; take out all the meat and slice it thinly. Reserve the meat, the coral, and the tomalley (the green stuff – it does not look very good but adds excellent flavour; take care to throw away the little sac at the front of the head).

5. Sauté the onion, garlic, carrots, and celery in the olive oil over medium heat until the vegetables are soft. Add the cumin, coriander, and hot pepper flakes. Stir for a few minutes. Now add the tomatoes, the beans, oregano, orange peel, and the reserved lobster and bean stocks. (If you did not cook the lobsters yourself, use water.) Bring the soup to a boil, reduce the heat to simmer, and cook for 1 hour, stirring occasionally.

6. Remove ½ cup of the beans and reserve. Discard the strips of orange peel. Transfer the rest to the work bowl of a food processor (in batches if necessary) and process until smooth. Add the reserved beans, bring to a simmer, and check seasoning.

7. Combine coriander, garlic, olive oil, salt, and the almonds in the work bowl of a food processor or blender. Process until you have a chunky paste.

8. Press the reserved coral and tomalley through a fine sieve into a small bowl; stir in the crème fraîche.

9.   To serve: Add water to the soup if you think it needs thinning. Bring the soup to a simmer. Add the sliced lobster meat to the soup. Cook for 3 minutes to heat through. Ladle into heated soup plates; garnish with streaks of crème fraîche and coriander pesto.

Variations: Black Bean and Shrimp Soup; Black Bean and Crab Soup

Serves 8.

1 lb	**small shrimp**, peeled and deveined OR
¾ lb	**lump crab leg meat**, thawed

1.   Make the soup and corriander pesto as described above; add water in place of the lobster cooking liquid. Bring the soup to a simmer, add the shrimp or crab meat and allow to heat through. Serve in warmed bowls, garnished with the coriander pesto and the crème fraîche.

Potato, Leek, and Stilton Soup

Serves 10.

10 cups	**Chicken Stock** (see page 226)
5 Tbs	**unsalted butter** (see page 23)
3	**leeks**, chopped (white part only)
3	**white onions**, chopped
3 cloves	**garlic**, crushed
1 Tbs	**chopped fresh thyme** OR
½ tsp	**dried**
5 medium	**potatoes**, peeled and diced
4 Tbs	**flour**
2 tsp	**salt**
1 tsp	**ground pepper**
1 cup	**whipping cream**
8 oz	**crumbled Stilton cheese**

1.   Bring the chicken stock to a boil; set aside on the back of the stove.

2.   Melt the butter in a large saucepan; put in the onions and leeks and cook over medium-low heat until translucent. Add the garlic, thyme, and chopped potatoes; sprinkle in the flour, then pour in the hot chicken stock. Bring to a boil, stirring occasionally; reduce the heat to simmer and cook for 1½ hours, until the potatoes are very soft.

3.   Transfer (in batches) to the work bowl of your food processor or blender. Process until smooth, pour into a large bowl, then return to the pot when it is all done. *(May be done up to 2 days ahead to this point, or may be frozen.)*

4.   Reheat the soup and stir in the cream. Just before serving, add the crumbled Stilton and stir until dissolved.

BEET CONSOMMÉ

Serves 4.

4¼ cups	**Chicken Stock** (see page 226)
1 large	**beet**, peeled and grated
1 tsp	**fresh ginger**, julienned
	salt and **pepper**

FOR GARNISH

½ small	**daikon radish**
4	**chives**, chopped

1.   Bring the chicken consommé to a boil; stir in the grated beet and ginger. Cook over medium heat for 5 to 7 minutes, until it has taken on a bright beet colour. Strain through a fine sieve. *(May be done ahead to this point.)*

2.   To serve: Slice the daikon radish thinly, and cut the slices into decorative shapes – stars, fish, crescents, and so on. Reheat the soup to simmering, season to taste, ladle into consommé cups, and float the radish shapes and chives on top.

CALDO VERDE

A substantial country soup from Portugal. Follow it with a green salad and some cheese (Spanish Manchego is now available here) and you have a good, simple dinner.

Serves 8.

4 Tbs	**extra virgin olive oil** (see page 133)
3 medium	**onions**, finely sliced
2 lbs	**potatoes**, peeled and thinly sliced
10 cups	**Chicken Stock** (see page 226)
1 tsp	**salt**
1 lb	**kale** OR **collard greens**, washed
½ lb	**chorizo sausage**, preferably smoked, OR **kielbasa** **Olio Santo** (see page 230)

1.   In a large pot, sauté the onions in the olive oil until very soft but not browned. Add the sliced potatoes, stock, and salt and bring to a boil. Turn the heat down to a merry bubble and cook until the potatoes are very tender – about 1 hour.

2.   Take the pot off the heat; transfer the soup in batches to the work bowl of your food processor or blender; process to a purée and set aside in a large bowl. When all the soup is puréed, return to the pot and bring to a simmer. *(May be done ahead to this point.)*

3.   Wash the greens and shred them very finely, then put them into the soup. If using fresh chorizo, drop the whole sausages into the soup and cook for 5 minutes – this will firm them up enough to be sliced. Then remove them, cut them into ¼″ slices, and put them back in the soup. If using smoked sausage, remove the skin, slice, and drop into the soup. Simmer for 20 minutes after the greens go in: the sausages need only 10 minutes in total.

4.   To serve: Ladle into bowls and pass the "olio santo" so that everyone can add a tablespoon or two to the soup.

GAZPACHO

Serves 6.

2 cups	**Tomato Concassé** (see page 228)
½ cup	**finely diced English cucumber**
½ cup	**finely diced green pepper**
½ tsp	**finely chopped garlic**
¼ cup	**finely chopped red onion**
½ tsp	**salt**
1 Tbs	**red wine vinegar**
¼ tsp	**black pepper**
½ tsp	**red pepper flakes**
2 cups	**cold water**
1 Tbs	**finely chopped parsley**
1 Tbs	**chopped fresh coriander**
2 Tbs	**extra virgin olive oil** (see page 133)
2 cups	**small croutons**, from day-old white bread (see below)

1. Chop all the vegetables finely – it can be done in the food processor, but be careful not to reduce them to a purée as the soup should have some texture. Combine them all in a large bowl.

2. Add the salt, vinegar, pepper, hot pepper flakes, water, parsley, coriander, and olive oil. *Stir well and set aside in the refrigerator for 1 hour (this can be done up to a day ahead).*

3. To serve: Divide the croutons between 6 soup bowls; spoon the soup on top.

BUTTER

To salt or not to salt? There is certainly nothing nobler about using unsalted butter in cooking; but there are a few arguments in its favour, particularly when making pastry: The salt in butter absorbs water; salted butter, as a result, has a higher water content than unsalted, and this water will make the flour in your recipe sticky and more difficult to work with.

The salt also imparts its flavour to the dish; if the recipe calls for just a tablespoon or two of butter, it doesn't really matter whether you use salted or not – a little salt adds spice, even to sweet recipes. But if the recipe requires a larger quantity of butter, try to use unsalted butter – the recipe will work better and the end result will taste better.

If you check the moisture content on the package of unsalted butter, you will find that it is significantly lower than on a package of salted butter. This is why it costs more: butter is more expensive than salt and water.

CROUTONS

Croutons for gazpacho are traditionally made from stale bread cut into small cubes and sprinkled on the soup by the guests. You may if you like use croutons that have been toasted, either with or without olive oil. To toast: Spread the croutons on a large baking sheet and bake in a 350° F oven for about 10 minutes, turning occasionally. If using olive oil, pour a few tablespoons of oil onto the baking sheet and toss the croutons in the oil until lightly coated before you put them in the oven to bake.

HORS-D'OEUVRE & FIRST COURSES

HORS-D'OEUVRE

"Hors-d'oeuvre" is a French word that means "outside the work", most commonly referring to cooking that is not part of the main work of the dinner, and there is no plural form – in French. Unfortunately for the French, the word is widely used as a noun in English, and the plural form is very much in evidence. It is such a convenient word to cover all of the small bits of food that people eat before dinner, and no other word does quite so well.

Hors-d'oeuvres – what should they be like? They should be interesting, visually attractive, easy to eat, complementary to the dinner that is to follow, and light. From the kitchen's point of view, they should also be easy to make. Sadly this last consideration does not fit with all the others. Hors-d'oeuvres are generally time-consuming, fiddly, and a lot of work. In most cases they can be made ahead, so at least the work can be done at your convenience; and if your party is not too formal, dips provide an excellent solution. (For more formal parties, dips are not as popular as they used to be.) For cocktail parties you need a wider array of bite-sized bits.

Putting out a tray of pâté or salmon mousse with crackers works well at a small party; at larger gatherings, and particularly where space is a consideration, it will be hard for people to navigate to the tray, and most of the guests will not get an opportunity to try the pâté or mousse. Again, in this situation, passing around trays of individual hors-d'oeuvres is the best solution.

It is worth remembering that there are now available some excellent frozen hors-d'oeuvres, most of them wrapped in either phyllo or tart pastry. They are designed to be heated in the oven for 15 to 20 minutes, and then served warm. I would not use these alone; but if, for example, you were to make a dip and prepare some shrimp yourself, these would add a nice professional touch to round out the menu.

TARAMASALATA

This Greek appetizer goes wonderfully well with a summer evening, a cold bottle of white wine, and a bowl of black olives. In Greece it is served with warm pita bread; a package of pita chips would be a good alternative – or Manoucher's long bread.

Serves 8 as an hors-d'oeuvre.

½ loaf	**day-old white bread**
	milk OR **water**
8 oz jar	**tarama** OR **smoked cod roe**
1 clove	**garlic**, crushed
1 Tbs	**lemon juice**
1 cup	**olive oil**
½ cup	**whipping cream**

MANOUCHER'S BREAD

Manoucher makes some of the best bread you can buy in Toronto. It is chewy, and doughy, with a real old-fashioned bread flavour, and it comes in several shapes and sizes: a long bread that looks like a French stick, called Manoucher's baguette; a shorter version of the same bread, which is stuffed with sheep's milk cheese and fresh herbs; and a long, flat bread that looks like a paddle – called the "long bread," it is excellent with taramasalata.

1.   Remove the crusts from the bread; cut it into chunks and soak it in milk or water for 5 minutes. Squeeze out as much of the liquid as you can, and transfer to the work bowl of your food processor.

2.   Add the tarama, crushed garlic clove, and lemon juice and process until somewhat smooth. With the motor running, pour the olive oil slowly down the feed tube, followed by the cream. It should have a good "dip" consistency (not too thick).

3.   Tarama varies greatly in consistency and saltiness; adjust the seasonings and texture by adding lemon juice, salt, pepper, oil, or cream. *(May be prepared 2 days before serving.)*

SMOKED CHICKEN BREAST WRAPPED IN SNOW PEAS

Makes 20.

1	**boneless smoked chicken breast** (OR duck, pheasant, or guinea fowl)
2 tsp	**oyster sauce** (see page 114)
pinch of	**salt**
pinch of	**black pepper**
20 large	**snow peas**
2 tsp	**black sesame seeds**

1.   Cut the chicken-breast meat into ½" cubes. Place in a bowl with the oyster sauce, salt, and pepper and toss to coat with the marinade. Leave to marinate until ready to assemble.

2.   Bring a pot of water to a boil.

3.   Trim the snow peas and remove the strings; cook in the boiling water just until they turn bright green. Drain and refresh under cold water.

4.   To serve: Wrap a snow pea around a chunk of chicken, skewer it with a toothpick, and sprinkle with sesame seeds.

BEEF OR CHICKEN SATAY

Makes about 25 skewers.

2 lbs	**beef tenderloin** OR
5	**boneless chicken breasts**, skin removed
package	**bamboo skewers** (at least 25)
1 cup	**Peanut** OR **Springroll Sauce** (see page 225 or 229)

FOR THE MARINADE

4 oz	**coconut milk**
3 tsp	**curry powder**
2 tsp	**oyster sauce** (see page 114)
1 clove	**garlic**, crushed
¼ cup	**vegetable oil**
pinch of	**salt** and **pepper**

1.   Combine coconut milk, curry powder, oyster sauce, garlic, oil, and salt and pepper in a medium bowl. Mix well.

2.   Cut the beef into strips 3″ by ¾″ by ¾″ (more or less). Put the strips into the marinade; let stand for at least 1 hour (may be refrigerated overnight). If using chicken, cut each breast across into 5 equal (more or less) pieces; marinate as above.

3.   Spear the beef (or chicken) onto a skewer, so that the skewer runs the length of the meat. Place it on a solid surface, lay a piece of plastic wrap over it, and pound it lightly so that the meat is somewhat flattened. Set aside in the fridge until ready to bake. *(May be done a day ahead to this point.)*

4.   Preheat the oven to 375°F.

5.   Lay the skewers on a baking sheet; they should not touch each other. Bake in the preheated oven for 5 to 7 minutes (depending on how well done you like them). Serve with peanut or springroll sauce.

GUACAMOLE

Guacamole and salsa make a very good pair. Serve with corn chips.

Serves 8.

4 ripe	**avocadoes**
1 large	**tomato**
3 cloves	**garlic**, crushed
1 Tbs	**coriander leaves**
1 Tbs	**lemon juice**
6 drops	**Tabasco Sauce**
1 tsp	**salt**
½ tsp	**black pepper**
¼ cup	**sour cream**

1.   Scoop all the flesh out of the avocadoes into the work bowl of your food processor.

2.   Peel the tomato: Pour boiling water over it and let sit for 20 seconds; take it out and slip the skin off (it may need longer than this – if so put it back in the water). Remove the seeds and the hard core. Transfer the pulp to the food processor; process with the avocado until quite smooth.

3.   Add the crushed garlic, coriander, lemon juice, Tabasco, salt, pepper, and sour cream. Process again until well combined. Refrigerate until ready to serve.

BACON-WRAPPED FILET WITH BEARNAISE MAYONNAISE

A simple and very popular hors-d'oeuvre.

Makes 24 little filets.

1¼ lbs	**beef tenderloin**, cut in 1″ cubes
1 Tbs	**Dijon mustard**
1 clove	**garlic**, crushed
4 Tbs	**olive oil**
¼ tsp	**salt**
¼ tsp	**black pepper**
12 strips	**side bacon**
24	**toothpicks**, without frills
½ cup	**Bearnaise Mayonnaise** (see page 228)

1.   Prepare the marinade: Combine the mustard, garlic, oil, salt, and pepper in a bowl large enough to hold the beef. Mix well. Add the beef cubes and toss well to coat thoroughly. Marinate for at least 1 hour at room temperature, or refrigerate overnight.

2.   Partially cook the bacon until the fat has started to run – it must not be at all crispy. (*EITHER* bake it on a baking sheet in a preheated 375°F oven for about 7 minutes, *OR* fry it on top of the stove.) Drain on paper towel and allow to cool.

3.   Cut each piece of bacon in half. Wrap each half around a cube of beef and secure with a toothpick pushed all the way through. (*May be prepared a day ahead, or frozen if you wish. If frozen, thaw the beef and allow to come to room temperature.*)

4.   Preheat the oven to 375°F.

5.   Arrange the cubes, not touching, on a baking sheet. Bake in the preheated oven for 12 minutes.

6.   To serve: Arrange the little filets on a serving tray with a small bowl of Bearnaise mayonnaise in the middle for dipping.

HEARTS OF PALM WITH PROSCIUTTO

Makes 16.

8 slices	**prosciutto**, quite thin (see page 53)
2	**palm hearts**, from a can
16 sprigs	**parsley**

FOR THE FILLING

½ lb	**cream cheese**
1 clove	**garlic**, crushed
1 tsp	**tarragon leaves**
1 tsp	**chopped dill**
1 Tbs	**lemon juice**
⅛ tsp	**salt**
⅛ tsp	**black pepper**

1.   Combine the cream cheese, crushed garlic, tarragon, dill, lemon juice, salt, and pepper in a bowl and mix well.

2.   Cut each slice of prosciutto in half across; cut each heart of palm into 8 pieces, lengthwise. Spread the filling over the prosciutto slices, then roll up around the heart of palm pieces. Stick a sprig of parsley into the end of each one.

CRAB DIP

This looks very good served with blue corn chips.

1 lb	**crab meat**, thawed and drained
¼ lb	**cream cheese**
2 Tbs	**Mayonnaise** (see page 227)
½ cup	**very finely chopped red pepper**
½ cup	**very finely chopped green pepper**
½ cup	**very finely chopped yellow pepper** (or use all one colour – no one will know)
2	**green onions**, finely chopped
1 clove	**garlic**, crushed (optional)
2 Tbs	**lemon juice**
⅛ tsp	**Tabasco Sauce**
⅛ tsp	**Worcestershire Sauce**
	salt and **black pepper**
3 Tbs	**chopped fresh dill**

1. Mash the cream cheese until it softens up; add the mayonnaise and stir well.

2. Put in the peppers, green onions, and garlic (if using it). Stir again.

3. Pour in the lemon juice, Tabasco, and Worcestershire. Mix together and taste for seasoning. Add salt and pepper if necessary.

4. Stir in the drained crab meat and the fresh dill. Allow to stand for ½ hour before serving to allow the flavours to blend. (It will keep in the fridge for 1 day.)

MARINATED SHRIMP WITH FENNEL

A good combination of taste and texture.

Serves 4.

20	**16/20 shrimp** (see page 48)
¼	**fennel bulb**

FOR THE MARINADE

½ cup	**lemon juice**
1 Tbs	**Dijon mustard**
5 Tbs	**olive oil**
½ tsp	**salt**
¼ tsp	**black pepper**
1 Tbs	**chopped fennel leaves**

1. Bring a pot of water to a boil; salt it and drop in the shrimp. Cook for 4 minutes, drain, and refresh under cold water. Peel and devein.

2. Combine lemon juice, mustard, olive oil, salt, pepper, and fennel leaves in a bowl large enough to hold the shrimp. Toss the shrimp in the marinade.

3. Cut the ¼ fennel bulb into pieces about ½" square; add them to the marinade. *Refrigerate for 4 hours, or overnight.*

4. To serve: Drain shrimp and fennel. Put one shrimp and one fennel piece on a toothpick and arrange on a platter.

GOUGÈRE PUFFS WITH STILTON AND PROSCIUTTO

Serves 12 as an hors-d'oeuvre.

1 recipe	**Choux Pastry** (see page 231)
1 cup	**finely crumbled Stilton cheese**
3 Tbs	**finely chopped prosciutto** (see page 53)
½ tsp	**black pepper**

1.   Make the choux pastry – be sure to use the recipe without sugar! Allow to cool.

2.   Preheat the oven to 375°F. Butter and flour a baking sheet – or line one with parchment paper.

3.   Stir the crumbled Stilton, the chopped prosciutto, and black pepper into the cooled choux pastry. With a teaspoon (or piping bag) place ¾" mounds of pastry mixture on the baking sheet, about 1" apart. Smooth the tops with a pastry brush dipped in beaten egg – or you can do it with your fingers.

4.   Bake for 15 minutes, until puffed and a deep golden brown – if you take them out too soon they will collapse as they cool and loose some of their good looks.

NOTE: This recipe may also be baked as one large puff. Draw a 9" circle on the baking sheet: Spread the choux paste (with flavourings mixed in) inside the circle. Bake for 40 minutes until golden brown. Cut into wedges with a serrated knife.

SALSA

A spicy dip for summer days when the tomatoes are good; you can make it all year but it's just not the same (better than doing without, however).

8 ripe	**tomatoes**
½	**green pepper**
½	**red pepper**
½	**yellow pepper** (yes, you may use all the same colour)
½	**red onion**
4 cloves	**garlic**, peeled and crushed
½ tsp	**hot pepper flakes**
1 to 2 Tbs	**coriander leaves**
1 tsp	**salt**
½ tsp	**black pepper**
1 Tbs	**olive oil**

1.   Seed the tomatoes; core and seed the peppers, then cut into large chunks; peel the half onion and cut into chunks; crush the garlic clove.

2.   Combine all of the ingredients in the work bowl of your food processor; process using the pulse action until reduced to small dice; do not process to the point where it becomes a purée.

3.   Serve with corn chips.

SMOKED SALMON MOUSSE

This mousse has a very good balance between texture (it is not at all rubbery), lightness (as a feather), and flavour (it really tastes of smoked salmon): and so it should – it took us a long time to get it right. Obviously the flavour of the smoked salmon is critical, so buy a good quality. Ask your retailer if they have scraps – unless they are lucky enough to be buying square fish (relatives of the ones they make fish sticks from) they probably will.

Serves 15 as an hors-d'oeuvre.

1 Tbs	**gelatin** (1 envelope)
¼ cup	**cold water**
½ cup	**boiling water**
6 oz	**smoked salmon**
4 oz	**cream cheese**
1 Tbs	**lemon juice**
dash of	**Tabasco Sauce**
¼ tsp	**paprika** (optional)
½ tsp	**salt**
2 Tbs	**finely chopped dill**
1 large	**egg white**
½ cup	**whipping cream**

1. Pour the cold water into a small bowl and sprinkle the gelatin over it; allow it to dissolve. Then pour on the boiling water and stir until the gelatin is melted.

2. In the work bowl of a food processor, combine the salmon, cream cheese, and lemon juice. Process until you have a smooth, pink purée.

3. Add Tabasco, paprika (if using it), salt, and the dill; process just to blend. Pour in the melted gelatin; process again until you have a smooth, soupy mixture. Refrigerate to let it start to set.

4. Line a loaf pan with plastic wrap; leave enough hanging over the edges to cover the top later.

5. Beat the egg white (with a tiny pinch of cream of tartar if you have it) until firm.

6. Beat the cream to soft peaks; do not overbeat or it will be hard to fold in.

7. Remove the salmon from the fridge; it's best if it is just starting to set; don't worry if it is not, as long as it is cold. Add the beaten egg white to the salmon and fold it in (you may have to stir more than fold, but try not to knock all of the air out). Then add the whipped cream and fold it in too. Pour or spoon the mixture into the lined loaf pan, fold the extra wrap over the top, refrigerate for at least 4 hours.

8. Unmould gently, using the plastic wrap to coax it out of the pan onto a platter.

9. Decorate the top with sprigs of dill and lemon slices; serve with crackers.

ESCARGOTS WITH ROQUEFORT IN PUFF PASTRY

Makes 48 little puffs.

1 can (12) **extra large escargots**
1 lb   **Puff Pastry**
          (see page 231)

FOR THE FILLING
½ cup   **crumbled Roquefort**
          OR **Stilton**
2 tsp   **finely chopped parsley**
¼ cup   **cream cheese**
1 tsp   **butter**, at room
          temperature
          (see page 23)
2 small
  cloves **garlic**, crushed
1 Tbs   **lemon juice**
¼ tsp   **salt**
⅛ tsp   **black pepper**
1   **egg**, beaten, for glaze

1. Make the filling: Mix the Roquefort, parsley, cream cheese, butter, crushed garlic, lemon juice, salt, and pepper in a small bowl. Transfer to a pastry bag fitted with a small plain tip, if you have one (it's a bit easier than working with a teaspoon).

2. Divide the puff pastry in half; roll each half out to a rectangle about 14" by 14"; it should be about ⅛" thick. Set one sheet aside; lay the other on your work surface.

3. Either pipe or spoon little mounds (about ½" across) of filling onto the pastry in a grid pattern, about 2" apart.

4. Cut each escargot in 4; press one piece of escargot on top of each little mound. Top each snail with a bit more filling.

5. Brush the beaten egg on the pastry around each snail. Drape the second sheet of pastry over the first, and press down carefully to seal the two sheets of pastry together around every mound.

6. Find a pastry cutter that fits comfortably over each mound, and leaves a little border all round. Remove the rounds, and seal the edges well by pressing with the tines of a fork.

7. Brush with egg wash. Set aside in the fridge until ready to bake.

8. Preheat the oven to 375°F.

9. Arrange puffs on the baking sheet. Bake for 15 to 20 minutes, until golden brown.

BRUSCHETTA

Serves 6 as an hors-d'oeuvre, 3 as a first course.

6 1" slices **crusty Italian bread**
          (a dense chewy bread
          is best)
2 cloves **garlic**, peeled
6 leaves **fresh basil**
½ – 1 cup **extra virgin olive oil**
          (see page 133)
1 tsp   **coarsely ground black
          pepper**

1. Grill the bread on both sides, using a barbecue or oven broiler – if you can make grill marks, so much the better.

2. Rub the surface of the bread with garlic cloves and the basil leaves – do it quickly while the bread is still warm.

3. Drizzle with the extra virgin oil and sprinkle with black pepper. Serve.

First Courses

I find first courses one of the hardest problems in planning a dinner. Because what you choose for the main course often ends up being relatively unadventurous, there is more pressure for the first course to be imaginative – and, of course, good. And from a practical point of view, a first course should not require so much last-half-hour attention that you are tied to the kitchen.

I remember an almost perfect (when measured by these standards) first course, which enjoyed an intense but relatively brief popularity when I was growing up in Scotland. It consisted of (canned) beef consommé mixed with a little sherry, poured into a glass serving bowl and chilled. Once it was firm a layer of (lumpfish) caviar was spread over the top; the whole thing was then covered with whipped cream. There was a much-talked-about occasion when someone made it with Beluga caviar (I was not on the guest list that night); but I never heard of anyone who used home-made consommé.

Strange as it sounds it is none the less quite good. But it does not stand up to repetition in the same way, for example, that steak does, or pasta. The more unusual a first course the less often you can repeat it; you can make the same main course time after time (provided that it is not sweetbreads or oxtails) and no one will think any the worse of you.

Your first-course repertoire should be a bit larger than your main-course list. But not all your first-course favourites need be new and different. When casting around for first-course inspiration do not overlook the tried-and-true favourites – smoked salmon (and particularly smoked trout; it is delicious with whipped cream flavoured with horseradish and a bit of mustard); tomatoes and bocconcini; prosciutto with melon or figs; or seviche. You would not want to serve them every time; but they are so good that you shouldn't ignore them just because they are, like many good main courses, relatively tame. You can probably remember a few dinners where you would have settled for something plain, simple, and good.

GOAT CHEESE OR **CHÈVRE**
Cheese made from goats' milk is called "chèvre" (from the French word for goat).
Chèvre is available in a range of textures, degrees of ripeness, and strengths of flavour. The mildest are the fresh cream chèvres, which are like regular cream cheese but made with goats' rather than cows' milk. They are generally not ripened, but some may be slightly ripe. Good ones are **Montrachet** from France, **Chevrai** from the Woolwich Dairy in Elmira, Ontario, and **Snowgoat** from Quebec, which is made from a combination of cows' and goats' milk, and so is a bit milder.
A bit stronger in flavour are the French chèvres **Crottin de Chavignol** and **Riblaire**. Depending on their ripeness, they range from mild and creamy to quite hard and strongly flavoured. A medium-ripe cheese of either of these kinds is the best choice for a warm goat-cheese salad, because they don't break up too much when sautéed or baked. And the flavour of Crottin de Chavignol is hard to beat. However, you may also use a firm, fresh cream chèvre if you prefer a milder flavour.
In the hard chèvres, **Bellissimo** from the Woolwich Dairy has a very good flavour and is not too strong. It is a good choice when you want a chèvre to grate.

Mussels on the Half Shell with Coriander and Tomato Sauce

Serves 6 as a first course.

2 lbs	**mussels**, scrubbed and bearded (see page 86)
¼ cup	**white wine** OR **vermouth**
2 cloves	**garlic**, finely sliced
1 28 oz can	**Italian plum tomatoes**
½ tsp	**hot pepper flakes**
¼ cup	**chopped coriander leaves**
1 Tbs	**olive oil**

FOR GARNISH

Additional	**coriander leaves**

1. Combine the mussels, white wine, and garlic in a large pot with a good-fitting lid. Bring to a boil over high heat; reduce heat to medium and steam for 7 minutes, until the mussels are well opened. Remove pot from heat, take out the mussels and set aside.

2. Strain the mussel liquid through cheesecloth or paper towel, return it to the pot and reduce over high heat to ¼ cup.

3. Drain the canned tomatoes, seed them as well as you can, and chop them coarsely. Add them to the mussel liquid with the hot pepper flakes and simmer for 15 to 20 minutes. Remove from the heat and allow to cool.

4. Remove the mussel meat from the shells, saving half the shells. Lay the half shells on the plates and put a mussel in each.

5. Add the olive oil and chopped coriander leaves to the tomato mixture; mix well and spoon over the mussels. Garnish with coriander leaves. Serve cold.

Scallops and Fennel with Peppercorns

Serves 6 as a first course.

24	**large scallops**, thawed
1½ cups	**champagne** OR **very dry white wine**
2½ Tbs	**chopped garlic chives**
2 tsp	**pink peppercorns**
½ tsp	**green peppercorns**
3 Tbs	**butter** (see page 23)
1	**large fennel bulb**, thinly sliced
3 Tbs	**Pernod**
1½ cups	**whipping cream**
3	**egg yolks**, beaten

1. Pour the champagne into a (non-aluminum) saucepan; add the scallops and bring to a boil over medium-low heat. As soon as it boils, lift out the scallops, put in the chives and the peppercorns, turn up the heat, and reduce the liquid to about ¾ cup.

2. Slice the fennel bulb lengthwise into thin strips. Heat the butter in a frying pan and sauté the fennel for 2 minutes. Then add the Pernod and light it – be careful to keep your face out of the way.

3. Remove the fennel, pour in the cream, and bring to a boil. Take the pan off the heat, and stir in the beaten egg yolks.

4. Add the scallops and fennel and allow them to heat through; but do not return the pan to the heat, or the eggs will curdle. Serve on warm plates.

THAI BEEF TARTARE

Very finely chopped raw beef tenderloin wrapped in lettuce leaves with Oriental herbs and spices – a truly great combination.

Serves 6 to 8 as a hors-d'oeuvre or first course.

1 recipe	**Thai Beef Salad** (see page 112) without flank steak
1 lb	**beef tenderloin**

1.   Prepare the salad ingredients: follow steps 3 and 5 on page 112.

2.   Cut the beef tenderloin into small cubes; place in the freezer until just starting to freeze. Chop by hand as finely as possible; or use a food processor until the meat is finely chopped but not pasty.

CHOPPING BY HAND: This is not a make-work project; it simply gives a better result than grinding or processing, both of which squeeze the natural juices out of the meat while it is being chopped, making the end result less tender.

3.   Serve on a platter with lettuce leaves around the edge, the meat in the centre, and the salad around the meat. The guests roll up the meat and salad in the lettuce leaves.

SHRIMPS, SCALLOPS, AND SQUID IN A CREAMY TARRAGON DRESSING

An attractive cold first course.

Serves 4.

OPTIONAL COURT BOUILLON FOR COOKING THE SEAFOOD

½	**carrot**
½ stick	**celery**
½	**lemon**
8	**peppercorns**
16	**16/20 shrimp** (see page 48)
16	**good-size scallops**
4	**small squid**
20	**snow peas** OR **asparagus tips**
4 leaves	**Boston lettuce**
4 leaves	**radicchio lettuce**
1	**red pepper**
1	**yellow pepper**
4	**cherry tomatoes** (not essential)

1.   Prepare the seafood: Bring a pot of water to a boil and add the carrot, celery, lemon, and peppercorns if you wish. Put in the shrimp and cook for 2 minutes, then scoop out with a skimmer or slotted spoon and allow to cool; cook the scallops for one minute. Clean the squid (if not already done) and cut into rings about ¼" wide. Blanch in the water for 30 seconds, then drain and cool. Peel and devein the shrimp; cut the scallops in half.

2.   Prepare the vegetables: Bring another pot of water to the boil and blanch the snow peas (2 minutes) or asparagus (5 minutes). Remove with the slotted spoon and refresh under cold water. Set aside to drain.

3.   Cut the peppers into thin strips and blanch them in the same water for 1 minute. Drain and refresh.

FOR THE DRESSING
FOR THE DRESSING
1¼ cups **Mayonnaise**
     (see page 227)
1½ Tbs **tarragon** OR
        white wine vinegar
1½ Tbs **grainy mustard**
2 Tbs **chopped fresh
        tarragon**
1 small
   clove **garlic**, crushed
juice of 1 **lemon**
        salt and **pepper**

4. Prepare the dressing: Mix together the mayonnaise, tarragon vinegar, mustard, fresh tarragon, minced garlic, and lemon juice. Season to taste with salt and pepper. *(May be prepared up to 12 hours ahead to this point.)*

5. Final assembly: Set one Boston and one radicchio leaf on each plate to form a cup, slightly to one side of the centre. Fan the snow peas (or asparagus) on the other side. Toss the seafood in the dressing; divide it between the four lettuce cups. Garnish with the pepper strips and cherry tomatoes.

VEAL CARPACCIO

Serves 4.

6 to 8 oz **veal tenderloin**
chunk of **Parmesan cheese**
½ tsp   **freshly ground black
          pepper**

FOR THE DRESSING
1 clove **garlic**, cut in half
¼ tsp   **salt**
1 Tbs   **lemon juice**
4 Tbs   **extra virgin olive oil**
          (see page 133)

1. Cut the veal into 8 thin slices about ¼" thick. The best way is to have the butcher cut it on the meat slicer. The next-best way is to put the veal in the freezer until it firms up (but does not freeze), then slice it thinly with sharp knife.

2. Place each slice between two sheets of waxed paper or plastic wrap and pound it with a blunt instrument; then roll with a rolling pin until it is very thin and almost transparent. Leave the veal in the waxed paper; cover with plastic wrap and refrigerate until ready to proceed. *(May be prepared a few hours ahead to this point.)*

3. Stir the garlic, salt, and lemon juice together in a small bowl until the salt dissolves. Slowly beat in the olive oil.

4. Arrange the veal on the serving plates or platter: Remove the top layer of waxed paper and press the exposed piece of veal onto the plate; use the first piece of paper you removed to smooth the veal out on the plate. This operation is a little tricky as the meat is so thin that it can tear.

5. Use a vegetable peeler to cut shavings from the chunk of Parmesan – the longer the better.

6. To serve: Pour the dressing over and scatter with Parmesan and grated pepper.

VEAL AND BEEF CARPACCIO

Serves 4.

¼ lb	**veal tenderloin**
¼ lb	**beef tenderloin**
1 recipe	**Veal Carpaccio Dressing** (see page 35)
½ cup	**Creamy Shallot Dressing** (see page 226)
chunk of	**Parmesan cheese**

1.   Slice, pound, and flatten the veal and the beef. (See page 35 for instructions.)

2.   Prepare the veal carpaccio dressing and the creamy shallot dressing.

3.   To serve: Lay the beef on one side of the plate and the veal on the other. Spoon the creamy shallot dressing over the beef, and drizzle the veal dressing over the veal. Sprinkle with the shaved Parmesan.

QUAIL EGGS IN CUCUMBER NESTS

Serves 4 as a first course.

12 slices	**English cucumber**, ½″ thick
12	**fresh quail eggs**
3 Tbs	**butter**, at room temperature (see page 23)
1 Tbs	**fresh basil leaves**, cut in strips
2 tsp	**very finely chopped green onion**
1 tsp	**Dijon mustard**
1 tsp	**finely chopped parsley**

1.   Scoop out the cucumber rounds with a melon baller to make a little cup out of each, taking care not to cut through the bottom.

2.   Butter a large plate; set the cucumber slices on it.

3.   With a small sharp knife, cut the pointed end off a quail egg and pour the egg into the cucumber cup. (It's almost impossible to crack a quail egg the same way you would a hen egg.) Repeat with the rest of the eggs.

4.   Choose a large pot that the plate can sit on without tipping in; fill it half way with water and bring to a boil. Butter a large piece of foil; tightly cover the plate with the quail eggs, butter-side down.

5.   Set the plate on top of the pot and steam for 15 minutes.

6.   While the eggs are steaming, make the basil butter: combine the soft butter, basil, green onion, mustard, and parsley in a small bowl. Mix well.

7.   Remove the plate from the steamer (using gloves!). Uncover, dot the nests with the basil butter, and serve – with toast points if you like.

ARTICHOKES STUFFED WITH HERBS AND PARMESAN

You eat these artichokes in the traditional way, pulling off one leaf at a time and dipping it in the stuffing. When all the leaves are off, you cut away the choke and attack the bottom and the rest of the stuffing with a knife and fork.

Serves 4.

4 large	**fresh globe artichokes**
½	**lemon**
1 cup	**dry white wine**
½ cup	**water**

FOR THE STUFFING

1 cup	**finely chopped parsley**
1 cup	**finely chopped mint leaves**
¼ cup	**finely chopped fresh dill**
2 tsp	**finely chopped fresh thyme**
½ cup	**finely chopped fresh basil**
1 Tbs	**finely chopped garlic**
4 cups	**fresh white breadcrumbs**
½ cup	**extra virgin olive oil** (see page 133)
½ tsp	**salt**
1 cup	**grated Parmesan cheese**

1.   Put a large pot of water on to boil.

2.   Preheat the oven to 350° F.

3.   With a sharp knife, cut 1″ off the tops of the artichokes. Pull off any blemished leaves. Cut the stem close to the artichoke so that it will stand upright. With scissors, cut off the points of any leaves that still have them. Rub all the cut areas with the half lemon.

4.   When the water comes to a boil, put in the artichokes and the half lemon, and cook for 20 minutes. Drain, then stand the artichokes upside down so that the water can drain out.

5.   Make the stuffing by mixing all the herbs, breadcrumbs, oil, garlic, and Parmesan together.

6.   Set an artichoke right-side up on your work surface; spread the leaves open with your fingers to expose up the centre; fill the cavity with the stuffing mixture, pushing it between the leaves and packing it down. When all the artichokes are done, set them upright in a baking dish or roasting pan. Pour the white wine and water around them, cover the dish tightly with aluminum foil; bake in the preheated oven for 1½ hours, basting occasionally with the cooking liquid.

7.   Serve hot, at room temperature, or cold, with some of the cooking liquid spooned around them.

SPINACH SALAD WITH SWEET AND SOUR ONIONS AND CAMEMBERT FRITTERS

Deep-fried wedges of Camembert on spinach leaves with caramelized onions – a very good first-course salad.

Serves 4.

1 cup	**finely sliced onions**
1 Tbs	**olive oil**
1 Tbs	**red wine vinegar**
¼ tsp	**sugar**
1	**egg**
1 Tbs	**water**
½ cup	**flour**
1 cup	**breadcrumbs**
1	**Camembert cheese**, about 8 oz
3 cups	**vegetable oil**, for frying
1 package	**fresh spinach**, (10 oz) washed and dried

FOR THE DRESSING

¼ tsp	**salt**
2 tsp	**red wine vinegar**
1 tsp	**Dijon mustard**
6 Tbs	**extra virgin olive oil** (see page 133)

1. Sauté the onions on very low heat until they have given off all their water (about 20 minutes). Then turn up the heat and stir constantly until they start to turn light brown. Add 1 Tbs of vinegar and the sugar; stir until the vinegar has evaporated. Set aside to cool. Do not refrigerate.

2. Make the dressing: In a small bowl combine the salt, 2 tsp vinegar, and Dijon mustard. Slowly beat in the olive oil until it forms an emulsion.

3. Beat the egg and water together in a small bowl. Spread out the flour and breadcrumbs on separate plates.

4. Cut the Camembert into 12 wedges. One at a time, spear a wedge on a skewer or fork; roll it in the flour, then dip in the egg and roll in the breadcrumbs. Dip again in the egg and roll again in the breadcrumbs, making sure that the corners are well coated. Set to dry for 30 minutes on a plate sprinkled with crumbs.

5. Heat the oil in a deep, heavy pot to 350° F (see page 85). Fry the fritters 4 at a time until golden brown. Set aside on paper towel to drain. *(May be prepared up to 4 hours ahead to this point.)*

6. Preheat the oven to 350° F.

7. Reheat the fritters, uncovered, in the hot oven for 10 minutes.

8. Place the dried spinach in a large bowl and toss with the dressing.

9. To serve: Divide the spinach between 4 plates. Set 3 warm fritters on each serving. Sprinkle the onions over the top and serve immediately.

ARUGULA SALAD WITH WARM GORGONZOLA AND WALNUT TOASTS

Arugula (also called Rocket in North America) is a slightly bitter, aromatic herb that makes a wonderful addition to a green salad. In this recipe, it is used alone; the pronounced flavour of the herb is balanced by the strong flavours of the dressing and the Gorgonzola. A very classy salad to serve as the first course at an Italian dinner; or it could be the salad course after a plain roasted or grilled main course.

Serves 4.

3 bunches	**arugula**, stemmed, washed, and dried
1 clove	**garlic**, cut in half
1 Tbs	**balsamic vinegar** (see page 138)
¼ tsp	**salt**
3 Tbs	**extra virgin olive oil** (see page 133)
1 Tbs	**walnut oil**
12 slices	**bread** (should be quite substantial; Italian, Portuguese, sourdough, or even rye would be good)
6 Tbs	**crumbled Gorgonzola** (make sure it's not bitter)
3 Tbs	**coarsely chopped walnuts**

1. Wash and dry the arugula; put into a large salad bowl.

2. Mix the garlic clove, vinegar, and salt in a small bowl until the salt starts to dissolve. Slowly beat the oils into the vinegar; set aside.

3. Cut the bread slices into triangles about 3" on each side; lightly toast them on both sides.

4. Spread the toasts with Gorgonzola; press the walnut pieces into the cheese. *(May be prepared 30 minutes ahead to this point.)*

5. Remove the pieces of garlic clove from the dressing and pour it over the arugula. Toss well and divide between 4 plates.

6. Place Gorgonzola triangles under broiler or in very hot oven until hot – but try not to let the toast get too crispy. Place 3 toasts on top of each salad. Serve.

SMOKED SALMON MOUSSE WITH WATERCRESS MAYONNAISE

A light, elegant, and very attractive first course, especially in the summer.

Serves 8 as a first course.

1 recipe	**Smoked Salmon Mousse** (see page 30)
1 cup	**Mayonnaise** (see page 227)
1 bunch	**watercress**, large stems removed
2 to 4 Tbs	**yoghurt** OR **sour cream**
½	**lemon**, sliced

1. Prepare the mousse according to the recipe. Unmould and cut into ½" to ¾" slices. Lay one slice on each serving plate.

2. Make the mayonnaise; while it is still in the processor, add the washed and dried watercress leaves. Process until finely chopped. Add the yoghurt or sour cream, a tablespoon at a time, until it reaches a pouring consistency – like thick cream. Spoon the mayonnaise around the mousse, and garnish with a slice of lemon.

BOCCONCINI WITH RED AND YELLOW TOMATOES

A colourful variation on one of the simplest and best ways to start a summer dinner. This is the time to use your really good extra virgin olive oil; some people like to add a little balsamic vinegar – it goes wonderfully well with tomatoes.

Serves 2.

1 ripe	**red tomato**
1 ripe	**yellow tomato**
2	**bocconcini cheese** (buffalo-milk, from Italy if possible; you will only need 1)
3 Tbs	**extra virgin olive oil** (see page 133)
6 leaves	**fresh basil**, finely sliced **salt** and **freshly ground pepper**

1. Slice the tomatoes across into ¼″ slices; slice the bocconcini about the same thickness.

2. Arrange the slices on a platter or directly on serving plates, alternating red tomato, yellow tomato, bocconcini. Drizzle the extra virgin oil over everything, sprinkle with the sliced basil leaves. Pass the salt and pepper grinder.

KAREN'S PÂTÉ

We quite often get approached by people who have their own recipe for chicken-liver pâté and would like us to sell it in the shop. From time to time (Karen would say "invariably") I am persuaded to carry the pâté. In self-defence, Karen developed her own chicken-liver pâté: it is smooth and creamy, with just the right amount of chicken-liver taste (well, what else could I say?). I must confess that it also sells quite well.

3½ cups	**finely sliced white onions**
½ cup	**finely sliced shallots**
¾ cup	**finely sliced green onions**
3 Tbs	**oil**
¾ lb	**chicken livers**, cleaned
2 tsp	**salt**
½ tsp	**black pepper**
¾ cup	**unsalted butter**, softened (see page 23)
1 Tbs	**green peppercorns**, in brine

1. Preheat the oven to 375° F.

2. On low heat, sauté the onions, shallots, and green onions in the oil until soft and beginning to turn golden; this will take 20 to 30 minutes.

3. Clean and trim the livers; lay them out on a cookie sheet that will hold them without crowding. Bake for 15 minutes. Remove from oven, drain in a colander, and allow to cool.

4. Pour the cooked onions into the same colander and allow them to drain along with the livers.

5. Transfer the cooled livers and onions to the work bowl of a food processor; add the salt and pepper and process until very smooth. Add the softened butter and process until smooth again. Add the green peppercorns and pulse once or twice to distribute them (do not mash them – they should remain whole).

6. Line a 4-cup loaf pan with plastic wrap, letting enough hang over the edges to completely enclose the pâté later. Scrape the pâté into the pan; rap the pan several times on your work surface to remove air pockets. Smooth over the top with a spatula. *Cover with the plastic wrap and refrigerate for 4 hours, or overnight.*

7. To serve: Ease the pâté out of the pan with the plastic wrap on to a serving plate. Serve with crackers before dinner; or with fresh white toast as a first course.

WARM GOAT CHEESE SALAD WITH OLIVE TOASTS

Serves 4.

1 bunch	**watercress**
1 head	**escarole**
5 Tbs	**extra virgin olive oil** (see page 133)
2 cloves	**garlic**, sliced thin
¼ tsp	**salt**
2 tsp	**red wine vinegar**
¼ tsp	**black pepper**
½ lb	**soft unripened goat cheese** (see page 32)
12	**sage leaves**, in good condition
a bit more	**extra virgin olive oil**
12 slices	**French** OR **Italian stick**
4 Tbs	**black olive paste**

1. Wash and dry the watercress and escarole. Remove the large stems from the watercress; tear the escarole into bite-sized pieces; put the greens in a large bowl.

2. Sauté the garlic in the oil until pale gold. Remove from the heat; take out the garlic from the oil and put it in a small bowl. Add the salt to it and mash them together (it doesn't matter if it's a bit chunky). Stir in the vinegar, then slowly beat in the oil that the garlic was cooked in. Set aside.

3. Preheat the oven to 350°F.

4. Cut the goat cheese into 4 slices; lay them on a baking sheet. Press 3 sage leaves onto each slice and drizzle with a little oil.

5. Toast the bread rounds lightly (it's better if they are not too crispy).

6. Bake the cheese in the preheated oven for 4 minutes. While it is baking, spread the olive paste on the toasts: it looks good if you just cover half of one side with the paste, but feel free to do it the way you like. Toss the greens with dressing; divide them between 4 plates, carefully place one piece of cheese on each salad, surround it with 3 toasts, and serve immediately.

GOAT CHEESE BAKED IN PARCHMENT ON A ZUCCHINI LATTICE

This makes a light and dramatically attractive first course for a dinner party – it tastes good and it's surprisingly easy. It is made ahead of time, and alleviates some of the last-moment panic.

Serves 4.

6	**small zucchini**
1 Tbs	**extra virgin olive oil** (see page 133)
¼	**roasted red pepper** (see page 47)
¼	**roasted yellow pepper**
2 sheets	**parchment paper,** 18" by 26"
	salt and **pepper**

FOR THE GOAT CHEESE AND MARINADE

¼ lb	**goat cheese**, semi-ripened (see page 32)
4 Tbs	**extra virgin olive oil**
½ tsp	**finely chopped garlic**
½ tsp	**freshly ground black pepper**
1 tsp	**chopped fresh rosemary leaves**
1 tsp	**chopped fresh oregano** (or your own selection of herbs)

1. Preheat the oven to 350°F.

2. Prepare the zucchini: Trim off the ends, then cut each zucchini in half lengthwise, and each half in thin strips lengthwise. You should have 40 strips, each one about 3½" long by ⅓" wide.

3. Lightly oil a baking sheet; lay the zucchini slices on it, cover them with aluminum foil, and bake in the preheated oven for 8 minutes. Remove from the oven, take off the foil, and allow to cool.

4. Slice the peppers into very thin slices. Set aside. (You may blanch the thinly sliced peppers in boiling water for 1 minute instead of roasting if you prefer.)

5. Combine the olive oil, garlic, pepper, rosemary, and oregano in a medium bowl. Cut the cheese into two slices, then cut each slice in half (since most goat cheeses are cylindrical, you will end up with 4 half-moon-shaped pieces). Put them in the marinade and roll them around until well coated. Let them marinate while you do the lattices.

6. Cut out the parchment paper (see page 77). Now make the zucchini lattices: Lay 4 zucchini strips side by side in the middle of the paper, with about ⅓" between them. Take 4 or 5 more strips and weave them between the first four at right angles; it is slightly fiddly (but worth it). Set the first one aside while you make the rest.

7. Lay one piece of goat cheese on each zucchini lattice; scatter the pepper strips over the cheese, and pour over the marinade. Fold up the parchment envelopes. Set aside but do not refrigerate. *(May be prepared up to 6 hours ahead to this point.)*

8. Preheat the oven to 350°F.

9. Bake the parchment parcels in the preheated oven for 12 minutes.

10. To serve: Place the parcels on plates; cut them open with scissors (or unfold if using the Christmas-cracker method) so that the contents are exposed, and serve immediately with crusty bread.

Shrimp Wrapped in Chinese Cabbage with Beurre Blanc

This makes a good first course for a dinner; it is very attractive, and almost all the work can be done ahead. Although shrimp is expensive, you need only serve 3 shrimp per person.

Serves 4.

12	**16/20 shrimp**, peeled and deveined (see page 48)
1 tsp	**salt**
1 Tbs	**Dijon mustard**
2 tsp	**grainy mustard**
1 clove	**garlic**, crushed
4 Tbs	**lemon juice**
1 Tbs	**fresh tarragon** OR **basil**, chopped
3 drops	**Worcestershire Sauce**
12 leaves	**Chinese cabbage**
½ tsp	**salt**
¼ cup	**white wine**
1 recipe	**Beurre Blanc** (see page 224)

1. Bring a pot of water to a boil; salt it and put in the shrimp; cook for 1 minute only (they get cooked more later). Drain and refresh under cold water.

2. Combine the mustards, garlic, lemon juice, fresh herbs, and Worcestershire Sauce in a bowl. Mix well; add the cooled shrimp and toss to coat with the marinade. Refrigerate for a least 1 hour, or for up to 18 hours.

3. Bring a large pot of water to a boil. Add the salt, then plunge in the cabbage leaves. Cook for 1 minute; remove and refresh under cold water. Lay on paper towel to dry.

4. Lay a cabbage leaf flat on your work surface. Cut out the hard stem part. Place a shrimp in the middle of the leaf and wrap it up so that it is completely enclosed in a neat cabbage package. Do the same with the rest of the shrimp.

5. Place the shrimp packages in a pan or dish that can go in the oven, and pour in the wine. Cover the pan tightly with foil or its lid. *(May be prepared up to 12 hours ahead to this point.)*

6. Preheat the oven to 375°F.

7. Bake the shrimp in the preheated oven for 20 minutes.

8. Prepare the beurre blanc. NOTE: You may reduce the shrimp cooking liquid and use it instead of the wine in the beurre blanc.

9. To serve: Lift the shrimp from the baking dish onto paper towel to absorb the excess water. Transfer to warm plates, surround with the beurre blanc, and serve immediately.

WATERCRESS SALAD WITH CHICKEN LIVERS, BACON, AND HONEY MUSTARD DRESSING

Serves 4.

FOR THE SALAD AND DRESSING

2 bunches	**watercress,** large stems removed
1 Tbs	**honey**
2 tsp	**Dijon mustard**
1 tsp	**red wine vinegar**
¼ tsp	**salt**
2 Tbs	**extra virgin olive oil** (see page 133)
2 Tbs	**vegetable oil**
1 lb	**chicken livers**, cleaned
16 slices	**bacon**
1 cup	**finely sliced onion**
½ tsp	**salt**
¼ tsp	**black pepper**
12 large	**sage leaves**, sliced
2 Tbs	**sherry**

1. Wash and dry the watercress and put it in a large bowl.

2. Mix together the honey, mustard, vinegar, and salt; slowly beat in the oils. Set aside.

3. Trim all membrane and green spots from the chicken livers; cut each liver into 8 pieces. Set aside.

4. Cut the bacon slices in half. Heat a heavy frying pan on medium heat; fry the bacon until crisp, then remove from the pan. Pour off all the bacon fat except for 1 Tbs.

5. Add the sliced onions to the pan and sauté until lightly browned. Transfer to a plate, and put the pan back on the heat.

6. Turn the heat up to high; add the livers to the pan and cook until they feel firm to the touch – still pink inside (if they get hard they will be well done). Add the salt, pepper, sherry, the sliced sage leaves, bacon, and onions. Stir for a moment to get everything heated through.

7. To serve: Toss the watercress with the dressing, then divide between 4 plates; spoon the livers and bacon on top and serve immediately.

SEVICHE

A very refreshing summer first course in which the fish is effectively cooked by the action of the lime juice. You must start at least 24 hours ahead – longer if you wish.

Serves 6 as a first course.

1 lb	**sea scallops**
1 lb	**firm white fish** (Monkfish, sea bass, red snapper, etc. – all skin and bones removed)
¾ cup	**lime juice**
¼ cup	**olive oil**
	salt and **black pepper**
½ tsp	**chili paste** (Harissa, OR Oriental)
3 Tbs	**chopped coriander leaves**
½ tsp	**finely chopped fresh green chili** (optional: OR use any hot green chili)

FOR GARNISH

1	**roasted red pepper** (optional: see page 47)

1.   Slice the scallops into ⅛″ to ³⁄₁₆″ slices – they may be either rounds (if you cut across the grain) or slices (if you cut with the grain).

2.   Cut the fish into ½″ cubes. Combine the fish and scallops in a stainless-steel or porcelain bowl. Mix the lemon juice, olive oil, and chili paste together, pour over the fish, and toss well. *Cover and refrigerate for 24 hours or longer (up to 48 hours.)*

3.   Remove from fridge, add the chopped coriander and optional chili pepper. Season with salt and pepper. Serve on a lettuce leaf (or see serving suggestion below); garnish with strips of roasted red peppers.

VARIATION: SEVICHE IN AVOCADO HALVES

An attractive presentation of seviche – it also makes a little go a long way.

Serves 12 as a first course.

1 recipe	**Seviche** (see above)
6 ripe	**avocado pears** (Haas preferably)

1.   Prepare seviche as described above.

2.   When you are ready to serve, cut avocadoes in half, remove the stone and fill the cavity with seviche – the lime juice will help to prevent the flesh from turning brown.

PASTA, RISOTTO & GNOCCHI

FRESH AND DRIED PASTA

In North America, ever since we fell in love with fresh pasta, we have had a tendency to use it in every pasta recipe we come across. In Italy, where they have had more experience with these things, they have discovered over the years that for some dishes you will get better results using dried pasta than fresh. Really good fresh pasta is light all the way through, firm but evenly textured, with only a slight bite to it. It goes particularly well with creamy and heavier sauces and is generally used in wider widths (fettucine, papardelle), in some shapes (orechiette), and especially in filled pastas (ravioli, tortellini, and agnolotti).

Dried pasta has a firmer texture than fresh pasta and has a little more resistance at the very centre; it usually has a stronger flavour. As a general rule, a fine pasta such as capellini, spaghettini and spaghetti is much better dried than fresh. For one thing, it is very hard to find fresh pasta that will hold together when cut this finely. And even if it does hold, it will not have the firm texture and the slightly harder centre "nerve" that is so important for thin pasta. This "nerve" is what you are paying for when you buy expensive dried pasta – the ability of a pasta to hold a firm centre even after it has been sitting in the sauce on your plate for 5 or 10 minutes.

You can, of course, use whatever pasta you like, with whatever sauce you like. There are certain combinations of pasta and sauce that have withstood the test of time and are now established traditions: spaghetti carbonara (with pancetta, ham, eggs, and Parmesan cheese) and alle vongole (with clams), fettucine Alfredo (with cream and butter), and papardelle alla lepre (with hare sauce). But these are traditions not rules, and you can mix sauce and pasta to suit your taste.

HOW TO COOK PASTA

You cook fresh pasta and dried pasta in the same way; the latter just cooks longer. Put a large pot of water on to boil over high heat; for ½ pound of dried pasta or ¾ pound of fresh (enough for 3 people) you should have about 4 quarts (almost 4 litres) of water. When the water boils add salt – about 1 Tbs per 4 quarts. You can, if you wish, add 2 Tbs of oil – it may not do much to prevent the pasta sticking together, but it does help stop it boiling over. With the water at a full boil, put in the pasta. Separate fresh pasta a bit as it goes in. Hold dried pasta together in a bunch (or two if the bunch is more than an inch across) and push it down at an angle where the bottom of the pan joins the sides. As you press the pasta will curve around the bottom and you will be able to put it in without its breaking. Stir the pasta to stop it sticking to the bottom of the pan and to separate the dried pasta strands.

When it comes back to the boil, start timing. Fresh pasta takes from 2 to 5 minutes (some filled pasta takes longer, particularly tortellini); dried pasta takes from about 6 to 10 minutes. Most packages give approximate times but the only way to truly tell is by testing it. Lift out a strand and try it. Drain the pasta just before you think it is done because it will continue to cook a little after you drain it. Drain it in a large colander; DO NOT REFRESH IT IN COLD (or any other kind of) WATER – This is a capital offence in Italy; in Canada you will escape with your life, but not your reputation.

ROASTING PEPPERS
On a gas stove
Turn on the gas flame and place the pepper directly on the burner. The skin will get charred completely black – this is what you want. Turn the pepper with tongs from time to time, until it is completely charred all over. Remove from the heat and allow to cool. When cool, slip the charred skin off with the your fingers (it is a bit messy, but very effective). You can wipe it with a cloth to remove the last bits. Remove the core and seeds and proceed with the recipe.

On an electric stove
Turn an element on to high until it gets red hot. Choose a pepper with as even an exterior as possible. Put the pepper directly onto the element; it will become completely charred and blackened – not so evenly as it would on a gas stove, but it will still work. Turn with tongs until blackened all over. Proceed as outlined above.

BLACK FETTUCINE WITH SHRIMPS AND A LEMON CHAMPAGNE SAUCE

A very dramatic presentation; read the recipe and work out how you plan to serve it before you start.

Serves 6 as a first course, 4 as a main course.

12 spears	**asparagus**
½	**red pepper**
½	**yellow pepper**
1 Tbs	**butter** (see page 23)
4 Tbs	**finely chopped shallots**
24	**16/20 shrimp**, peeled and deveined (see below)
1 cup	**champagne** OR **dry white wine**
4 cups	**whipping cream**
3 Tbs	**lemon juice**
1½ Tbs	**very finely chopped lemon zest**
1 tsp	**salt**
⅛ tsp	**pepper**
1 lb	**black (squid ink) fettucine**

SHRIMP SIZES

Shrimp are sorted so that all the shrimp in a box are more or less the same size. The numbers – for example, 16/20 – refer to the number of shrimp required to make up one pound (in this case between 16 and 20 shrimp). The larger the shrimp the smaller the number; 4/6 is the largest regularly available (they weigh almost ¼ pound each); 51/60 is about as small as you will find – except for peeled salad shrimp.

---

1. Make the sauce first: Sauté the shallots in butter until translucent; add the peeled and deveined shrimp and sauté for 2 minutes until they change colour. Take out the shrimp and set aside.

2. Pour the champagne into the pan and reduce over high heat to 2 or 3 Tbs. Pour in the whipping cream, and cook down until it coats the back of a spoon heavily (you should have about 1½ to 2 cups of sauce). Add the lemon juice, lemon zest, salt, and pepper. Set aside.

3. Bring a large pot of water to a boil. Peel the asparagus (if large) and cut into 2″ lengths. Blanch in the boiling water for 4 minutes; scoop out and refresh under cold water. Cut the peppers into strips, blanch for 1 minute and refresh. Dry them well. *(May be prepared up to 12 hours ahead to this point.)*

4. Reheat the cream sauce over a low heat.

5. Bring a large pot of water to a boil; salt it and put in the pasta. Cook until just al dente (2 to 5 minutes for fresh; 6 to 10 for dried). Drain.

6. To serve: For the most dramatic presentation, serve the white sauce over the black pasta, with the shrimp and vegetables standing out on top. As soon as the pasta is ready, toss it in butter and oil in the pan in which it was cooked; this will stop the pasta sticking together. At the same time, heat a frying pan, add 1 Tbs butter, and sauté the vegetables and shrimp until heated through (about 3 minutes). Put the pasta on the warm plates, pour over the sauce, and arrange the shrimp and vegetables on top.

7. For a less-dramatic presentation (one that is less fiddly at the last moment), reheat the sauce, add the shrimp and vegetables until heated through, then put the drained pasta into the sauce and toss it well. Transfer to the heated plates and serve.

FETTUCINE WITH ASPARAGUS, PROSCIUTTO, GORGONZOLA, AND CREAM

A deliciously rich and creamy pasta dish. Good for a winter lunch or first course for dinner.

Serves 4.

1 Tbs	**butter** (see page 23)
3 Tbs	**finely diced prosciutto** (see page 53)
2 cups	**whipping cream**
8 oz	**Gorgonzola cheese**, cut in ½″ cubes
½ tsp	**salt**
½ tsp	**black pepper**
8 oz	**asparagus**, peeled and cut into 1″ pieces (see below)
2 tsp	**salt**
1 lb	**fresh fettucine**

1. Put a large pot of water on to boil.

2. Sauté prosciutto in the butter until lightly brown. Add the cream; boil over high heat until reduced to 1 cup.

3. Add the Gorgonzola and stir until it melts; stir in the salt and pepper; keep warm.

4. Add 2 tsp salt to the pasta water; add the asparagus pieces; bring the water back to a boil and cook for 1 minute.

5. Now add the fettucine to the asparagus; bring the water back to the boil again and cook for 2 to 3 minutes, until just done. Drain everything but do not rinse.

6. Bring the sauce to a boil; add the pasta to the sauce and toss everything together well. Serve.

PEELING ASPARAGUS

Some would say that only fanatics peel asparagus; in fact, peeling it is more economical, because you can eat so much more of the stem; and it certainly makes for a more attractive presentation. However, it's probably only worth peeling medium and thick stalks; the very thin ones are tender enough as is. With a good vegetable or potato peeler it is not difficult: Lay the asparagus flat on your cutting board; hold the tip end and peel away from you, towards the stem, taking a good amount off (about as much as you would peel off a potato). Rotate the asparagus so that you peel it all round. Finally, break or cut off the bottom of the stem, where it is clearly too woody to be any good. Prepared this way, the stem needs no more cooking time than the tips, and the stalks can be cooked lying on their sides.

SPAGHETTINI WITH RAPINI, GARLIC, AND OLIVE OIL

A pasta dish for those who like the pronounced flavours of country food.

Serves 6 to 8 as a first course, 4 as a main course.

½ cup	**extra virgin olive oil** (see page 133)
2 cloves	**garlic**, sliced
2	**anchovy filets**, finely chopped
¼ tsp	**red pepper flakes**
2 tsp	**salt**
1 lb	**dried spaghettini**
2 lbs	**rapini**, large stems removed, flowers and leaves reserved, washed, and drained

1. Put a large pot of water on to boil.

2. Sauté the garlic in the olive oil until it turns pale gold: don't overcook, as it burns easily. Add the chopped anchovy filets and stir until they dissolve. Then add the red pepper flakes.

3. Add 2 tsp salt to the boiling water. Put in the pasta, bring the water back to a boil, and cook for 4 minutes.

4. Add the rapini leaves and flowers to the pasta pot. Cook another 3 to 5 minutes, until barely done. Remove ½ cup of the cooking liquid and reserve. Drain the pasta and rapini – do not rinse.

5. Pour the olive oil and anchovy mixture into the pasta cooking pot; set over medium-high heat. Add the reserved pasta cooking water, then the pasta and rapini. Cook, stirring constantly, until the water is absorbed and the oil starts to sizzle. Serve on warmed plates.

BUCKWHEAT LINGUINI WITH PUTANESCA SAUCE

Serves 6 as a first course, 4 as a main course.

1½ lbs	**fresh buckwheat linguini** OR
1 lb	**dried wholewheat spaghetti**
2 tsp	**salt**
2 Tbs	**olive oil**
½ cups	**Parmesan cheese**, freshly grated

FOR THE SAUCE

2 cups	**Basic Tomato Sauce** (see page 223)
¼ cup	**olive oil**
½ cup	**finely chopped onion**

1. Prepare the tomato sauce, following the recipe; frozen, bottled, or canned sauce may be used if you don't have time.

2. Sauté onion, garlic, and pancetta until the garlic is pale gold.

3. Add the capers, olives, sundried tomatoes, tomato sauce, and pepper flakes; bring the mixture to a boil. Reduce the heat and cook, stirring occasionally, for 15 minutes.

4. Bring a large pot of water to a boil; add salt and oil. Put in the pasta, bring back to a boil, and cook until just done (2 to 5 minutes for fresh; 6 to 10 minutes for dried).

1 tsp	**finely chopped garlic**
¼ cup	**finely chopped pancetta** OR **prosciutto** (see page 53)
1 Tbs	**capers**, drained
⅓ cup	**black olives**, pitted and halved
⅓ cup	**green olives**, pitted and halved
2 Tbs	**sundried tomatoes**, chopped
½ tsp	**dried red pepper flakes**

5. Drain the pasta, but do not rinse. Pour the sauce into a large heated bowl, add the pasta, and stir to coat. You can put the pasta directly into the sauce pot, if not serving at the table.

6. Serve with freshly grated Parmesan cheese.

PENNE WITH SMOTHERED SCALLOPS, TOMATOES, AND BASIL

"Smothering" refers to the way the scallops are cooked by putting them in the pot with the hot pasta and sauce. The end result has the heavenly aroma of tomato, garlic, olive oil, and basil; and the scallops are cooked to perfection.

Serves 6 as a first course, 4 as a main course.

2 28 oz cans	**Italian tomatoes**
1 lb	**sea scallops**, thawed
⅔ cup	**extra virgin olive oil** (see page 133)
1 Tbs	**finely chopped garlic**
¼ tsp	**hot pepper flakes**
1 tsp	**salt**
1 tsp	**Grated Lemon Zest** (see page 237)
1 lb	**dried penne**
½ cup	**fresh basil leaves**
2 Tbs	**chopped Italian parsley**
4 Tbs	**freshly grated Parmesan cheese**

1. Put a large pot of water on to boil.

2. Drain the tomatoes and remove most of the seeds; cut off the hard stem ends and chop the flesh coarsely.

3. Slice the scallops into thin rounds, about ¼″ thick. Place in a small bowl with the grated lemon rind, and set aside.

4. Sauté the garlic in the oil over medium heat until very pale gold – do not let it burn. Add the chopped tomatoes, salt, and hot pepper flakes. Simmer over low heat for 5 minutes.

5. When the water boils, salt it and put in the pasta. Bring back to a boil and cook for 7 to 9 minutes, until barely done. Drain and add immediately to the pasta sauce. Stir to coat with the sauce. Add the basil leaves, chopped parsley, and scallops, and stir gently.

6. Cover the pot with a piece of aluminum foil and then with the lid, so that no steam can escape. Remove the pot from the heat, and let it stand for 3 or 4 minutes – no peeking!

7. Remove the lid, stir in the Parmesan, and serve immediately on hot plates.

TORTELLINI WITH CREAM AND SPICY SAUSAGE

A quick and simple supper.

Serves 6 as a first course, 4 as a main course.

4	**hot Italian sausages** (about 1 lb)
1 Tbs	**butter** (see page 23)
1 lb	**tortellini**, veal or cheese
2 cups	**whipping cream**
1 cup	**grated Parmesan cheese**

1. Put a large pan of water on to boil.

2. With a sharp knife, slit the sausage skins down one side; carefully remove the skins from the meat and discard. Chop the meat finely (I know it's already ground, but it still somehow manages to stick together).

3. Melt the butter in a large frying pan or saucepan and sauté the sausage meat until it changes colour. Add the cream, bring it to a boil, reduce the heat, and simmer until slightly thickened.

4. Add salt to the water, put in the tortellini, bring it back to the boil and cook for 10 to 12 minutes, until tender. Drain well.

5. Add ½ cup of Parmesan cheese to the cream and sausage; stir to incorporate, then add the drained tortellini. Stir for a minute or two until heated through. Serve in warm soup plates. Pass the rest of the Parmesan cheese separately.

VEGETABLE LASAGNE WITH BUTTERNUT SQUASH

I am not sure why people speak of lasagna in such an off-hand manner. There is certainly nothing off-hand about preparing it; it involves at least three quite time-consuming steps. But a good lasagna is well worth expending a few calories on – and this one is particularly good.

Serves 8 or more.

3 Tbs	**olive oil**
½ cup	**finely chopped onion**
½ cup	**chopped prosciutto** (see page 53)
4 cups	**peeled and diced butternut squash**
2 Tbs	**finely chopped Italian parsley**
1 tsp	**salt**
½ tsp	**black pepper**
8 sheets	**fresh pasta**, 10″ by 12″ (red-pepper pasta would be a good choice)

1. Sauté the onion and prosciutto in the oil until the prosciutto changes colour. Add the squash and stir well. Reduce the heat to low, cover tightly and cook until the squash is tender but not mushy (about 40 minutes). Stir in the parsley, salt, and pepper, and set aside to cool.

2. Bring a large pot of water to the boil, salt it, then cook 2 sheets of pasta at a time until tender (about 2 to 4 minutes, depending on thickness). When cooked, remove the pasta to a large pan of iced water to cool.

3 cups	**Béchamel Sauce** (see page 224)
3 cups	**Basic Tomato Sauce** (see page 223)
1 cup	**freshly grated Romano cheese** (use Parmesan if you can't find it)

PROSCIUTTO
Prosciutto is a fresh leg of pork that is dry-cured with salt and spices. It is not smoked. It is boned and then left to hang in a cool, dry place for 3 to 6 months. In Europe it is called Parma ham, after the geographical centre of its production. Pancetta is side of pork cured in the same way; and capicolla is the boned shoulder.

---

3.   Choose a baking dish close to the same size as the pasta. Spread ⅓ cup of tomato sauce on the bottom of the baking dish; dry the pasta and lay it on top. Spread with ⅓ cup tomato sauce, then about ⅐ of the squash, followed by ⅓ cup of béchamel, and 4 Tbs of grated cheese. Keep layering in this order until all the pasta sheets are used up; cover the top layer with béchamel and dot with tomato sauce. *(May be prepared up to 2 days ahead to this point.)*

4.   Preheat the oven to 350° F.

5.   Cover the lasagna tightly with foil; bake for 20 minutes, then remove the tin foil and bake for 25 minutes longer. Remove from the oven and allow to set for 15 minutes in a warm place before serving.

SPAGHETTINI "FENICE" WITH TOMATOES, GARLIC, AND BASIL

A very simple but intensely flavoured tomato sauce for fine dried pasta, given to me by Luigi of "La Fenice" restaurant. In the summer you can make it with very ripe fresh tomatoes. At any time of year the Italian canned ones give an excellent result.

Serves 6 as a first course; 4 as a main course.

2 28 oz cans	**Italian plum tomatoes**
¾ cup	**extra virgin olive oil** (see page 133)
1 tsp	**chopped garlic**
18 leaves	**fresh basil**, washed
1 lb	**dried spaghettini**

1.   Put a large pot of water on to boil.

2.   Drain the tomatoes and remove as many of the seeds as you can. Chop the tomatoes coarsely and set aside.

3.   Heat the olive oil in heavy pan; add the chopped garlic and cook over medium heat until pale golden brown; quickly put in the tomatoes (this will stop the garlic browning any further) and continue to cook for 2 minutes. Throw in the washed whole basil leaves and stir.

4.   Salt the pasta water, put in the spaghettini and cook for about 4 minutes (depending on thickness) until "al dente". Drain well and pour into the tomato sauce. Toss to coat the pasta with the sauce and serve in warmed soup plates. It does not really need Parmesan cheese.

Tagliatelle with Fresh Salmon, Crème Fraîche, and Chives

This rich and elegant pasta dish has a wonderful, fresh salmon flavour. The salmon is cut in such thin strips that the heat of the pasta is enough to cook it.

Serves 6 as a first course, 4 as a main course.

10 oz	**fresh salmon**, skin and bones removed
1½ cups	**Crème Fraîche** (see page 226)
1 tsp	**salt**
2	**egg yolks**
½ cup	**Crème Fraîche**
½ cup	**freshly grated Parmesan cheese**
4 Tbs	**finely chopped chives**
1 tsp	**finely chopped lemon zest** (see page 237)
1 tsp	**black pepper**, ground
1 Tbs	**Italian parsley**
2 tsp	**salt**
1 Tbs	**oil**
1 pound	**fresh tagliatelle** (could be a mix of flavours – spinach, saffron, and red pepper would be very good)

1. Put a large pot of water on to boil.

2. Cut the salmon into thin slices, then cut each slice into strips.

3. Choose a saucepan large enough to hold the cooked pasta. Bring 1½ cups of crème fraîche to a boil, add the salt, and turn down the heat to a simmer.

4. In a small bowl, beat the egg yolks with ½ cup crème fraîche; add the Parmesan, chives, lemon zest, pepper, and parsley; and stir to mix. Set aside.

5. Add 2 tsp salt and the oil to the boiling water. Put in the pasta, bring the water back to the boil and cook until just done (3 to 5 minutes for fresh pasta). Drain in a large colander.

6. Immediately, add hot pasta to the pan of simmering crème fraîche. Stir to coat with the sauce. Then add the egg and cream mixture, and stir to mix. Finally, add the salmon strips and stir gently.

7. Serve immediately in warm plates or bowls.

PASTA SALADS

While pasta salads are not part of the Italian repertoire, they can be delicious. Dried pasta will work better than fresh because it will hold a firm texture longer.

SALAD OF CONCHIGLIE WITH TUNA

Conchiglie are shell-shaped pasta.

Serves 6.

1 lb	**dried shell pasta**
3 Tbs	**red wine vinegar**
¼ tsp	**salt**
½ tsp	**black pepper**
2	**anchovy filets**, chopped
1 tsp	**finely chopped garlic**
1 cup	**extra virgin olive oil** (see page 133)
1 Tbs	**capers**, drained
1 Tbs	**black olive paste**
1 cup	**pitted green olives**
1 cup	**coarsely chopped parsley**
½ cup	**basil leaves**, finely sliced
2 cans	**tuna**, packed in water
½	**English cucumber**
½ cup	**freshly grated Parmesan cheese**

1. Bring a large pot of water to a boil; add salt and cook the shells until tender. Drain and cool under cold water. Drain again.

2. Stir together the vinegar, salt, pepper, anchovies, and garlic. Slowly beat in the olive oil. Stir in the capers, olive paste, pitted olives, parsley, basil, and tuna. Toss this mixture with the cooled pasta, and allow to sit for ½ hour for the flavours to blend. *(May be made up to a day ahead; refrigerate.)*

3. Cut the cucumber in half lengthwise, scoop out the seeds, and then slice across into thin half-moons. Add the cucumber and Parmesan to the salad, toss again and serve.

FUSILLI WITH TOMATO BUTTERMILK DRESSING

Our regular pasta salad in the store; creamy but not excessively rich.

Serves 8.

5 large	**ripe tomatoes**
1 cup	**Mayonnaise** (see page 227)
1 tsp	**salt**
¼ tsp	**black pepper**
1½ tsp	**finely chopped garlic**
1¼ cups	**buttermilk**
1 lb	**dried fusilli** (stands up better to sitting in sauce)
1 large	**tomato**, cut into ½" cubes
½ cup	**fresh basil leaves**, washed

1. Place the tomatoes in the work bowl of a food processor; process until completely puréed.

2. Add the mayonnaise, salt, pepper, garlic, and buttermilk. Process again until you have a smooth sauce.

3. Bring a large pot of water to a boil; salt it. Put in the pasta and cook, stirring occasionally to stop the strands sticking together, for 8 to 10 minutes, until al dente. Drain and rinse under cold water; allow to drain.

4. When the pasta is drained, combine with the dressing in a large bowl. Slice the basil leaves finely; add them and the tomatoes to the dressing. Allow to sit for 30 minutes before serving for the flavours to blend.

THAI BEEF NOODLE SALAD

A really excellent and very popular salad.

Serves 4.

2 Tbs	**vegetable oil**
2 tsp	**finely chopped garlic**
½ lb	**capellini noodles**, broken in half
½ cup	**Springroll Sauce** (see page 229)
2 Tbs	**lemon juice**
1 Tbs	**Thai fish sauce** (see page 114)
1 lb	**flank steak**
1 Tbs	**oyster sauce** (see page 114)
1 tsp	**black pepper**
4	**green onions**, cut into 3″ lengths
½	**English cucumber**, peeled and seeded, cut in 2″ lengths
½ cup	**fresh coriander leaves**
½ cup	**fresh mint leaves**

1. Sauté the garlic in the oil over low heat until just golden; remove from the heat and allow to cool.

2. Bring a large pot of water to a boil; cook the noodles until just tender. Drain and transfer to a large bowl. Pour in the garlic oil and toss to coat. Add the springroll sauce, lemon juice, and fish sauce; toss again.

3. Preheat the broiler or barbecue for 15 minutes.

4. Rub the flank steak with the oyster sauce and black pepper. Broil or barbecue until cooked rare (no more than medium rare, if you must). Allow to cool for 20 minutes.

5. Cut the green onions into 3″ lengths, then lengthwise into thin strips; cut the cucumber halves into 2″ lengths, then into thin strips lengthwise. Add them to the noodles, along with the coriander and mint leaves.

6. Slice the flank steak lengthwise (with the grain) into 1″ strips, then across the grain into very thin slices; add them to the noodles. Toss well. (*This may be made ahead; it will keep for 2 days in the fridge.*)

PENNE WITH CHICKEN, SHRIMP, AND ROUILLE

A cold pasta dish that makes an excellent summer lunch; rouille is a red pepper and garlic mayonnaise that is delicious with fish and seafood.

Serves 4.

½ lb	**penne**
2	**boneless chicken breasts**
2 cups	**small shrimp**, peeled and deveined

1. Roast, peel, and seed the red peppers (see page 47).

2. Place 2 of the peppers in the work bowl of a food processor and process with the salt until smoothly puréed. Add the pepper, garlic, mayonnaise, balsamic vinegar, and Tabasco; process again until smooth. Scoop it out into a large mixing bowl.

3. Bring a large pot of water to a boil; salt it and put in the pasta. Bring back to a boil and cook for 7 to 9 minutes until cooked. Drain and refresh under cold water. Toss the pasta as it cools so that it doesn't stick together.

FOR THE ROUILLE

4 large	**red peppers**
1½ tsp	**salt**
¼ tsp	**ground black pepper**
1 tsp	**finely chopped garlic**
1½ cups	**Mayonnaise** (see page 227)
2 Tbs	**balsamic vinegar** (see page 138)
8 drops	**Tabasco Sauce**

4. Cook the chicken breasts: They can be poached in simmering (not boiling!) water for 8 minutes; *or* placed on a baking sheet covered with foil and baked for 17 minutes in a 350°F oven; *or* you can use left-over chicken as long as it is not greasy. Cut into thin slices.

5. Cook the shrimp (if not pre-cooked): Poach in lightly salted water for 2 minutes. Drain and cool.

6. Cut the remaining 2 roasted red peppers into strips.

7. Combine the chicken, shrimp, and peppers with the sauce. Stir so that everything is well coated. Allow to stand for 30 minutes so that the flavours can develop. Serve with a good French or Italian bread.

SINGAPORE SHRIMP NOODLE SALAD

A very good and colourful salad; you can use chicken, pork, or shrimp – or any combination thereof.

Serves 6.

1 lb	**dried linguini,** broken in half
2 tsp	**salt**
½ cup	**vegetable oil**
2 Tbs	**curry powder**
2 Tbs	**oyster sauce** (see page 114)
2 Tbs	**lemon juice**
3 cups	**cooked salad shrimp**
½ cup	**red pepper julienne strips**
½ cup	**green pepper julienne strips**
½ cup	**carrot julienne strips**
¾ cup	**green onion julienne strips**
¼ cup	**coarsely chopped coriander leaves**

1. Bring a large pot of water to a boil; add the salt and cook the noodles until "al dente"; drain and cool under cold water. (In normal circumstances this is a crime of the worst description; Italians will tell you that a pasta salad is not a normal circumstance.)

2. Heat the curry powder and oil over low heat until the curry smells fragrant. Remove from the heat and allow to cool.

3. Pour the curry-oil mixture, oyster sauce, and lemon juice over the cooled noodles and toss well. Put in the shrimp, red and green pepper strips, carrot strips, green onion, and coriander leaves. Toss the salad well.

Pasta E Fagioli (Pasta and Beans)

The very antithesis of nouvelle cuisine; but one of the very best examples of Italian country cooking. It is more a soup than a pasta dish and should be eaten with a spoon out of a (large) bowl.

Serves 6 to 8.

1½ cups	**fresh Romano beans** OR
1 large can	**Romano beans** OR
¾ cup	**dried Romano beans**
½ cup	**finely chopped carrot**
½ cup	**finely chopped celery**
1 cup	**finely chopped onion**
1 tsp	**finely chopped garlic**
1 Tbs	**finely chopped parsley**
2 Tbs	**extra virgin olive oil** (see page 133)
10 cups	**chicken** OR **beef stock**
28 oz can	**Italian plum tomatoes**
1 slice	**prosciutto,** ¼" thick (see page 53)
1 piece	**Parmesan cheese rind**
½ lb	**short dried pasta**
	salt and **pepper**
Serve with	**grated Romano cheese** (use Parmesan if not available)
	Olio Santo (see page 230) OR
	extra virgin olive oil

1. If using dried beans, soak them overnight in cold water in a large bowl. The next day, cover with fresh water, bring to a boil, and simmer until tender, 1½ to 3 hours (the time will depend on the age of the beans).

2. If using fresh beans, cover with cold water, bring them to a boil, and cook at a steady boil until the beans are tender (30 to 45 minutes). Drain and set aside.

3. Sauté the diced carrots, celery, onion, garlic, and parsley in the oil until lightly browned.

4. Drain the canned tomatoes, and push them through a sieve; add them to the vegetables, along with the stock, slice of prosciutto, and Parmesan rind. Bring to a boil, then reduce the heat to a simmer. Cook for 1 hour, stirring occasionally.

5. If using fresh or dried beans, add them now and simmer for 1 hour longer. If using canned beans, add them after it has simmered for the full 2 hours.

6. Bring a large pot of water to a boil, salt it, and add the pasta; cook until "al dente". Drain them and add to the soup. Cook until heated through.

7. Serve in deep bowls; pass the cheese and the "olio santo" (or straight extra virgin olive oil) – everybody adds a couple of tablespoons to the soup.

RISOTTO

Risotto is one of the great dishes of the world. It deserves to have the popularity that pasta now has – and perhaps one day it will. The only thing that stands in its way is that it is a little time-consuming to prepare, and requires a bit of experience to cook it properly.

The trick to risotto is knowing what the consistency of the finished dish should be. Once you know that, you can make a perfect risotto every time. The best way that I can describe it is that it should look like a rather loose rice pudding. It should not be too soupy, but that is certainly better than being too dry. It is really not at all difficult to make; you just keep cooking it and adding more stock until the rice is done.

Once made, it must be eaten right away: it is almost impossible to keep a risotto standing, because the rice continues to absorb liquid and the consistency changes even as you look at it. Some recipes will tell you that you can keep it warm for half an hour or so; but it is not the same as eating straight from the stove. This is a dish for good friends who will sit down when you tell them to and appreciate that what you have made is not just another plate of rice.

RISOTTO WITH PORCINI MUSHROOMS

You can make this risotto with or without the saffron; personally I think the saffron adds the touch of perfection.

Serves 4.

1 oz	**dried porcini mushrooms** (see page 83)
1 recipe	**Risotto Milanese** (see page 60)

1. Put the porcini in a small bowl, pour boiling water over them, and allow to soak for 20 minutes. Remove the mushrooms, rinse them under warm water, and cut off any parts that are very hard. Chop them coarsely. Strain the soaking liquid through cheesecloth or a paper filter into a saucepan.

2. Pour the chicken stock into the saucepan with the mushroom liquid, add the onion and saffron, and proceed with the recipe for Risotto Milanese. The chopped porcini should be added to the risotto about halfway through the cooking.

RISOTTO MILANESE

The classic version from Milan, flavoured with saffron and chicken stock. Since the rice absorbs so much liquid the flavour of your stock is important. But please, make it with good old stock cubes if that is all you have – stock-cube risotto is a lot better than none at all.

Serves 4 as a first course or accompaniment to the main course.

5 cups	**Chicken Stock** (see page 226)
1 medium	**onion**, peeled
¼ gram	**saffron**
1 clove	**garlic**, finely chopped
1 medium	**onion**, finely chopped
1 Tbs	**butter** (see page 23)
1¼ cups	**Arborio rice** (see page 61)
½ cup	**freshly grated Parmesan**

1. Bring the chicken stock to a boil in a saucepan; add the onion and the saffron. Keep it simmering over low heat while you proceed with the recipe.

2. In a good-size heavy-bottom pot, sauté the garlic and onion in butter over medium heat until translucent; add the rice and stir to coat with the butter.

3. Ladle about 1 cup of the hot stock into the rice and stir until it stops bubbling. Let it cook for a minute or two, stir again, and add more stock as soon as the first batch has been almost absorbed.

4. Keep stirring, cooking, and adding more stock; the heat should be high enough that it bubbles all the time, but not so high that it is continually sticking to the bottom of the pan (some sticking is inevitable, particularly towards the end).

5. Add the liquid in smaller amounts as you go on. If you run out of stock before the risotto is done, finish it with plain water.

6. The total cooking time will be about 30 minutes; you can only tell if it is done by testing it. There should be just the slightest "bite" to the very centre of the grain – but it should not be hard.

7. Serve immediately with freshly grated Parmesan cheese. It may be simple – but there are few things like it.

RISOTTO WITH BEETS

A risotto with a beautiful deep red colour. For more detailed instructions on how to make it, refer to the recipe for Risotto Milanese (page 60).

Serves 4 as a main course, or 6 as a first.

1 Tbs	**butter** (see page 23)
1 Tbs	**olive oil**
1 medium	**white onion,** finely chopped
1½ cups	**finely chopped beets,** raw
2 cups	**Arborio rice** (see below)
8 cups	**Chicken Stock** (see page 226)
1 tsp	**salt**
2 tsp	**Grated Lemon Zest** (see page 237)
4 Tbs	**Crème Fraîche** (see page 226) OR **whipping cream**
½ cup	**freshly grated** **Parmesan**

1. Sauté the onion in the butter and oil until translucent. Add the finely diced beets and stir to coat. Cover with the lid, turn down the heat, and cook gently until the beets are almost tender (about 15 minutes).

2. Bring the chicken stock to a simmer on the back of the stove. Stir the rice into the beets, turn the heat up to medium, and start to add the stock.

3. Follow steps 3 to 6 in the Risotto Milanese recipe (page 60), adding stock and stirring until the rice is done. Bear in mind that you are going to stir in Parmesan cheese just before you serve, and it will absorb quite a bit of liquid, so keep it more soupy than normal.

4. Stir in the crème fraîche (or whipping cream), lemon rind, and Parmesan cheese. Serve immediately.

ARBORIO RICE

Arborio rice is a short-grain rice grown in the Po valley in northern Italy. It is valued for its ability to absorb a large amount of liquid without the rice becoming mushy. If the liquid has a nice flavour, then so will the rice. "Superfino" is the best grade of Arborio. There are also other rices that have similar qualities, such as Vialone, but they are not easy to find, and are little, if any, better than Arborio.

GNOCCHI

Gnocchi, like pasta, is a word that covers a multitude of things. Broadly speaking, gnocchi are made from either potatoes or flour (wheat or semolina), butter, eggs, and milk. They range from light and delicate potato puffs to quite solid semolina cakes. They are usually baked before serving, often with a sauce (although this may be nothing more complicated than melted butter and cheese). They may be served as a first course, or as the accompaniment to the meat course.

GNOCCHI PARISIENNE

This is one of the lightest gnocchi recipes, more French in style (as its name implies) than Italian. The recipe is very similar to that for Choux Pastry (see page 231).

Serves 4 as a main course; 6 as a first.

1 cup	**milk**
6 Tbs	**butter**
	(see page 23)
1 cup	**all-purpose flour**
½ tsp	**salt**
¼ tsp	**pepper**
pinch of	**nutmeg**
5 large	**eggs**

FOR THE SAUCE

2 tsp	**butter**
2 Tbs	**finely chopped shallots**
1 clove	**finely chopped garlic**
¼ cup	**white wine**
4 cups	**whipping cream**
	salt and **pepper**
pinch of	**nutmeg**
¼ cup	**grated Gruyère cheese**
¼ cup	**grated Parmesan cheese**

1. Bring the milk, butter, salt, pepper, and nutmeg to a boil in a saucepan over medium heat. As soon as it boils, put in the flour all at once. Stir until the mixture comes away from the sides of the pan and starts to form a ball. Remove from the heat and allow to cool. (This mixture is called a panade.)

2. Bring a large pot of water to a boil; salt it. Spoon the panade into a piping bag fitted with a ½" plain tip. Pipe 2" lengths directly into the water, using a knife to cut them off. Cook until they float up to the surface, then scoop them out with a slotted spoon, and drain on paper towel.

3. Make the sauce: Sauté the shallot and garlic in butter over medium heat until soft and translucent. Turn up the heat and pour in the white wine; cook until reduced to 2 or 3 Tbs. Pour in the whipping cream and reduce until it coats the back of a spoon heavily. Season with nutmeg, salt, and pepper. Set aside.

4. Preheat the oven to 375° F. Butter a large baking dish.

5. Arrange the drained gnocchi in the baking dish. Pour over the cream sauce, and sprinkle the grated cheeses on top. Bake in preheated oven for 20 minutes, until the cheese is melted and the gnocchi have puffed.

GNOCCHI ALLA ROMANA

Makes 10 to 12 gnocchi—enough for 3 for a first course or as an accompaniment to the main course.

2 cups	**milk**
1 cup	**semolina flour** OR **Cream of Wheat**
1 tsp	**salt**
¼ tsp	**pepper**
pinch of	**nutmeg**
1	**egg yolk**
1 Tbs	**butter** (see page 23)
½ cup	**grated Parmesan cheese**
½ cup	**grated Gruyère cheese**

1.   Rinse out a saucepan with water, pour in the milk, and bring to a boil; pour in the semolina (or Cream of Wheat), salt, pepper, and nutmeg. Cook over medium heat, stirring constantly until the panade (which is what the mixture is called) comes away from the side of the pan and starts to form a ball. Remove from the heat, and beat in the egg yolk, butter, and Parmesan.

2.   Turn the panade out of the pan onto a baking sheet; with a wet spatula or palette knife spread it as evenly as you can, about ½″ thick. Allow to cool.

3.   Cut the gnocchi into shapes (circles are traditional; squares are more economical) about 2″ across. They should be quite firm.

4.   *EITHER* melt the butter in a frying pan and sauté the gnocchi on both sides until lightly browned; *OR* arrange circles or squares in a baking dish; dot with butter and sprinkle with cheese. Bake in 400°F oven for 15 minutes.

5.   To serve: They may be served directly from the frying pan; or arrange the sautéed gnocchi on a baking sheet. Sprinkle with the grated Gruyère and broil until lightly browned.

PIZZA & FLATBREADS

Pizza is no longer just for kids. It has come upscale in a big way; today you can find gourmet pizza in restaurants, fast-food outlets, and even for home delivery. There is no doubt that some of the topping combinations require an act of faith from the eater (there being no logical foundation for them), but the same could be said of sausages, pancakes, and maple syrup – a combination unknown in England when I was growing up. When I was served it on a plane years ago, I thought it was just one more eccentricity of airline cuisine. I have since converted. So, why not mango and smoked salmon pizza?

With all this good pizza available, it is reasonable to question whether there is any point in making it yourself. When you are looking for a quick snack after the movies, probably not. But if you are having, say, a group of friends around to watch some movies on TV, or if you find yourself with a rainy afternoon and kids to entertain, pizza is a very good solution.

Pizza is not at all difficult to make. But it requires a bit of preparation time because the dough is yeast-based and must be set aside to rise. Even though pizza can't be made on the spur of the moment, so much of the work can be done ahead that it does work well for a party – and the variety of combinations possible means it will appeal to everyone.

Commercial pizza ovens are very hot and very dry; traditionally they are wood-fired, with an open front. The reason is not simply one of aesthetics; the worst enemy of pizza is steam and if you have a very hot, open oven that allows all the steam to escape, your crust will be crisp and dry. The steam problem is the main reason why a special technique is required to make good pizza at home. Karen has worked out a two-stage method of baking that gives you a crisp and evenly baked crust without using a baking stone or the very high heat of a commercial pizza oven.

There is an initial ten-minute baking period before the cheese goes on, which allows the steam produced by the topping to escape and hardens the crust enough so that it can be easily removed from the pan. The final baking is done directly on the oven rack: the crust stays crisp, and the cheese has just enough time to melt without becoming hard, stringy, or bitter.

You can make the dough ahead, so that all you need do at the last minute is assemble the pizza. If you do plan to make the dough in advance, you can roll it out and refrigerate it on the pans until you're ready to use it: it will be fine for at least 8 hours in a cold fridge. It can also be frozen in the pizza shape, but this method requires you to have more than one pan (unless you are highly organized and are prepared to freeze them one at a time, taking them off the pan and putting them into bags when they are hard). Alternatively you can make the dough and let it proof in the fridge either overnight or for the whole day. When it comes time to use the dough, take it out, let it come to room temperature, then roll it out and continue with the recipe.

BASIC PIZZA DOUGH

Makes 1 16" or 2 9" pizzas.

1½ cup	**water,** lukewarm, about 110°F
½ tsp	**sugar**
1½ tsp	**active dry yeast**
½ tsp	**salt**
¼ cup	**olive oil**
½ cup	**semolina flour** (optional)
2½ to 3 cups	**unbleached white flour,** either all-purpose or hard **flour,** for kneading surface
2 Tbs	**olive oil**

1. Stir sugar and water together in a large bowl.

2. Sprinkle the yeast on top of the water. The yeast will dissolve and bubble to the surface (about 5 to 10 minutes).

3. Stir in the salt, oil, and semolina, if you are using it. If not, use more plain flour in Step 4.

4. Beat in the flour, one cup at a time, until the mixture is too stiff to beat any more.

5. Spread about a cup of flour onto your kneading surface and scrape the dough out of the bowl onto it. Start kneading the dough, adding flour as needed, to make a pliable, resilient dough. (Total active kneading time is about 10 minutes.)

IF THE DOUGH BECOMES TOO HARD TO WORK
Let the dough sit for a few minutes. This allows the gluten that you have developed by kneading to relax. It should then be easier to work.

IF YOU HAVE ADDED TOO MUCH FLOUR AND THE DOUGH IS STIFF AND DRY
Brush the flour on your surface aside, spread the surface lightly with oil, and continue to knead.

6. Wash out the bowl in which you made the dough, and pour in the oil. Put in the dough and roll it around so that it is oiled all over. Cover loosely with plastic wrap or a clean cloth.

7. Allow to rise in a warm place for two to three hours until dough has doubled in bulk. Punch down the dough and proceed with the pizza.

TO FREEZE PIZZA DOUGH: The dough may be frozen at this point. Punch it down, wrap well in plastic wrap, then in a plastic bag.

TO THAW: Remove the dough from the freezer. Loosen the outer plastic bag, and allow to thaw at room temperature for 8 hours.

BASIC PIZZA WITH TOMATO AND MOZZARELLA

1 recipe	**Basic Pizza Dough** (see page 65)
2 Tbs	**extra virgin olive oil** (see page 133)
2 Tbs	**semolina flour**
4 Tbs	**Basic Tomato Sauce** (see page 223)
12 oz	**full-fat mozzarella,** shredded (see below)

1.   Preheat oven to 400° F.

2.   Knead the pizza dough for a few minutes until smooth.

3.   Lightly but thoroughly oil baking sheet OR sprinkle with semolina.

4.   Place dough on a flat surface (you can do it directly on the baking sheet) and roll it out. If it becomes too springy and hard to roll, let it sit a few minutes. Use your hands to pat and stretch it into place on the baking sheet. *(May be done ahead to this point.)*

5.   Spread tomato sauce over pizza. Place pizza on lower rack of hot oven. Bake for 10 minutes, or until dough can be easily lifted off the pan.

6.   Leave dough on the pan and remove from oven. Quickly sprinkle with cheese.

7.   With a spatula, lift and slide the dough off the pan directly onto the oven rack.

8.   Bake for 15 to 20 minutes. Check the underside of the crust from time to time. Slide back onto baking sheet, and remove from oven.

9.   Allow to cool for 10 minutes before cutting.

MOZZARELLA

In Italy, mozzarella was traditionally made from buffalo milk; in fact, "mozzarella di bufala" can still be bought in cheese shops in Italy – and from time to time in Canada. It doesn't look very much like what you and I think of as mozzarella: it is a very white, very soft ball about 3″ in diameter; it is stored in water to preserve freshness, but even so it has a shelf life of two weeks or less. This cheese is almost never heated or cooked, but is at its best sliced and eaten with fresh tomatoes, extra virgin oil, and fresh basil.

Mozzarella that is used for cooking is quite a different animal; it must have a quite high fat content, so that it melts into a wonderfully rich and creamy mass. Low-fat mozzarella is a shapeless, tasteless, slightly rubbery cheese that separates into butter and a tough curd when cooked. Even if you insist on eating it (and there are lots of people who say that it's better than no cheese at all) don't try to cook with it. Choose a mozzarella with a butterfat content of at least 20 per cent, (preferably 25 per cent) of the total weight (the official Canadian formula).

The cheeses that are shaped like gourds, which can be found hanging in Italian cheese shops, are called Scamorze, and are very similar to mozzarella. Because they are made by hand by cheese makers who follow the old traditions, they are often better in both flavour and texture than regular mozzarella.

PIZZA VARIATIONS

Using the basic recipe, you can make any number of different pizzas. Here are a few suggestions.

PROSCIUTTO, BLACK OLIVE, AND ONION PIZZA

1 recipe	**Basic Pizza Dough** (see page 65)
4 Tbs	**Basic Tomato Sauce** (see page 223)
¼ cup	**black olives, pitted** (see page 69)
¼ lb	**prosciutto**, thinly sliced and cut into 1″ strips (see page 53)
2 cups	**thinly sliced red** OR **white onion**
12 oz	**full-fat mozzarella** shredded, (see page 66)

1. Preheat oven to 400° F.

2. Roll and press out dough onto baking sheet.

3. Spread tomato sauce over dough. Distribute onions, prosciutto, and olives evenly over the sauce.

4. Bake for 10 minutes, or until dough will come off baking sheet.

5. Slide pizza off baking sheet directly onto oven rack. Bake for 15 to 20 minutes more, until lightly browned.

"WHITE" PIZZA WITH KALE AND MOZZARELLA

A white pizza ("Pizza bianca" in Italian) is made without tomato sauce or tomatoes.

½ lb	**kale**, trimmed and washed
4 Tbs	**extra virgin olive oil** (see page 133)
1 tsp	**finely chopped garlic**
2	**anchovy filets**, chopped
1 recipe	**Basic Pizza Dough** (see page 65)
12 oz	**full-fat mozzarella** shredded (see page 66)

1. Preheat oven to 400° F.

2. Cook kale in plenty of boiling water for about 5 minutes. Drain and rinse under cold water. Squeeze out as much water with your hands as you can, then chop the kale finely.

3. Sauté the garlic in oil until it is pale gold.

4. Add anchovy filets to garlic and stir until dissolved.

5. Add the kale and stir well to coat with oil. *(May be made ahead to this point.)*

6. Roll out and press pizza dough onto baking sheet.

7. Spread kale over dough and bake for 10 minutes or until dough will lift off baking sheet.

8. Remove pizza from oven, sprinkle with cheese, and slide off pan directly onto oven rack. Bake for 15 to 20 minutes, or until lightly browned.

PIZZA WITH GOAT CHEESE AND SUNDRIED TOMATOES

1 Tbs	**olive oil**
½ tsp	**garlic**, finely chopped
3 Tbs	**finely chopped sundried tomato**
4 Tbs	**Basic Tomato Sauce** (see page 223)
2 Tbs	**black olive paste**
½ tsp	**black pepper**, ground
1 recipe	**Basic Pizza Dough** (see page 65)
½ lb	**firm chèvre** OR **cream-style chèvre**, cut into " cubes (see page 32)

1. Preheat oven to 400° F.

2. Sauté garlic in oil until light gold in colour.

3. Add sundried tomato, tomato sauce, olive paste, and pepper. Cook on low heat for 5 minutes until sauce is slightly thickened. Allow to cool. *(May be made ahead to this point.)*

4. Roll and press dough out onto baking sheet.

5. Spread sauce evenly over dough, then bake for 10 minutes, until comes away from pan easily.

6. Remove from oven and spread cheese over sauce. Slide off pan directly onto oven rack and bake for 15 to 20 minutes, until lightly browned.

CALZONE WITH SPINACH, RICOTTA, AND GENOA SALAMI

Calzone is a pizza that has been folded over and the edges sealed to make a closed pastry, like a turnover.

Makes 4.

10 oz	**fresh spinach**
1 Tbs	**olive oil**
¼ cup	**finely chopped white onion**
1 Tbs	**olive oil**
1 cup	**ricotta cheese**
¼ tsp	**salt**
3 Tbs	**grated Parmesan cheese**
2 Tbs	**grated Romano cheese** (use Parmesan if not available
1 recipe	**Basic Pizza Dough** (see page 65)
¼ lb	**Genoa salami**, thinly sliced
1 Tbs	**olive oil**

1. Preheat oven to 400° F.

2. Sauté spinach in oil until it wilts. Spread on a plate to cool, then squeeze out as much water as you can with your hands. Chop finely.

3. Sauté onion in oil until translucent. Place in a large bowl to cool.

4. Add spinach to onion in the bowl. Add ricotta, salt, and cheeses and stir well. *(May be prepared up to 1 day ahead to this point.)*

5. Divide dough into four. Sprinkle work surface with flour. Roll each piece of dough into a 6" circle. Allow dough to relax if it becomes too springy.

6. Cover dough with salami, leaving a 1" border around the edge.

7. Spread the filling mixture on top of the salami, again leaving the border all around.

8. Fold the calzone in half, pressing the edges together, and crimping the dough well to seal.

9.   Place calzone on a lightly oiled baking sheet, and brush tops with oil.

10.   Bake on lower rack of preheated oven for 15 minutes.

11.   Slide calzone off baking sheet onto oven rack and bake for 15 minutes more.

12.   Allow to cool for 10 minutes before serving.

"White" Pizza with Fresh Clams

2 lb	**fresh Manilla clams** (or any other small clam) (see page 86)
¼ cup	**white wine**
1 tsp	**finely chopped garlic**
4 Tbs	**olive oil**
¼ cup	**white wine**
2 Tbs	**chopped Italian parsley**
⅛ tsp	**red pepper flakes**
1 recipe	**Basic Pizza Dough** (see page 65)
4 Tbs	**grated Parmesan cheese**

1.   Preheat oven to 400°F.

2.   Scrub the clams well in several changes of water.

3.   Bring wine to a boil in a pot large enough to hold the clams. Add the clams and cover. Cook over medium heat for 7 to 10 minutes, shaking pot occasionally. When clams are open, remove from heat and set aside until clams are cool enough to handle.

4.   Remove clam meat and discard the shells. Strain clam cooking liquid through a sieve lined with cheese-cloth or paper towel.

5.   Sauté garlic in oil until it is pale gold.

6.   Add wine to garlic and boil until reduced by half. Add the strained clam liquor and reduce by half again.

7.   Remove from heat and stir in parsley and red pepper flakes. Allow to cool. *(May be prepared up to 1 day ahead to this point.)*

8.   Roll out and press dough onto baking sheet.

9.   Spread clam-juice mixture over the pizza dough. Bake for 10 minutes, until dough comes off baking sheet easily.

10.   Slide pizza off baking sheet onto oven rack. Bake for 15 minutes more.

11.   Remove pizza from oven; spread with clams and grated cheese. Return to oven and bake for 5 minutes more, until clams are heated through.

OLIVES

Green olives are picked before they are fully ripe; black olives are left to ripen on the tree – except in most of California, where they are picked young and ripened chemically (and taste like it).

CALAMATA: Large, purple-black olives from Greece. Sharper, spicier taste than most other black olives. The best olive for a Greek salad, but too acidic for pizza topping.

NIÇOISE: Small, fruity black olives from the south of France, often cured in oil. Good for pizza and for cooking.

INFORNATE: Oven-baked olives from Morocco with a very wrinkled skin. Dry-cured in oil. Excellent flavour and very meaty texture. Good for pizza.

GAETA: Medium-sized black olives from southern Italy; may be oil or brine-cured. Good for pizza.

Gorgonzola and Sweet Potato Pizza

This unlikely-sounding combination really works: it's one of our favourites.

1 cup	**thinly sliced sweet potato**
1 recipe	**Basic Pizza Dough** (see page 65)
½ cup	**thinly sliced red onion**
8 oz	**Gorgonzola**, cut into ½"cubes
1 Tbs	**olive oil**

1. Preheat oven to 400° F.

2. Cook sweet potato in boiling water until tender (20 to 25 minutes). Cut into thin slices and set aside to cool. *(May be made ahead to this point.)*

3. Roll out and press pizza dough onto baking sheet.

4. Arrange onions on dough, and spread sweet potato on top. Sprinkle with Gorgonzola pieces.

5. Drizzle olive oil over pizza.

6. Bake for 10 minutes, until pizza comes off baking sheet easily.

7. Slide pizza off baking sheet onto oven rack and bake for another 10 to 20 minutes.

THIN PIZZA AND FOCACCIA

Thin pizza and focaccia are more like bread than pizza. Although they are delicious on their own, they are at their best when served as an accompaniment to a robust pasta or soup and salad and go wonderfully well with meat grilled on a barbecue.

Thin Pizza with Garlic and Olive Oil

Makes 4.

1 recipe	**Basic Pizza Dough** (see page 65)
4 Tbs	**extra virgin olive oil** (see page 133)
2 tsp	**finely chopped garlic sea salt**, ground

1. Preheat oven to 400° F.

2. Divide dough into four. Roll and press dough into thin rounds, about ⅛" thick.

3. Mix oil and garlic together and spread over the dough.

4. Bake for 10 minutes on lower rack of preheated oven.

5. Slide pizza directly onto oven rack and bake for 10 minutes longer until crisp and golden brown.

6. Sprinkle lightly with salt.

ARMENIAN FLATBREAD

Making your own crackers may seem like carrying things too far. On the other hand it tastes delicious, is not difficult – and will impress your friends no end. It might just be worth it.

Makes 8 large crackers (or lavash).

2 cups	**warm water**
1 Tbs	**granulated sugar**
1 Tbs	**active dry yeast** OR **instant dry yeast**
2 cups	**all-purpose flour**
½ cup	**unsalted butter**, melted (see page 23)
2½ cups	**all-purpose flour**
1 Tbs	**oil**

1. Pour the warm water into a large bowl – it should be just about body temperature (the water not the bowl!). Sprinkle the yeast over it and allow it to dissolve. (If using instant yeast, follow the package directions – they work.) Allow the yeast to bubble up to the surface.

2. With a large spoon, beat in 2 cups of flour and melted butter until the mixture is smooth. Add more flour, ½ cup at a time, until the dough is fairly stiff but not dry.

3. Turn the dough onto your floured work surface, turn the bowl upside down over it, and allow it to rest for 15 minutes.

4. Sprinkle more flour on the work surface; knead the dough for about 8 minutes, adding flour as necessary to prevent it from sticking.

5. Pour oil into a large bowl; roll the dough around in it until well coated. Cover the bowl with plastic wrap and allow to rise in a warm place for about 1½ hours, until doubled in bulk.

6. Preheat the oven to 375°F. Lightly butter a cookie sheet.

7. Turn the dough onto your work surface, punch it down and divide into 8 pieces. Put one piece on your work surface; set the rest aside covered with plastic.

8. Lightly flour the work surface; roll out each piece of dough into a 12″ circle. Roll it around your rolling pin and unroll onto the greased cookie sheet.

9. Bake in preheated oven for 10 to 12 minutes, until the top bubbles up, the bottom begins to brown, and the bread is crisp. Remove from the oven and cool on a rack.

10. Roll out the second lavash while the first is baking. Transfer to the hot baking sheet and continue until all are baked.

11. Lavash will keep for several days if closely covered.

SWEDISH FLATBREAD

This tastes a bit like a flat scone; delicious with butter and strawberry jam. It is the reaction of the buttermilk with the soda that makes the bread rise; try to get it in the oven as quickly as possible after you combine these two ingredients.

2⅔ cups	**all-purpose flour**
¼ cup	**granulated sugar**
½ tsp	**baking soda**
¼ tsp	**salt**
½ cup	**unsalted butter** (see page 23)
1 cup	**buttermilk**

1. Preheat the oven to 400° F.

2. Sift the flour, sugar, soda, and salt into a large bowl.

3. With a pastry cutter, cut the butter into the flour until the mixture resembles coarse crumbs. You may do this in the food processor: place the flour mixture in the work bowl; pulse once or twice to aerate. Cut the butter into cubes and distribute them over the flour. Process only until the mixture looks like coarse meal (do *not* let it come together in a ball).

4. With a fork, stir in the buttermilk. Shape the dough into 1″ balls. Lightly flour your work surface; roll out each ball into a 4″ to 5″ circle.

5. Place the breads 1″ apart on an ungreased cookie sheet. Bake in the preheated oven for 3 to 5 minutes, until very light brown.

CHEDDAR CHEESE BISCUITS

Makes about 20 biscuits.

2 cups	**all-purpose flour**
1 cup	**grated old cheddar cheese**
2 tsp	**baking powder**
½ tsp	**baking soda**
½ cup	**butter**, cold (see page 23)
⅔ cup	**buttermilk**
1 tsp	**granulated sugar**
¼ tsp	**salt**
1 large	**egg yolk**
1 cup	**grated old cheddar cheese**

1. Preheat the oven to 400° F. Lightly butter 2 cookie sheets or line them with parchment.

2. In a medium bowl, combine the flour, 1 cup of cheese, the baking powder and soda. With a pastry cutter, cut in the cold butter until the mixture resembles a grainy meal. (You may do this in the food processor.) Put in flour, 1 cup of cheese, baking powder and and soda; pulse once or twice to aerate; cut the cold butter into cubes and distribute them over the flour. Process, using pulse action, only until the mixture resembles very coarse meal – don't over do it or the biscuits will be tough. (Transfer to a mixing bowl for the next step.)

3. Mix the sugar and salt into the buttermilk; whisk in the egg yolk. Add this to the dry ingredients and stir until the dough gathers into a ball (if necessary add more buttermilk 1 tsp at a time until it comes together).

4. Turn out the dough onto a lightly floured surface and knead for about 30 seconds, just until smooth. Gently roll it out to ½" thick. With a 2" cookie cutter (or thin-rimmed glass) cut into rounds (re-form the scraps until you have used it all up).

5. Transfer the rounds to the cookie sheets. Bake for 10 minutes in the preheated oven. Then remove from the oven, sprinkle the top of each biscuit with cheddar cheese, and return to the oven for 10 minutes more, until the biscuits are pale golden brown and the cheese has melted.

FOCACCIA WITH ONIONS AND FRESH ROSEMARY

½ cup	**thinly sliced Bermuda onions**
1 recipe	**Basic Pizza Dough** (see page 65)
1 Tbs	**fresh rosemary leaves**
2 Tbs	**extra virgin olive oil** (see page 133)

1. Preheat oven to 400°F.

2. Soak sliced onions in cold water for 30 minutes. Drain on paper towel.

3. Roll and press out dough onto baking sheet.

4. Sprinkle rosemary leaves over onions.

5. Drizzle with olive oil.

6. Bake in preheated oven for 10 minutes, until dough will come away from the pan easily.

7. Spread onions over dough, pressing them lightly into the dough with your fingers.

8. Slide focaccia off pan directly onto oven rack. Bake for 15 to 20 minutes longer, until golden brown.

FISH & SEAFOOD

Nothing suffers more being cooked improperly, or is subjected to it more often, than fish. We have all grown up with grey, overcooked, crumbling fish that had a suspiciously strong taste; it is not an experience we are in any hurry to repeat.

Surprisingly, no one has done more to repair this damage than our own Department of the Environment, with what is known as the "Canadian Fisheries 10-Minute Rule". As a rule of thumb, they say you should cook fish for 10 minutes per inch of thickness at the thickest part of the fish. The rule applies regardless of how you cook it – baking, barbecuing, frying, or poaching, it is more or less all the same – and of what shape the fish is – whole fish, steaks, boneless filets, all get the same 10 minutes per inch.

At the shop, we have an 8-minute rule; we find that 10 minutes is just a little too long when you take into account that the fish, particularly whole fish and thick cuts, will continue to cook in the middle after being removed from the heat. Of course, there are recipes where the cooking time is much longer than this, for example, when cold wine is poured over the fish just as it goes into the oven and it takes some time for the fish to get up to the cooking temperature.

A hint when you are barbecuing fish (which is an excellent way to cook it if you can overcome the problem of the fish sticking to the grill): Make sure the barbecue is very hot; you don't have to worry about flames when cooking fish because there is not enough fat to catch fire. Dry the fish, coat it with flour (seasoned if you like), and brush with oil just before you put it on the grill. This anti-stick method is not foolproof – sometimes a piece will stick, particularly when you are using whole fish – but you get a much better taste than with most of the other non-stick approaches. Laying foil over the grill and putting the fish on that does have its uses, especially if you put grilling herbs – fennel stalks are particularly good – onto the coals and cover the barbecue while the fish is cooking. The aroma of the smouldering herbs will permeate the fish.

Finally, fish that has not been frozen is clearly better than fish that has, provided of course that it is fresh. Sometimes frozen fish is all that you can find, and sometimes frozen is better than fresh. A fish supplier friend who has experimented extensively swears that it makes almost no difference whether you thaw frozen fish quickly or slowly. The big difference is in the freezing, particularly how much moisture the fish was allowed (or encouraged) to absorb before and during it.

HALIBUT WITH MUSCAT GRAPES IN MUSTARD

Muscat grapes are available in the late summer and early fall; if you are using regular seedless grapes, you could substitute a sweet dessert wine for the sherry.

Serves 4.

2 Tbs	**Dijon mustard**
1 Tbs	**soya sauce**
1 tsp	**honey**
2 tsp	**dry sherry**
4	**halibut filets** OR **steaks** about 6 oz each
½ lb	**muscat grapes**, halved and seeded OR **green seedless grapes**, halved

1.   Mix the mustard, soya sauce, honey, and sherry together. Brush or spoon half of it onto the halibut; toss the halved grapes with the rest.

2.   Heat the broiler or barbecue for 15 minutes.

3.   Broil (or barbecue) for 4 minutes on each side.

4.   Serve on heated plates, with the grapes alongside.

SEARED SALMON IN DOLCE-FORTE SAUCE

This sweet and sharp sauce also goes well with barbecued or grilled salmon.

Serves 4.

FOR THE SAUCE

2 Tbs	**golden raisins**
4 Tbs	**balsamic vinegar** (see page 138)
2 Tbs	**fish stock, Chicken Stock** (see page 226), OR **water**
6 Tbs	**finely sliced shallots**
3 Tbs	**extra virgin olive oil** (see page 133)
6	**anchovy stuffed green olives** (use green olives and 1 anchovy filet if you don't have these)
2 Tbs	**capers**
4	**salmon filets**, about 6 oz each

1.   Put raisins, vinegar, and stock (or water) in a small pan; bring to the boil over high heat. Cover tightly and set aside.

2.   Sauté the sliced shallots in oil until golden; add them to the raisins. Chop the olives and capers and add them as well. Keep the sauce warm.

3.   Place a cast-iron frying pan over high heat; allow to heat for 5 minutes.

4.   Salt the salmon filets lightly. Place them in the very hot pan; cover (use foil if there is no lid) and cook for 3 minutes.

5.   Uncover, turn the salmon over, replace the cover, and cook for 2 more minutes. The salmon should be brown and crispy on the outside, but still very tender in the middle.

6.   Serve the salmon on heated plates; spoon the warm sauce over it.

WHOLE RED SNAPPER BAKED IN BANANA LEAVES

You can find banana leaves in most food stores in Chinatown, in the freezer section (fortunately for you the writing on the package is in English). The leaves give the fish a wonderfully fresh, nutty flavour.

Serves 4.

1 large	**red snapper**, about 3½ lbs, scaled and gutted
3 Tbs	**fine julienne strips of ginger**
4 Tbs	**soya sauce**
1 package	**banana leaves**, thawed
4 slices	**lemon**
½ cup	**julienne strips of green onion**

1. Make 3 diagonal cuts on each side of the fish. Mix the ginger and soya sauce together.

2. Remove the banana leaves from the package and unfold them. Cut 3 pieces each 2 feet long with scissors. (Rewrap any leftover leaves in plastic wrap and then foil, and refreeze; they will be fine.) Wash and dry the leaves.

3. Lay 2 of the banana leaves side by side with a small overlap on your work surface; lay the third piece across the middle of the first two, at right angles. Spread 2 Tbs of the soya-ginger mixture over the middle of the top leaf and lay the fish on top of it, as close to the centre as possible. Tuck the lemon slices into the cavity of the fish, and spread the remaining soya-ginger mixture on top of the fish. Now fold the ends of the top leaf over the fish; then wrap the two overlapping leaves tightly around the fish, making a neat package (it's not as complicated as it sounds).

4. Preheat the oven to 350° F.

5. Place the wrapped-up fish in a baking dish and cover the dish tightly with foil. Bake in the preheated oven for 30 minutes.

6. To serve: Remove the foil and gently lift the fish onto a serving platter. Cut through the banana leaves with scissors, and open up the package. Sprinkle with the julienned green onions and serve immediately.

SALMON IN PARCHMENT

A great presentation for salmon that allows you to do other things up to at the last minute, like talk to your friends. The vegetables are included in the package.

Serves 4.

8	**asparagus spears** peeled and cut in 2" pieces
1	**carrot** cut in julienne strips
a few	**French green beans** (or other fine beans)
1	**leek**, cleaned and cut in julienne strips
1 Tbs	**butter** (see page 23)
2 sheets	**parchment paper**, 18" by 26"
4	**salmon filets**, about 6 oz each **salt** and **pepper**
¼ cup	**white wine**

1.   Bring a large pot of water to a boil; salt it and throw in the asparagus spears; cook for 2 minutes, then fish them out with a strainer or slotted spoon and refresh under cold water; drain. Repeat with the carrot sticks and beans.

2.   Melt the butter in a pan; add the leek strips and sauté lightly; add the rest of the vegetables and toss to coat with the butter. Remove from the heat and set aside.

3.   Preheat the oven to 400° F.

4.   Prepare the parchment-paper packages (see box): lay a piece of salmon in each; divide the vegetables between the four packages, laying them on top of and around the salmon. Season with salt and pepper; spoon 2 Tbs white wine over each and seal up the packages. Set them on a baking sheet.

5.   Bake in preheated oven for 12 minutes. Remove from the oven and serve immediately. Let each guest open his or her own package.

MAKING PARCHMENT ENVELOPES
There are two approaches to making parchment envelopes – the purist's and the Christmas cracker approach. You do not need to ask which one I favour.
The Purist's Approach
These instructions assume a full-size sheet of parchment (17½" by 25½"). If you use a different size, try to end up with the finished sizes shown. Cut the sheets of parchment in half (each piece will be approx 18" by 13"). The objective of these instructions is to make a heart-shaped piece of paper, with a fold down the centre.
1.   Fold each half in half (the folded piece will measure 13" by 9").
2.   Practise this with a sheet of scrap paper before you attack the parchment. Lay one folded piece of paper on your cutting board, with the fold edge to your left. With the tip of a sharp knife, draw half a heart, starting at the fold edge, about ⅓ down from the top. Make it as large as the paper will allow. Pull off the excess paper, open it up and you should have a heart shape.
3.   Place the salmon (or whatever else you want to cook) in the middle of one side of the heart; fold the top flap over and line it up directly over the bottom. Now fold the edges together so that the package is sealed. Beginning at the place where you started to cut, fold over a 1½" long strip of edge; make a second fold, starting about ⅔ of the way up the first fold: the second fold seals the open end of the first. Continue folding all the way round the edge; when you reach the end twist the tail to seal it. The package is ready.
The Christmas-Cracker Approach
The pieces of parchment should be about the same size as for the first method. Lay out a piece of parchment on your work surface; put the salmon in the middle, lengthwise. Fold first one long edge then the other edge over the salmon so that it is completely enclosed. Now twist the ends to seal them, and make the whole thing look like a Christmas cracker. Could anything be simpler? No. But is it the pure essence of the parchment envelope? It certainly is not.

FRESH SALMON WITH HOT TARTARE SAUCE

The hot tartare sauce makes an interesting change from Hollandaise. The sauce is made while the salmon is cooking in the oven.

Serves 4.

4	**salmon filets**, about 6 oz each, skin and bones removed
½ cup	**dry white white wine** OR **dry vermouth**

FOR THE SAUCE

3 Tbs	**butter** (see page 23)
½ cup	**finely chopped green onions**
2 Tbs	**finely chopped cornichons** (sour pickles)
2 tsp	**capers**
½ cup	**Crème Fraîche** (see page 226)
1 Tbs	**Dijon mustard**
4 Tbs	**Italian parsley,** chopped **salt** **freshly ground black pepper**

1. Preheat the oven to 350°F.

2. Arrange the salmon in one layer in a baking dish in which it fits snugly without overlapping.

3. Warm the wine or vermouth in a small (non-corrodable) saucepan; pour it over the salmon. Cover the dish tightly with foil and bake in the preheated oven for 15 minutes.

4. Sauté the green onions in butter until wilted; add the cornichons and capers. Remove from the heat.

5. Take the salmon dish out of the oven; remove the salmon to a plate, cover loosely with the foil, and put back in the turned-off oven while you finish the sauce.

6. Pour the salmon cooking liquid into the pan with the green onions and capers; turn heat up to high and reduce to ¼ cup. Add the mustard and crème fraîche and continue to cook over high heat until the sauce thickens slightly. Season to taste with salt and pepper. Stir in the parsley.

7. Place the salmon filets on warmed plates; spoon the sauce around and serve.

OVEN-POACHED SALMON WITH BEURRE BLANC

Serves 4.

4	**salmon filets**, about 6 oz
	salt and **pepper** (white is best)
1 cup	**white wine**
3 Tbs	**lemon juice**
	water
1 recipe	**Beurre Blanc** (see page 224)

1. Preheat the oven to 350° F.

2. Choose a baking dish large enough to hold the salmon filets in one layer; butter it generously, or line with parchment. Lay the salmon filets in the dish; season them with salt and pepper; pour in the wine and lemon juice, and enough water to just cover the fish. Cover the dish tightly with foil. Place in the preheated oven and bake for 30 minutes.

3. While the salmon is cooking, make the beurre blanc.

4. Remove the baking dish from the oven. Lift the salmon out onto paper towels to remove excess water; transfer to warm plates, spoon some of the beurre blanc over the fish and pass the rest separately.

COLD POACHED SALMON WITH DILL MAYONNAISE

Serves 6.

6	**salmon filets**, about 6 oz each
1	**bay leaf**
8	**peppercorns**
1 cup	**white wine** (optional)
2 slices	**lemon**
2 stalks	**lemon grass**, cut in half (optional: see page 114)
1 cup	**Dill Mayonnaise** (see page 227)

1. Fill a large frying pan with water; add the bay leaf, peppercorns, lemon slices, and optional white wine and lemon grass. Bring to a boil, add the salt, reduce the heat to a simmer and put in the salmon. Poach at a bare simmer for 6 to 10 minutes, depending on thickness (about 8 minutes to the inch).

2. Lift out carefully and allow to cool. Decorate the top with lemon slices or strips of red pepper; serve with dill mayonnaise.

NOTE: The texture of the salmon will be better if it is not refrigerated between cooking and serving.

SALMON EN CROUTE

Salmon "en croute" makes a very impressive presentation, particularly at a buffet where your guests can see it in all its glory. Believe it or not, it is simple to do: just follow the instructions and banish from your head any anxiety about working with puff pastry. Make sure that you buy the salmon in the correct form; you need one whole side (half a fish), with the skin removed, and all the little lateral bones taken out. You can make this recipe with less than a whole side for a small party, but a 6" piece of fish (for 4 people) would be the lower limit.

Serves 10.

2 pack-ages	**fresh spinach**
2 large	**eggs**
pinch of	**ground nutmeg**
	salt and **pepper**
2 lbs	**Puff Pastry**, thawed but cold (see page 231)
1	**egg**, beaten
1 whole side	**salmon**, all skin and bones removed
1 recipe	**Hollandaise Sauce** (see page 229)

1. Wash the spinach and remove the large stems. Place it in a large pot with just the water that clings to the leaves. Cook covered over medium heat until the spinach is wilted. Drain, refresh under cold water, and leave to cool.

2. When cool, squeeze out as much water with your hands as you can, chop the spinach coarsely, and transfer it to the work bowl of the food processor. Add the eggs, nutmeg, salt, and pepper; then process until quite finely chopped. Set aside.

3. Divide the puff pastry in two; on a lightly floured work surface, roll out each piece to a rectangle approximately 10" wide and about 4" longer than the side of salmon (it should be large enough that the salmon can lie on it with a clear border of 1½" all round). The pastry should be ⅛" to ³/₁₆" thick. Lay one piece (the larger if there is a choice) on a large baking sheet, covered with parchment (preferably) or foil; set the other aside.

4. Lay the salmon on the pastry (what used to be) skin-side down, and centred so as to leave an even border all round. With a spatula spread the spinach mixture evenly over the top of the salmon and smooth it out.

5. Dampen the exposed edges of pastry around the salmon with water. Drape the second sheet of puff pastry over the salmon, shaping the top pastry sheet around the fish and pressing it firmly against the bottom pastry sheet to seal it. Now comes the good part: With a sharp knife, trim the excess pastry from around the salmon, making the whole package into the shape of a fish. Cut two small holes for steam to escape in the top; with the point of a knife you can score gills, scales, and fins on the top of the pastry. Then brush with the beaten egg and refrigerate until ready to bake.

(May be prepared up to a day ahead to this point.)

6. Preheat the oven to 425° F.

7. Brush the pastry with egg glaze if there is any left. Bake in the centre of the preheated oven for 15 minutes; then turn the oven down to 350° F and bake for 20 minutes more. Remove from the oven and allow to sit in a warm place for 15 minutes before serving. Cut in ¾″ slices with a serrated knife. Serve with Hollandaise sauce. May also be served at room temperature with mayonnaise.

FRESH TUNA WITH EGGPLANT CAVIAR

Serves 6.

6	**fresh tuna steaks** about 6 oz each
1 Tbs	**extra virgin olive oil** (see page 133)
1 tsp	**salt**
½ tsp	**black pepper**, ground
1 tsp	**fresh thyme leaves**, chopped
1	**red pepper**, roasted (see page 47)
1	**yellow pepper**, roasted
1	**green pepper**, roasted

FOR THE EGGPLANT CAVIAR

1 lb	**eggplant**, small and firm
½ tsp	**salt**
1 Tbs	**lemon juice**
2 Tbs	**Crème Fraîche** (see page 226) OR **whipping cream**
1 tsp	**finely chopped garlic**
1 Tbs	**finely chopped greeen onion**
1 Tbs	**olive oil**

1. Sprinkle the tuna with oil, salt, pepper, and thyme. Set aside to marinate (refrigerate if marinating, for more than 1 hour).

2. Chop 1 Tbs of each colour roasted pepper, to be used in Step 8 below.

3. Preheat oven to 350° F.

4. Place eggplant directly on gas burner or under broiler until skin is charred, turning as necessary.

5. Transfer to preheated oven and bake for 30 to 40 minutes until very soft. Remove from oven and allow to cool.

6. Peel off the skin and remove any large deposits of seeds. Sprinkle with salt and place in a colander to drain for an hour.

7. Squeeze to remove excess water. Place flesh in work bowl of food processor and purée. Add lemon juice and crème fraîche and blend again.

8. Transfer to a mixing bowl, add the chopped garlic, green onion, olive oil, and the chopped peppers from Step 2; stir well to mix. Refrigerate until required.

9. Preheat barbecue or broiler.

10. Barbecue or broil the tuna for 3 or 4 minutes on each side: do not overcook.

11. Sauté the pepper strips in oil until warmed through.

12. Serve the tuna on warm plates, with a dollop of eggplant caviar on top, surrounded by the peppers.

SALMON COULIBIAC

Salmon En Croute (pages 80-81) was really just a warm-up for this recipe; there are several more steps here, but none is really complicated and the end result is very impressive.

Serves 10.

FOR THE RICE MIXTURE

⅔ cup	**long-grain white rice**
⅓ cup	**wild rice**
⅓ cup	**Weehani rice** (optional – use more wild rice if you don't have this)
½ oz	**dried wild mushrooms** (Trompettes de la mort [cheaper]; or Morels [a lot pricier] – see page 83)
2 Tbs	**butter** (see page 23)
½ cup	**finely chopped shallots**
2 cups	**sliced regular mushrooms**
2 cups	**sliced oyster mushrooms**
½ cup	**white wine**
2 Tbs	**lemon juice**
4 cups	**whipping cream**
4 Tbs	**chopped fresh dill** **salt** and **pepper**
2 lbs	**Puff Pastry**, thawed (see page 231)
1 side	**salmon**, skin and bones removed
2 Tbs	**lemon juice** **salt** and **pepper**
8	**hard-boiled eggs**
1½ cups	**finely chopped parsley**
1	**egg**, beaten

1.   Prepare the rice mixture first. Cook the rices separately – *EITHER* cook in large pots of boiling water until just tender (about 12 minutes for white rice; 40 minutes for both wild and Weehani), drain and allow to cool; *OR* cook in tightly covered saucepans with the amount of water indicated on the package (about 2 cups per cup of rice for white rice; 2½ cups per cup for wild and Weehani) until all the water is absorbed and the rice is tender; remove from heat and allow to cool.

2.   While the rice is cooking, place dried mushrooms in a small bowl, and pour in just enough boiling water to cover. Allow to soak for 20 minutes; then remove mushrooms and slice them. Strain the soaking liquid through cheesecloth or paper towel (or paper coffee filter) and reserve.

3.   Sauté the shallots in butter until translucent. Add the sliced oyster, regular, and wild mushrooms and cook until the juices run. Turn up the heat to medium-high, pour in the white wine and lemon juice; reduce to ¼ cup. Pour in the reserved mushroom soaking liquid and reduce again to ¼ cup.

4.   Pour in the cream and reduce the sauce to 2 cups. Add the dill and lemon juice, and salt and pepper to taste.

5.   Combine all the cooked rice in a large bowl; pour the sauce over the rice, mix well, and allow to cool.

6.   When the rice mixture is cool, proceed with the assembly. Divide the puff pastry in two. On a lightly floured surface, roll out each piece to a rectangle about 10″ wide and 4″ longer than the side of salmon – about 24″ overall. The pastry should be ⅛″ to ³⁄₁₆ ″ thick.

7.   Cut the side of salmon in half lengthwise; you will have two filets, each about 20″ long by 3″ to 4″ wide at their widest part. Slice the hard-boiled eggs into ¼″ slices.

DRIED MUSHROOMS

Dried mushrooms are quite different from their fresh counterparts. Dried morels, for example, have a slightly smokey, a much more intense and darker flavour than fresh morels. They are neither better nor worse – just different. Most recipes call for dried mushrooms not just because the season for fresh ones is so short, but because fresh ones will not give the same effect.

The mushrooms that you will find most easily in dried form are morels, cepes (called porcini in Italy), chanterelles and trompettes de la mort. They are none of them cheap, but morels are the most expensive and the most prized; trompettes make not a bad substitute, since both are so-called black mushrooms. They have a great affinity with a cream sauce.

To rehydrate, pour a small amount of boiling water over the mushrooms and let them soak for 20 minutes. Take them out and rinse out any sand under running water. Save the soaking liquid for use in the sauce or soup.

8. Lay one piece of pastry on a large baking sheet (use the narrower one if there is a difference). Do *not* do all this on the work surface: you will have a terrible time trying to lift it onto the baking sheet afterwards.

9. Spread ⅓ of the rice mixture over the bottom pastry, leaving a 1½″ border all round. Arrange half the hard-boiled egg slices on the rice; sprinkle with ½ the chopped parsley and lay 1 piece of salmon on top of the eggs. Cover the salmon with half the remaining rice; make the top as level as possible (build up the sides so that there is not a big hump down the centre). Then put on the rest of the egg slices, sprinkle with the rest of the parsley, lay on the second piece of salmon, and finally, add the last of the rice. Again, try to make the surface a rounded hillock rather than a craggy mountain.

10. Dampen the exposed pastry border with water and drape the second piece of pastry over the top, pressing the edges well together to seal them. With a sharp knife, trim off the excess pastry all round, but leave a border of at least ¾″ of double-thickness pastry. You can make the pastry fish shaped by varying the width of the border to create fins, a tail, and a mouth. Brush the whole thing with the beaten egg, cut two holes (about ⅓″ across) for steam to escape during cooking, and draw on fish scales, gills, and so on, with the tip of a sharp knife if you wish – you've come so far, you might as well! *(May be prepared up to 1 day ahead to this point. Keep refrigerated.)*

11. Preheat the oven to 425°F.

12. Bake the coulibiac in the middle of your preheated oven for 20 minutes, then turn the oven down to 375°F and cook for another 30 minutes. Remove from the oven and allow to rest for 20 minutes in a warm place before serving (it can wait for up to an hour, which allows it to firm up and makes it much easier to carve – but, of course, it won't be so hot).

13. Cut into slices about ¾″ to 1″ thick with a serrated knife.

SEA BASS WITH MUSSELS

This is quick and simple to prepare; be careful not to overcook the fish.

Serves 4.

2 Tbs	**butter** (see page 23)
1 small	**white onion**, chopped
1 cup	**white wine**
2 lbs	**mussels**, cleaned and bearded (see page 86)
2 lbs	**sea bass** OR **grouper** OR **snapper filets**
2 Tbs	**oil**
2 Tbs	**butter**
¾ cup	**whipping cream**
	lemon juice
	salt and **pepper**

1. Melt the butter in a saucepan large enough to hold the mussels. Add the onion and cook over medium heat until translucent. Add the white wine and let it come to a boil; put in the mussels and cover the pot. Steam for 5 minutes, or until the mussels are fully open.

2. Remove the mussels to a large bowl; strain the liquid and reserve it. When they are cool, remove most of the mussels from their shells, leaving a dozen intact for garnish.

3. Dry the fish filets on paper towel. Heat the oil in a large frying pan over medium-high heat. Add the butter, then the fish. Fry for about 2 minutes on each side, then transfer to a dish in a warm oven.

4. Pour the strained mussel liquid into the frying pan to deglaze it; reduce it over medium-high heat to about ½ cup. Pour in the cream, bring it to a boil, and let it cook down until the sauce is slightly thickened (enough to coat heavily the back of a spoon).

5. Adjust the seasoning: If it's too salty, add some lemon juice. Add the mussel meats (and any liquid that has collected) to the sauce; let them get hot.

6. To serve: Arrange the fish filets on warm plates or serving platter; pour the sauce around and decorate with the whole mussels.

CRAB CAKES

Makes 6 to 12 large or 36 cocktail-sized.

FOR THE CRAB CAKES

¾ cup	**milk**
5 Tbs	**butter**
	(see page 23)
¼ cup	**finely chopped onion**
¼ cup	**finely chopped celery**
6 Tbs	**flour**
2 large	**egg yolks**
¼ tsp	**black pepper**
8 drops	**Tabasco Sauce**
12 oz	**crab meat**, thawed and drained
2 tsp	**parsley**, finely chopped

FOR FRYING

(See below)

1 cup	**flour**
1½ cups	**breadcrumbs**
2 Tbs	**water**
1	**egg**
3 cups	**vegetable oil**

DEEP FRYING IN OIL

Oil for frying meat, fish, and vegetables should be between 320°F and 360°F – the lower temperature for meat, the high one for vegetables, and somewhere in between for fish and seafood. Of course the best way to check the temperature is with a thermometer. But if you don't have one, there are a couple of ways to get reasonably close: when oil gets to frying temperature a blue haze will rise from the surface; if you go on heating it beyond this point, it will start to smoke; this means that it is burning and the oil is no longer any good. The second way to check is to drop in a cube of day-old bread; if it turns golden brown in about 1 minute, the oil is at the right temperature.

---

1. Bring the milk to a simmer in a small saucepan, then remove from the heat.

2. Melt the butter in a heavy pan over medium heat. Add the onions and celery; the vegetables will absorb the butter; keep cooking them, stirring steadily, until the butter is released again. Now add 6 Tbs flour; cook over low heat for 5 minutes, stirring from time to time; take care not to brown the flour.

3. Add the hot milk to the vegetables. Heat, stirring constantly, until a smooth thick paste is formed and the mixture boils. It should be quite thick; it may look oily – if so don't worry. Remove the pan from the heat.

4. Beat the egg yolks into the sauce one at a time. Add the pepper, Tabasco, crab meat, and the parsley; stir thoroughly to combine everything. Spread the mixture on a large plate or baking sheet to cool completely.

5. With your hands, form the mixture into 6 to 12 large cakes, or about 36 cocktail-sized ones.

6. Spread out the flour and breadcrumbs on separate plates. Beat the egg with the water in a shallow bowl.

7. Roll each cake in the flour, dip it in the egg and then into the crumbs; press the crumbs firmly onto the cakes. Shake off any excess, and set the cakes aside on a cookie sheet spread with crumbs. *(May be prepared up to 24 hours ahead to this point, if refrigerated.)*

8. Heat the oil in a large frying pan to 350°F.

9. Gently slip the cakes into the hot oil and fry until golden on one side; turn and fry the other side. Drain the cooked cakes on paper towel in a 250°F oven. Don't fry too many cakes at one time or the oil temperature will drop and they will get greasy.

10. Serve with Coriander Mayonnaise (see page 228) or Jalapeño Tartare Sauce (page 227); or try hot tartare sauce (see page 78).

SEAFOOD SALAD

Seafood salad has the best flavour if it is served slightly warm – at the very least not chilled. You can make it in advance, but it will have the tenderest texture if you don't have to refrigerate it. If you do, let it come to room temperature before you serve. This recipe has a few steps to it, but is quite simple and does not take long.

1 large	**red pepper**
2 lbs	**mussels** (see below)
¼ cup	**white wine**
½ lb	**medium shrimp** (see page 48)
1 clove	**garlic**, finely chopped
¼ cup	**extra virgin olive oil** (see page 133)
¾ lb	**squid**, preferably small
½ lb	**sea scallops**
½ cup	**extra virgin olive oil**
¼ cup	**lemon juice**
1 Tbs	**coriander leaves**, chopped
3 Tbs	**Italian parsley**, chopped
	salt and **black pepper**

SHELLFISH SEASONS

The traditional rule about oysters is not to eat them in months that do not have an "R" in them – i.e., May to August, which is the breeding season. The reasons were gastronomic, not conservationist: oysters loose their clean tangy taste in the breeding season and take on a milky quality. Today, for reasons of conservation, the consumption of shellfish is not encouraged during the summer months. With cultivated species, like mussels, it is not so important; but with lobster and other types still in their natural habitat, the law generally prohibits taking them during the breeding season. The lobster season is arranged by the authorities to move around the coast, closing in one area as it opens in the next: thus, everyone gets a share of the lucrative lobster market, a glut is avoided, the price holds, and the lobster lives on to be caught another day.

1. Roast the red pepper (see page 47). Let it cool then remove the skin. Cut away the stem and discard the seeds. Cut the flesh into thin strips. Set aside.

2. Combine the mussels and white wine in a covered pot. Set over medium-high heat and steam for 7 minutes or until the mussels are fully open. Remove from the heat and set aside.

3. Bring a pot of water to a boil. Add salt then put in the shrimp. Cook for 2 minutes only. Drain and allow to cool. Then peel, devein if necessary, and set aside.

4. Prepare the squid and scallops. Clean the squid by pulling off the head; cut off the tentacles just below the eyes. Keep the tentacles and discard the head and anything inside the body, including the hard cartilage. Under running water peel off the purple membrane covering the body. Wash every thing well. Leave the tentacles whole; cut the body across into rings about ¼" wide. Set aside.

5. Cut the scallops into slices about ¼" thick; you can cut them either way – across the grain, into rounds, or with the grain, in slices. Set aside.

6. Chop the garlic finely. Pour the olive oil into a large frying pan and cook the garlic over medium-high heat until just starting to brown. As soon as it starts to turn colour, put in all the squid pieces, and stir-fry for 1 minute, until the squid turns white. Immediately remove the pan from the heat and put in the scallop slices. Cover the pan (with foil if there is no lid) and let them cook in the residual heat.

7. To assemble: Remove most of the mussels from their shells and place in a large bowl, leaving about 16 good-looking ones in the shell. Transfer the squid and scallops to the bowl, leaving behind most of the liquid. Put in the shrimp and the roasted red pepper strips. Pour over the extra virgin oil and the lemon juice and toss gently – be careful not to break up the mussels. Add freshly ground black pepper, a little salt, the chopped parsley and coriander. Transfer to a serving platter and arrange the whole mussels around the edge, as decoration.

THAI SQUID SALAD

2 lbs	**squid**, cleaned
3 Tbs	**lemon grass** (see page 114)
¾ cup	**coriander leaves**
1 cup	**fresh mint**
½ cup	**finely sliced green onions**
4 Tbs	**toasted rice powder**

FOR THE DRESSING

2 Tbs	**vegetable oil**
2 tsp	**finely chopped garlic**
½ cup	**Springroll Sauce** (see page 229)
2 Tbs	**lemon juice**
1 Tbs	**Thai fish sauce** "Squid Brand" (see page 114)

1. Clean the squid and cut into 3/8″ rings.

2. Bring a large pot of water to a boil; put in the squid rings and cook only until they turn opaque (about 30 seconds). Drain, shaking to remove the excess water.

3. Make the dressing: Sauté the garlic in the oil until very pale gold; pour into a bowl and allow to cool. When cool add the springroll sauce, lemon juice, and fish sauce.

4. Remove dry top and outer fibrous covering from the lemon grass. Chop finely and grind (in a mortar, coffee grinder, or food processor). Add the coriander, mint, onions, and rice powder, and toss together in a large bowl with the squid.

5. Pour over the dressing and toss everything well together.

SHRIMP WRAPPED IN PROSCIUTTO

Excellent on the barbecue; soak the skewers in water for an hour or more so that they won't burn during cooking.

Makes 16 appetizers; or serves 4 as a first course.

16	**16/20 shrimp** (see page 48)
2 Tbs	**lemon juice**
2 Tbs	**extra virgin olive oil** (see page 133) **salt** and **pepper**
8 slices	**prosciutto** (see page 53)
16	**skewers**, soaked in water

1. Peel the shrimp but leave their tails on. Put them in a small bowl and pour on the lemon juice, olive oil, salt, and black pepper. Leave to marinate for an hour, or overnight in the refrigerator.

2. Cut each slice of prosciutto in half across. Wrap the prosciutto around each of the shrimp and thread onto the soaked skewers.

3. Preheat the grill for 15 minutes.

4. Grill the shrimp for 2 to 3 minutes on each side over high heat. The prosciutto should get well browned.

CHICKEN & DUCK

For years cooks have done terrible things to chicken, to the point where its reputation is quite ruined, making it hard to consider seriously as something to serve at an important dinner. This is too bad since chicken is such an adaptable meat, able to be fitted into almost any situation and to acquit itself with distinction. It can be dressed up for a formal dinner, or down for a family supper. However it is cooked, it need never be tough, tasteless or a discredit to its kind.

When buying chicken, it is worth considering spending the extra money to buy free-range or organic birds; they really do have more flavour. If you can't find these, or don't want to spend the money, try to find chickens with yellow skins (called "New York style"). These are the same broiler chickens you will find elsewhere, but they have been scalded at a lower temperature to remove the feathers. As a result fewer layers of skin have been taken off, and the remaining skin has a yellowish tinge. While it is true that the skin is not the most healthy part of the bird to eat, it *is* much the most flavourful. It imparts its flavour to the meat as it cooks, so, if you feel you must remove it, do it after the bird is cooked.

When cooking chicken, use as gentle a heat as possible. Intense heat hardens the proteins in the meat, making it tough. This rule applies to all methods of cooking chicken; even on a grill or barbecue, use a lower heat with chicken than you would with meat or fish.

The other thing to bear in mind when cooking chicken is not to over-cook it. One of the problems, of course, is that the legs need more cooking than the breast (obviously a consideration only when you are cooking a whole chicken). Most people are surprised when we tell them how long to cook a breast: a boneless breast needs only 10 minutes in a gently simmering liquid, or 18 minutes in a 350°F oven (it takes longer for the chicken to get up to cooking temperature in the oven). A leg will take almost twice as long – about 18 minutes poaching or 35 minutes in the oven. If the chicken is to be reheated later, it should be slightly undercooked at the first stage (just a little pink in the middle). Do not be concerned: after it has been reheated all trace of pinkness will be gone.

Duck is much more of a challenge to cook than chicken. It is practically impossible to cook a whole duck and get a good result, because the legs take so much longer than the breast. By far the best way is to separate the legs from the breast, as we do in both the recipes in this section. Duck breast can also tolerate a higher cooking temperature than the legs, particularly if, like the French, you prefer the breast to be quite pink – or deep red, as many do. Doneness is largely a question of taste, although it is true, with duck as with any tender cut, that the meat will be juicier if you serve it pink in the middle.

THAI BARBECUE CHICKEN

A great dish for informal summer entertaining.

Serves 6.

6	**fresh coriander roots**, washed
1 tsp	**black pepper**
3 Tbs	**Thai fish sauce** ("Squid Brand") (see page 114)
1 Tbs	**oyster sauce** (see page 114)
2 cloves	**garlic**, crushed
6	**chicken breasts**, boneless but skin on (boneless thighs may be used)
½ lb	**capellini noodles** OR **Japanese somen**
1 head	**leaf** OR **Boston lettuce**
1	**English cucumber**, sliced **coriander leaves** **mint sprigs** **Springroll Sauce** (see page 229)

1. Remove the leaves from the coriander roots and reserve them for later. Chop the roots coarsely; transfer to the work bowl of a food processor or blender. Add the pepper, fish sauce, oyster sauce, and garlic. Process to a fine paste.

2. Put the chicken pieces in a bowl, pour the coriander paste over them, and stir to coat well. Cover with plastic wrap and refrigerate overnight.

3. Bring a large pot of water to a boil; salt it and add the noodles. Cook until just tender, drain, refresh under cold water, and allow to cool.

4. Preheat the broiler or barbecue.

5. Broil the chicken skin side down (or barbecue skin side up) for 5 minutes; then turn and cook until the skin is crispy – *don't* overcook it.

6. Wash and dry the lettuce leaves; leave them whole. Arrange the lettuce leaves, cucumber slices, coriander, and mint sprigs on a large platter.

7. Cut the chicken into ½" strips; mound it in the middle of the platter.

8. How to eat it: Take a lettuce leaf; on it place a piece of chicken, a slice of cucumber, some coriander and mint leaves, and some noodles. Roll it up and tuck in the ends. Dip in the springroll sauce, and eat – it's different and very good.

VARIATION ON THAI BARBECUE CHICKEN

Use the Thai marinade to prepare chicken quarters for the barbecue or broiler.

	marinade ingredients, as above
	chicken, cut in quarters

1. Prepare the marinade; pour it over the chicken pieces, toss well to coat thoroughly, and refrigerate overnight.

2. Preheat the broiler, or barbecue, or the oven to 375°F.

3. Cook the chicken as above; cooking time will be about 25 minutes for broiler or barbecue; 35 minutes in the preheated oven.

PESTO-STUFFED CHICKEN BREASTS

This dish has become very popular with our catering customers. All of the work can be done ahead; but its presentation is quite different from most other made-ahead dishes. The breasts are served whole, and are elegant enough for even the most formal dinner party. They have the added advantage that if you have to put dinner on hold for a while because one of your guests is held up, they will stay delicious and tender much longer than almost anything else.

Serves 6.

¾ cup	**pine nuts**
1 lb	**spinach**
2 Tbs	**finely chopped shallots**
2 Tbs	**butter** (see page 23)
½ cup	**ricotta cheese**
2 Tbs	**pesto sauce** (see below)
1	**egg yolk**
¼ tsp	**black pepper**
6	**chicken breasts**
3 slices	**prosciutto** (see page 53)

FOR THE SAUCE

3 Tbs	**butter**
½ lb	**mushrooms**, sliced
1 cup	**Chicken Stock** (see page 226)
¾ cup	**dry white wine**
¼ cup	**whipping cream**
3 Tbs	**butter**
3 Tbs	**lemon juice**
2 Tbs	**fresh basil**, chopped

PESTO SAUCE
To make your own pesto:
2 cloves garlic, crushed
½ cup pine nuts
¾ cup olive oil
½ cup grated Parmesan
1 large bunch basil leaves
½ tsp salt
Combine all ingredients in the work bowl of a food processor; process coarsely.

A wide range of packaged pesto sauces, including fresh, frozen, and in jars, is available. For this recipe we generally use Italian pesto sauce in a jar, although a fresh one is an excellent substitute, if you can find one.

---

1.   Preheat the oven to 350° F.

2.   Spread the pine nuts on a baking sheet; bake in the preheated oven for 5 minutes, or until lightly browned.

3.   Wash the spinach and remove the large stems; place it in a large saucepan with the water that clings to the leaves; cover and cook over medium heat until it is wilted. Drain in a colander and allow to cool. Then squeeze out as much water as you can. Chop the spinach, and put it in a medium bowl.

4.   Sauté the shallots in 2 Tbs butter until soft; add to the spinach.

5.   Add the pine nuts, ricotta, pesto, egg yolk, and pepper to the spinach; mix everything well together.

6.   Bone the chicken breasts and remove the skins; trim off any fat. Put the breasts, one at a time, between two sheets of parchment or waxed paper; with a blunt instrument flatten them to nearly twice their original area.

7.   Lay the chicken breasts out (what used to be) skin-side down. Place half a piece of prosciutto in the middle of each breast; divide the filling between the breasts, placing it on top of the prosciutto. Fold the edges of the chicken breasts up over the filling; reshape it as best you can into something that looks like a chicken breast (it will be a bit more mounded up). Set aside on a buttered baking sheet.

8.   Make the sauce: Melt 3 Tbs of butter in a frying pan over medium heat. Sauté the mushrooms for 3 minutes. Remove and set aside.

9.   Pour the chicken stock into the pan, turn the heat up to high, and cook until reduced to ¼ cup. Add the white wine and bring it to a boil. Reduce the sauce to about ½ cup. Now add the cream, bring to a boil, and reduce until lightly thickened; add the mushrooms. Set aside if not serving immediately. *(May be prepared up to 12 hours ahead to this point.)*

10. Preheat the oven to 375°F.

11. Melt 3 Tbs butter with the lemon juice. Pour it over the breasts. Bake in the preheated oven for 25 minutes, basting once or twice. Reheat the sauce while the chicken is baking.

12. Remove the cooked chicken to a warm serving platter or warm plates. Pour the juices from the baking dish into the sauce, and boil it up. Add the chopped basil, adjust the seasoning if necessary, and spoon it over and around the chicken.

CHICKEN WITH PORCINI MUSHROOMS

Porcini means "little pigs" in Italian; they are fat little mushrooms found in the autumn, and have a pronounced meaty taste. In France the same mushrooms are called "cepes" (you may even find them labelled "Boletus Edulis", which is their Latin name). Whatever you call them, they have a wonderful flavour. Gnocchi alla Romana (see page 63) would be an excellent accompaniment to this dish.

1 oz	**dried porcini mushrooms** OR **cepes** (see page 83)
2 cups	**boiling water**
4	**boneless chicken breasts**, OR **bone-in chicken breasts**, OR **bone-in chicken quarters**
1 Tbs	**olive oil**
1 Tbs	**butter** (see page 23)
1 clove	**finely chopped garlic**
½ cup	**whipping cream**

1. Place porcini in a small bowl; pour over them about 2 cups of boiling water, and leave to soak for about 15 minutes. Then remove the mushrooms and chop them coarsely; reserve the soaking liquid.

2. Heat the oil and butter in a large frying pan; dry the chicken well and sauté on both sides until golden brown. Remove from the pan and set aside.

3. Pour all but 1 tsp of oil from the pan; sauté the chopped garlic until golden, then add the chopped mushrooms. Put the chicken pieces back in the pan, skin side up, pour in ¼ cup of the mushroom-soaking liquid, cover the pan and cook on low heat (15 minutes for breasts, 20 minutes for chicken quarters).

4. Preheat the oven to 325°F.

5. Remove the chicken pieces to a plate and place in the preheated oven, skin-side up. Leave the mushroom pieces in the pan.

6. Strain (there may be bits of sand in it) the rest of the mushroom-soaking liquid into the pan. Turn up the heat to medium high and reduce to about ½ cup. Then add the whipping cream, bring to a boil, and cook until the sauce coats the back of a spoon nicely. Season to taste with salt and pepper.

7. Transfer the chicken pieces to serving plates, spoon the sauce around them, and serve.

CHICKEN WONDERFUL

Quick and simple; at least one person (not even related to me) thought it was very good!

Serves 2.

¼ lb	**sliced mushrooms** (optional)
2 Tbs	**butter** (see page 23)
2	**chicken breasts,** boneless (or bone-in)
1 Tbs	**butter**
¼ cup	**finely chopped shallot** OR **green onion** OR **white onion**
¼ cup	**white wine**
1 Tbs	**chopped fresh tarragon** (or other fresh herb)
½ cup	**whipping cream**

1.   If putting in mushrooms (they do make a good addition) melt the butter in a frying pan and sauté over medium-high heat until lightly browned. Remove from the pan and set aside.

2.   Dry the chicken breasts thoroughly; add more butter to the pan and sauté the breasts until pale golden brown on both sides. Remove the breasts while you sauté the onions, then return the breasts to the pan and add the white wine. Reduce the heat to low and cook, covered with the lid or foil, for about 10 minutes.

3.   Remove the chicken and turn up the heat to high; reduce the cooking liquid to 2 Tbs, then pour in the cream and bring to a boil. Add the tarragon (and the reserved mushrooms if using them); cook until lightly thickened. Put the chicken back in and allow to heat through.

CHICKEN IN PHYLLO WITH ORANGE GINGER SAUCE

Serves 6.

6	**boneless chicken breasts,** skin off
1 Tbs	**grated fresh ginger** **salt** and **pepper**
1 package	**phyllo pastry,** thawed
½ cup	**melted butter** (see page 23) pastry brush

FOR THE SAUCE

1 cup	**Chicken Stock** (see page 226)
1 cup	**orange juice**
1 Tbs	**honey**
1 Tbs	**grated fresh ginger**
½ cup	**whipping cream** **salt** and **pepper**

1.   Rub the skinless chicken breasts with the grated ginger, salt, and pepper. Make sure that the butter is warm.

2.   Open the phyllo package, unroll the pastry carefully, and lay it to one side of your work surface. Cover with a slightly damp (not dripping) towel to prevent it from drying out.

3.   Make sure that your work surface is dry (no water; melted butter is okay), lay one sheet of phyllo down on it and brush it all over with melted butter; lay a second sheet of phyllo directly over the first and brush it with butter. If you are using the flag method (see box), lay a third sheet over the first two and brush with butter. If using the oblong method, two sheets are enough. Wrap up the chicken following the directions shown in the box. Brush the outside with melted butter and set aside.

4. Make the sauce: Pour the chicken stock into a saucepan or frying pan; cook over high heat until reduced to ½ cup. Add the orange juice and reduce the sauce to 1 cup. Now put in the honey, grated ginger, and cream. Cook until the sauce is slightly reduced and thick enough to coat a spoon lightly. Add salt and pepper if necessary. *(May be prepared up to 24 hours ahead to this point, if refrigerated.)*

5. Preheat the oven to 375° F.

6. Lay the phyllo-covered chicken on a baking sheet. Bake in the preheated oven for 25 minutes, until the phyllo is golden.

7. Reheat the sauce over medium heat. To serve, set the chicken on a warm plate, and spoon some sauce around it.

WRAPPING WITH PHYLLO

Folding the Flag (makes a triangular package)

1. Cut the layered sheets of phyllo in half vertically. Set one half aside for another piece of chicken.

2. Lay the phyllo vertically (north and south to you) on the work surface. Take the top left-hand corner and fold it over to the right-hand edge of the phyllo (the folded-over piece will be triangular in shape).

3. Lift up the flap that you have just folded and tuck the chicken breast under it.

4. Now fold the chicken breast and the phyllo straight down towards you; the fold will be along the line made by the edge of the first fold.

5. Now fold to the left along the base of the triangle, keeping the package triangle-shaped. The next fold will be down towards you again (it's just like folding a flag).

6. Keep going till you get to the end; you will have a triangular package. Wrap the end around so that it all sticks to the package. Brush with melted butter.

An Oblong Package

1. For this you will use the full sheet, but two layers of phyllo thick, rather than three.

2. Lay the chicken breast diagonally across the lower left-hand corner of the sheet.

3. Wrap the triangle of phyllo sticking out at the bottom left-hand corner of the sheet up over the chicken, then flip the chicken over (towards the top right-hand corner), folding it into the phyllo as you do so.

4. Flip the chicken over again, folding more phyllo around it.

5. Fold the pastry to the right and the left of the chicken up over the chicken so that the package has neat ends.

6. Flip the chicken over once or twice more to completely enclose the chicken. Brush with melted butter and set aside.

CHICKEN STUFFED UNDER THE SKIN WITH PARMESAN SOUBISE

"Soubise" indicates that there are onions in the recipe; it works well with either a whole chicken, or with boneless breasts.

Serves 6.

4 Tbs	**butter**
2 slices	**prosciutto**, not too thin, chopped (see page 53)
4 cups	**finely sliced onions**
½ cup	**Arborio rice** (other rice may be used) (see page 61)
½ cup	**grated Parmesan cheese**
½ cup	**grated Romano cheese** (use Parmesan if not available)
1 Tbs	**chopped fresh sage**
1 Tbs	**chopped Italian parsley**
½ tsp	**salt**
¼ tsp	**black pepper**
1	**chicken** , 3 to 4 pounds OR
6	**boneless breasts**, with skin on
1 Tbs	**Dijon mustard**
2 bunches	**watercress**
2 Tbs	**lemon juice**

1.   Preheat the oven to 350° F.

2.   Choose a sauté pan that can also go in the oven. Sauté the prosciutto in butter until it changes colour; add the onions and sauté over medium-low heat until they are very soft and pale gold – do *not* brown. Set aside until the rice is ready.

3.   Bring a pot of water to a boil over high heat. Add the rice and cook for 3 minutes. Drain, and add it to the onions. Stir to ensure that the rice is well mixed in. Cover the pan tightly with foil, and bake in the pre-heated oven for 30 minutes. (If your pan can't go in the oven, transfer to a baking dish that can.)

4.   Remove from the oven and set aside. When cool, add the cheeses, sage and parsley, salt and pepper, and mix well together.

5.   *IF USING A WHOLE CHICKEN:* Split the chicken down the back with a heavy knife; set it breast up on your work surface, and hit it hard with the heel of your hand to flatten the breast bone.

6.   Loosen the skin by inserting your hand between the skin and the meat at the neck, and working it back to the thighs.

7.   Stuff the chicken under the skin, pushing all the way back so that it partially covers the thighs. Massage the skin on the outside to even out the stuffing.

8.   Set the chicken in a roasting pan, spread the mustard over the skin and bake in the preheated oven for 1 hour. Baste occasionally with the pan juices.

9.   Wash and dry the watercress and remove the large stems; place in a large bowl.

10.   When the chicken is done, remove from the oven, transfer to a serving platter and keep warm. Pour the fat from the pan and discard; pour in the lemon juice and scrape up all the brown bits. Pour this sauce over the watercress, and toss well. Carve the chicken and serve with the warm watercress salad.

5. *IF USING BONELESS CHICKEN BREASTS:* Lift the skin along one edge of the breast, leaving it attached along the other. Put the stuffing on the meat, but not all the way to the very edges, as it will come out as it cooks. Tuck the skin back over the stuffing and enclose it as best you can. Tie a couple of loops of string around the breast to hold everything in place; do not pull the string too tight.

6. Spread the mustard over the skin and bake in the preheated oven for 25 minutes.

7. Wash and dry the watercress; remove the large stems and place in a large bowl.

8. Remove chicken from the pan and keep warm. Pour off the fat from the pan, pour in the lemon juice and scrape up the brown bits. Pour this juice over the watercress and toss well. Serve the warm watercress salad alongside the chicken on warm plates.

CHICKEN FAT RICE

This is South-East Asian comfort food – homey, satisfying, and tastes like more.

Serves 6.

2½ cups	**short-grain Oriental rice**
2 Tbs	**chicken fat** OR **butter**
6 Tbs	**sliced shallots**
1 Tbs	**finely chopped garlic**
1 whole	**chicken**, cut in 12 pieces OR **12 chicken pieces**
5 cups	**Chicken Stock** (see page 226) OR **water**
1 tsp	**salt**
2 Tbs	**oyster sauce** (see page 114)
2 Tbs	**finely chopped green onions** **Springroll Sauce** (see page 229) **chopped fresh coriander**

1. Preheat the oven to 350° F.

2. Wash the rice and let it drain.

3. Sauté the shallots in chicken fat until it is pale gold. Add the garlic and sauté until the garlic is gold and the shallots are brown.

4. Add the chicken pieces; sauté until the chicken loses its raw look (it does not have to brown). Add the rice, stirring constantly until well coated with fat.

5. Add the chicken stock, salt, and oyster sauce; bring to a boil over high heat, stirring occasionally. Cover the pan tightly (use foil if there is no lid) and put in the oven. Bake for 15 minutes; then remove the lid, stir well, replace the lid, and bake for 15 minutes longer. Remove from the oven, and allow to sit covered for 10 more minutes.

6. To serve: Sprinkle with the chopped green onions. Serve with the springroll sauce to which you have added some chopped fresh coriander leaves.

CHICKEN AND HAM PIE WITH BISCUIT TOPPING

As the Duchess of Windsor used to say, you can never be too rich, too thin, or have too much puff pastry. But I have to admit that the biscuit top does make a nice change now and again.

Serves 6 to 8.

1	**chicken**, 3 to 4 pounds
1	**onion**
1	**carrot**
1	**celery stick**
1	**bouquet garni**
4 Tbs	**butter** (see page 23)
4 Tbs	**flour**
¼ cup	**whipping cream**
	salt and **pepper**
8 oz	**mushrooms**, quartered
2 Tbs	**butter**
8 oz	**mild ham**, in bite-sized pieces

FOR THE BISCUIT

2 cups	**all-purpose flour**
1 Tbs	**baking powder**
½ tsp	**salt**
1 Tbs	**sugar**
3 Tbs	**butter**
3 Tbs	**lard** OR **vegetable shortening**
½ cup	**grated Gruyère cheese**
1	**egg yolk**
¾ cup	**milk**

1. Put the chicken in a covered saucepan in which it fits comfortably. Add the onion, carrot, celery, and bouquet garni; pour in enough cold water to almost cover the chicken. Bring to a boil, uncovered, over medium-high heat. When it boils, skim the grey scum from the surface, turn the heat down to a simmer, cover the pan, and cook for 1 hour. Check from time to time that the water is just simmering. The chicken is done when the leg can be pulled off the bird quite easily.

2. Remove the chicken from the pot and set aside to cool; turn up the heat and reduce the cooking liquid to about 4 cups. Strain it into a bowl. Skim as much fat as you can from the surface.

3. When the chicken is cool, remove the skin and cut the meat into bite-sized chunks. Set aside.

4. In a medium saucepan, melt the butter and stir in the flour; cook over medium heat for 2 to 3 minutes, stirring; do *not* let it brown.

5. Off the heat, pour in about 2 cups of the reduced chicken cooking liquid. Return to the heat and stir until it boils. Add more liquid until the sauce is smooth, but still quite thick (bear in mind that it will thin out when the pie is baked). Remove the sauce from the heat and stir in the cream; season with salt and pepper.

6. Sauté the mushrooms in 2 Tbs butter over medium heat until lightly browned; add them to the sauce, along with the diced chicken and ham, and stir it all together. Transfer to a baking dish, and set aside while you put the topping together.

7. Preheat the oven to 350° F.

8. Sift the flour, baking powder, salt, and sugar into a large bowl. Cut the butter and lard or shortening into small (⅓″) cubes, and add to the flour. Work the fat into the flour by rubbing between the tips of your fingers, until only small lumps remain. Stir in the grated cheese.

9. Make a well in the centre of the flour; pour in the milk and the egg yolk. Stir with a fork until the liquid is absorbed. Turn out the dough onto your work surface; knead it a few times until it all has the same consistency; *don't* over do it.

10. On a lightly floured surface, roll out the dough ¾″ thick. Stamp into rounds with a 3″ cookie cutter (or a glass). Reform the scraps, roll them out, and cut out more rounds until the dough is all used up.

11. Place the biscuit rounds on top of the filling, close together but not overlapping.

12. Bake in the preheated oven for 40 minutes. Check the biscuit after 20 minutes. If it is browning too fast, cover loosely with foil until the filling is hot.

COLD BREAST OF CHICKEN WITH RED PEPPER SALSA

Serves 6.

6	**boneless chicken breasts**, skin off
¼ cup	**white wine**

FOR THE RED PEPPER SALSA

7	**red peppers**, cored and seeded
½	**red onion**, coarsely chopped
4 cloves	**garlic**, peeled
1 Tbs	**fresh coriander**
1 tsp	**salt**
½ tsp	**pepper**
1 Tbs	**olive oil**

1. Preheat the oven to 350° F.

2. Arrange the chicken breasts in a baking dish, pour on the wine, cover tightly with aluminum foil, and bake in the preheated oven for 20 minutes. Remove from the oven and allow to cool.

3. Make the salsa: Combine the red peppers, onion, garlic, coriander, salt, pepper, and oil in the work bowl of your food processor. Process using the pulse action until all the ingredients are chopped to small dice – but *stop* before they are reduced to a purée.

4. To serve: *EITHER* set the chicken breasts on serving plates and spoon the salsa over them *OR* spoon the salsa onto the plate, slice the chicken breast across into 6 or 7 slices, and arrange the slices on top of the salsa.

LEMON MUSTARD CHICKEN

Serves 4.

4	**chicken breasts**, bone in
juice of 1	**lemon**
1 clove	**garlic**, minced
2 Tbs	**Dijon mustard**
1 Tbs	**tarragon leaves**

1.   Preheat the oven to 375° F.

2.   In a small bowl, mix together the lemon juice, garlic, mustard, and tarragon (you can use another herb if you wish). Spread this mixture over the skin side of the chicken breasts.

3.   Bake the chicken breasts skin-side up in the preheated oven for 25 minutes, until lightly browned.

CHICKEN POT PIE

The whole lemon permeates the pie with its flavour – as well as supports the crust.

Serves 4.

4	**chicken breasts**, bone in
2	**whole chicken legs**, bone in
4 cups	**Chicken Stock** (see page 226)
1 cup	**dry white wine** OR **dry sherry**
2	**bay leaves**
5 Tbs	**butter** (see page 23)
10 Tbs	**flour**
1 cup	**onion**, cut in ½″ chunks
1 cup	**carrot**, cut in ½″ chunks
1 cup	**celery**, cut in ½″ chunks
½ lb	**asparagus**, trimmed & cut in 1″ pieces
1 tsp	**salt**
¼ tsp	**pepper**
1 Tbs	**finely chopped parsley**
1	**lemon**
1 lb	**Shortcrust** OR **Puff Pastry** (see page 233 or 231)
1	**egg yolk**
1 tsp	**water**

1.   Preheat the oven to 350° F.

2.   Place the chicken pieces in a baking dish large enough to hold them without overlapping. Bake for 15 minutes in the preheated oven.

3.   Bring the chicken stock and white wine or sherry to a boil with the bay leaves. Pour over the chicken, cover tightly with foil, and bake for 1 hour longer. Then remove from the oven and allow to cool.

4.   When the chicken is cool enough to handle, remove the skin and bones and discard; cut the meat into bite-sized chunks and set aside.

5.   Skim as much fat as you can from the chicken cooking liquid, discard the bay leaves. You will need 5 cups of liquid for Step 6 – add water if you don't have enough or reduce it over high heat if there is too much. Reheat it for Step 6.

6.   Melt the butter in a large heavy pot; whisk in the flour and cook over low heat for a few minutes without browning. Whisk in the hot cooking liquid and bring to a boil, stirring constantly (it should be quite thick). Add salt and pepper and put in the onion, carrot, celery, and asparagus. Turn the heat down to a simmer and cook for 5 minutes.

7. Remove from the heat, stir in the chicken pieces and the parsley. Pour the chicken mixture into your baking dish. Prick the lemon with a fork and stand it upright in the middle of the chicken. Set aside to cool (it should be quite cool when the pastry is put on).

8. Preheat the oven to 425°F.

9. On a lightly floured work surface, roll out the pastry to a rectangle large enough to cover the dish, with a bit of overlap. Brush the edges of the pie dish with water and drape the pastry over, pressing against the rim to seal it. Trim the edges, but leave about ½" overhanging the edge. (Decorate the top with pastry cut-outs if you wish.) Cut a couple of holes for the steam to escape; brush with the egg yolk beaten with 1 tsp of water. *(May be prepared up to 24 hours ahead to this point, or frozen.)*

10. Bake on a baking sheet (to catch the drips) in the preheated oven for 20 minutes; then turn the heat down to 375°F and bake for another 30 minutes, until the pastry is golden brown and the filling is hot.

COLD CHICKEN WITH AVOCADO MAYONNAISE

A light and attractive chicken dish for summer, or lunch parties year round.

Serves 6.

6	**boneless chicken breasts**, skin off
¼ cup	**white wine** OR **vermouth**
	salt and **pepper**
½ cup	**Mayonnaise** (see page 227)
½ cup	**sour cream** OR **Crème Fraîche** (see page 226)
1 ripe	**avocado** (dark bumpy-skinned Haas is best)
2 tsp	**lemon juice**
½ cup	**Tomato Concassé** (see page 228)
¼ cup	**very finely chopped green onion**
2 Tbs	**chopped fresh coriander**

1. Preheat the oven to 350°F.

2. Place the chicken breasts on a baking sheet; pour on the white wine, cover tightly with foil, and bake in the preheated oven for 20 minutes. Remove from the oven and allow to cool.

3. Peel the avocado; put it in the work bowl of the food processor; add the mayonnaise, sour cream (or crème fraîche), and lemon juice. Process until smooth. Transfer to a bowl, press plastic wrap down onto the surface, and refrigerate until serving time.

4. Remove the mayonnaise from the fridge, and stir in the tomato concassé, green onion, and coriander.

5. To serve: *EITHER* place the chicken breasts on plates or a platter and spoon over the avocado mayonnaise *OR* spoon the mayonnaise onto the plate, slice the chicken breast crosswise into 6 or 8 slices, and lay the slices on top of the mayonnaise.

ORIENTAL CHICKEN SALAD

An extravaganza of a salad with great consumer appeal. It has so much in it that it needs no accompaniment. Excellent for a summer buffet. You will see that there are a lot of ingredients; if you don't have one or two of them, just omit them – no one will know.

Serves 6 as a main course (more, if there are other dishes on the buffet).

FOR THE MARINADE

½ cup	**tahini** (sesame paste)
2 Tbs	**hot chili paste** OR **harissa**
2 Tbs	**soya sauce** OR **tamari**
2 Tbs	**oyster sauce** (see page 114)
4 cloves	**finely chopped garlic**
1″ piece	**ginger,** cut in slivers
¼ tsp	**salt**
¼ tsp	**black pepper**
1 Tbs	**brown sugar**
4 Tbs	**oil**
4 Tbs	**water**
6	**boneless chicken breasts**
	salt
12	**snow peas**, topped and tailed
1 med.	**zucchini**, Chinese cut
1 med.	**carrot**, Chinese cut
1 head	**broccoli**, in florets
½ head	**cauliflower**, in florets
½	**green pepper,** in julienne strips
½	**red pepper,** in julienne strips
1 bunch	**watercress,** large stems removed
1 head	**Boston lettuce**
½ head	**radicchio lettuce**
2	**Belgian endive**
½ cup	**roasted cashews**
1 pkg.	**alfalfa sprouts,** roots removed
2	**oranges**

1. Prepare the marinade: In a large bowl, combine tahini, chili paste, soya sauce, oyster sauce, garlic, ginger, salt, pepper, sugar, oil, and water; mix well together. Add the chicken breasts to the marinade, and allow to sit at room temperature for at least 1 hour. (May be refrigerated overnight.)

2. Preheat the oven to 375° F or light the barbecue.

3. Remove the chicken from the marinade, leaving as much as you can on the chicken. *EITHER* bake in preheated oven for 20 minutes *OR* barbecue over medium heat for 5 to 7 minutes on each side. Allow the chicken to cool.

4. Bring a large pot of water to a boil. One at a time, blanch the vegetables; scoop them out with a skimmer or slotted spoon when done, and refresh under cold water. The approximate blanching times after the water comes back to a boil are:

snow peas	2 minutes
zucchini	30 seconds
carrots	3 minutes
broccoli	2 minutes
cauliflower	2 minutes
peppers	30 seconds

5. Wash and dry the watercress and lettuces; tear them into bite-sized pieces and place in a large bowl. Cut the endive into 2″ pieces. Peel the oranges with a sharp knife, and cut into segments without pith. Remove the roots from the alfalfa sprouts. Put everything into the lettuce bowl, and add the cashews.

6. Make the dressing: Combine the sesame seeds, sesame oil, lemon and orange juices, vinegar, garlic, ginger, soya sauce, oil, salt, and pepper in a bowl, and mix very well to combine.

FOR THE DRESSING

1 Tbs	**black sesame seeds**
½ tsp	**sesame oil**
2 Tbs	**lemon juice**
1 cup	**orange juice**
2 Tbs	**red wine vinegar**
1 clove	**finely chopped garlic**
1 tsp	**grated ginger root**
1 tsp	**soya sauce** OR **tamari**
¼ cup	**vegetable oil**
¼ tsp	**salt**
¼ tsp	**black pepper**

FOR THE CRISPY WONTON

2 cups	**vegetable oil** for frying
1 pkg.	**wonton wrappers**

7. Heat the vegetable oil in a deep heavy pot to 360°F (see box on page 85). Fry the wonton wrappers until crispy. You can also use some types of Chinese noodle, but make sure that they are suitable for frying.

8. Add the vegetables to the salad ingredients; pour on the dressing and toss well. Transfer to a serving platter or bowl. Slice the chicken breasts and arrange them on top of the salad. Garnish with the crispy fried wonton wrappers.

CASSEROLE OF CHICKEN, LEMON, AND TARRAGON

Good fork food for a buffet dinner.

Serves 4.

4 large	**boneless chicken breasts**, skin removed
1 Tbs	**butter** (see page 23)
½ tsp	**salt**
¼ tsp	**pepper**
¼ cup	**white wine**
4 Tbs	**finely chopped shallots**
1 large	**leek**, white part only, in julienne
3 Tbs	**butter**
¼ cup	**flour**
2 oz	**white wine**
1¼ cups	**Chicken Stock** (see page 226)
¾ cup	**whipping cream**
1 Tbs	**lemon**
1 tsp	**lemon zest** (see page 237)
3 Tbs	**chopped fresh tarragon leaves**
½ tsp	**salt**
¼ tsp	**pepper**

1. Melt the butter in a frying pan over medium heat – do *not* let it brown. Dry the chicken breasts thoroughly; sauté only until they turn white – 1 minute on each side should do it (you want to firm up the outside of the breasts, but not to brown them). Remove the first ones from the pan while you sauté the rest. Return them all to the pan, pour in the wine, season with salt and pepper, and reduce the heat to low. Cover the pan and cook for 8 minutes.

2. Remove the breasts and allow to cool. Reserve the pan juices; measure them out and make up to 1¼ cups with chicken stock.

3. In a saucepan, melt the butter and sauté the shallots and leek until translucent; add the flour and cook for 2 minutes (it will not brown because of the moisture in the leeks; but make sure it does not stick to the bottom). Pour in the chicken cooking liquid and stock, bring to a boil, and allow to cook for 3 or 4 minutes, to get rid of the raw-flour taste. Pour in the cream and the lemon juice; add the zest and chopped tarragon. Bring to a boil, then reduce the heat to low.

4. Cut the chicken breasts across into ½" slices; add to the sauce and allow to heat through. Adjust the seasoning and serve.

CHICKEN WITH BROWN BUTTER, CAPERS, AND PARSLEY

2	**boneless chicken breasts**, skin off
2 Tbs	**white wine** OR **water**
2 Tbs	**butter** (see page 23)
2 tsp	**capers**, drained
1½ Tbs	**finely chopped parsley**
2 tsp	**lemon juice**

1.   Preheat the oven to 350°F.

2.   Place the chicken breasts in a baking dish, pour in the wine, cover tightly with foil, and bake in the preheated oven for 20 minutes. Remove and keep warm.

3.   Melt the butter over medium heat until it turns nut brown, but be careful that it does not burn. Add the juice, from the baked chicken (it will prevent the butter from browning any further), capers, lemon juice, and parsley. Pour over the chicken and serve immediately.

DUCK WITH GINGER AND BLACK BEAN SAUCE

This method of cooking duck, in which the meat is first marinated and then the legs cooked separately from the breast, is the best way of dealing with these difficult creatures.

Serves 4.

2	**ducks**, 3 to 3½ lb each
3 Tbs	**chopped fresh ginger**
2 Tbs	**finely sliced garlic**
½ tsp	**black pepper**, coarsely ground
2 Tbs	**sea salt**
6 cups	**duck stock** (see page 103) OR **Chicken Stock** (see page 226)
½ cup	**medium-dry sherry**
2 tsp	**oil**
2 Tbs	**fresh ginger**, cut in julienne strips
1 Tbs	**Chinese fermented black beans**, rinsed and drained
2 tsp	**honey**
½ cup	**scallions**, cut in julienne strips

1.   Cut the legs from the ducks. Lift the breast meat off the carcasses. You should have four legs and four breasts. With a sharp knife, score a diamond pattern on the skin side of the breasts, but do not cut right through to the meat.

2.   Combine ginger, garlic, pepper, and salt. In a shallow dish, layer the duck pieces with the spice mixture. Cover with plastic wrap and refrigerate overnight.

3.   Combine duck stock (see page 103) with sherry in a saucepan. Bring to a boil and reduce over high heat to 1½ cups.

4.   Preheat oven to 400°F.

5.   Sauté julienned ginger in oil until lightly browned. Add the black beans and cook until they sizzle. Add the reduced stock and bring to a boil. Remove from heat and add honey to taste. Set the sauce aside.

6.   Brush the spices from the duck pieces. Place the legs on a rack in a roasting pan. Roast in preheated oven for 40 minutes.

7. Heat a heavy frying pan over medium heat. Place duck breasts skin-side down and cook until well-browned and crisp on that side: pour off any fat as it renders. (Save it if you like fried potatoes; they are at their best done in duck fat.) Turn and cook lightly on the meat side. Remove from the pan and keep warm until the legs are done.

8. To serve: Reheat the sauce. Place one leg on each of four warm plates. Slice each breast into 4 or 5 pieces on the diagonal, and arrange around the leg. Pour the sauce around and garnish with the julienned scallions.

TO MAKE DUCK STOCK

1. Chop the duck carcasses into small pieces with a heavy knife. Arrange them in a single layer on a roasting pan and cook for 45 minutes in a 350°F oven, until bones are brown and crisp, turning occasionally.

2. Place the cooked bones in a stock pot and cover with water. Pour a little water into the roasting pan and scrape off all the brown bits; add them to the stock. Bring to a boil over high heat. Reduce to a simmer and skim the foam from the top. Reduce heat and simmer for 6 hours, adding water as needed to keep the bones covered. Strain the stock and refrigerate overnight. When cold, skim the solidified fat off the top.

DUCK WITH RADISH CAKES AND BEET AND APPLE PURÉE

Serves 4.

FOR THE DUCK

2	**ducks**, 3 to 3½ lb each
2 tsp	**fresh thyme leaves**
2 Tbs	**finely sliced garlic**
½ tsp	**black pepper**, coarsely ground
2 Tbs	**sea salt**, ground

FOR THE BEET AND APPLE PURÉE

¾ cup	**finely diced onion**
2 Tbs	**butter** (see page 23)
1½ cups	**finely sliced beets**
½ cups	**finely sliced apples**, cored and peeled
½ tsp	**salt**
½ cup	**water**

1. Remove the legs from the ducks. Lift the breasts off the carcasses. You should have four legs and four breasts. With a sharp knife score a diamond pattern on the skin side of the breasts, but don't cut all the way through to the meat.

2. Combine the thyme, garlic, salt, and pepper. In a shallow dish, layer the duck pieces with the spice mixture. Cover with plastic wrap and refrigerate for 4 hours, or overnight.

3. In a small pan, sauté the onions in butter until translucent.

4. Add the beets and apples, and stir well.

5. Add the water and salt. Bring to a boil, reduce heat to a simmer, cover tightly and cook for 30 minutes, stirring occasionally.

FOR THE RADISH CAKES

1½ cups	**finely grated white radish** (daikon) OR **turnip**
1½ tsp	**salt**
½ cup	**finely chopped onion**
1	**egg**
¼ cup	**flour**
¼ tsp	**black pepper**, ground
4 Tbs	**oil**

6. When tender, process to a purée in food processor or blender. Return to the pot and set aside.

7. Place grated radish and salt in a colander. Toss and allow to drain for 30 minutes or more.

8. Squeeze out as much water as possible with your hands and transfer to a bowl. Add the onion, egg, flour, and black pepper; beat lightly to combine.

FINAL ASSEMBLY

9. Preheat oven to 400°F.

10. Brush the spice mixture from the duck pieces. Place the duck legs on a rack in a roasting pan. Roast in preheated oven for 40 minutes.

11. Heat a heavy frying pan over medium heat. Cook duck skin-side down until brown and crispy; pour off any fat as it renders (keep it for frying potatoes). Turn duck and cook lightly on the meat side. Keep warm until everything else is ready.

12. Heat the 4 Tbs of oil in a heavy pan over medium-low heat. Drop tablespoons of the radish cake batter into the pan; flatten them slightly with the back of the spoon. Cook until golden brown, then turn and cook the other side. Drain on paper towels and keep warm.

13. Reheat the beet and apple purée over low heat.

14. Place one duck leg on each of four warm plates. Slice the breasts on the diagonal into 4 or 5 slices; arrange around the legs. Garnish with the radish cakes and the beet and apple purée.

NOTE:
This recipe works well for pork tenderloin (use 1 large or 2 small tenderloins). Marinate as for the duck. Roast in a 375°F oven for 30 minutes. Make the radish cakes and the beet and apple purée as described above.

BEEF, VEAL, LAMB & PORK

When I lived in England one of the (culinary) questions that provoked the best arguments was how to cook roast beef. There were a number of points of view, all loudly voiced, ranging between those who recommended putting the oven on "Clean" and cooking the beef for 5 minutes, then turning off the oven and letting the roast sit in it for two hours, to those who favoured getting up at 5:00 in the morning to put the beef in the oven to cook with just the pilot light till 8:00 at night. My mother was not keen to try either of those methods (and in any case, her oven was neither self-cleaning nor gas), so I am in no position to pass judgment. But the fall-out of this argument was that most regular people (including me) were thrown into a dither of anxiety about what we should be doing; we lost all confidence and no longer felt able to boil an egg let alone cook roast beef.

For many reasons, including the example set by mothers everywhere – though not yours or mine, of course – with an unfailing talent for producing meat done to a uniform grey colour, there is a lot of confusion about just how meat should be cooked. The meat in the recipes that follow falls fairly well into two categories: tender cuts cooked at a high temperature for a short time; and tough cuts cooked at a low temperature for a long time. You might expect the two methods to lead to the same result, but that is not so. A tender cut cooked quickly can be timed to give you meat done to the degree of doneness that you like. A tough cut cooked long and slowly is always going to reach more or less the same degree of doneness (generally known as overdone) but will be redeemed (indeed, elevated to heights that a tenderloin, however expertly cooked, can never achieve) by the wonderful gelatinous texture that develops with long cooking. Not a cook I know would trade away an oxtail stew for a loin of provimi veal – or for almost anything else.

The recipes for meats that need long and slow cooking should give you no problems – an extra half-hour of cooking will do no real harm – but it is important not to cook them too fast. High heat toughens proteins, so most of these meats are braised in well-flavoured liquids whose temperature, even when boiling, cannot go much over 212°F. All you need do is check to make sure that the liquids are just bubbling.

Cooking tender cuts of meat is not much more of a problem. First, always preheat the oven, grill, or barbecue: no one can produce good results putting meat into a cold oven (*pace* the pilot-light school). Most recipes call for the oven to be quite hot.

Second, decide how you like your meat cooked; all I will say is that you will get more of the natural juices if you cook it medium-rare; if you don't like natural juices, cook them away. On second thoughts, I will join Julia Child in putting in a plea for not overcooking pork. The organisms that cause the problems are effectively killed at 137° F; not even I would eat pork at that temperature. Most recipes call for it to be cooked to 165° F; all you gain with those last 30 degrees is an unnecessary margin of safety and what you loose is taste, texture, and juiciness. Wean yourself gently: cook your pork a little less each time. You will discover that cold roast pork, done slightly pink, is one of the best cold meats there is.

Next, put the meat in the oven (barbecue, grill, etc.); cook it for a little less than the time suggested in the recipe, then have a look at it. There are a few ways you can find out how done it is. The most reliable is to stick an instant-reading thermometer into the centre of the meat and let it adjust for 10 seconds; if your thermometer is reading more or less accurately this is what the temperatures mean:

Less than 110° F: Rare; deep red in the middle. Probably not done enough for most people (except for beef tenderloin).

110° F to 125° F: Medium rare; very pink in the middle. Good for beef, perhaps a little under for veal; too pink for lamb (for most tastes).

125° F to 140° F: Medium; still a bit pink in the middle (fine for lamb and veal; a bit overdone for beef).

Over 140° F: No comment.

Another not-quite-so reliable way to test doneness (but the only method used by professionals) is feel. As the proteins harden with cooking, the meat becomes firmer to the touch. Feel an uncooked piece of meat; it feels like a relaxed muscle (your bicep, for example), which is of course what it is. If you progressively tighten your arm muscles, you will feel the bicep become firmer, until finally it is very hard. Meat goes through the same stages as it cooks. Get into the habit of poking or pinching the meat to test its doneness. If you do this in tandem with a thermometer in the beginning you will gradually learn to associate a certain feel with the way you like your meat cooked.

Just one caution when using this method on a barbecue: Grilled meat is exposed to very intense heat on the outside, from the combination of hot coals and often flames as well. The outside becomes very hard because of the severe hardening of the proteins in this part of the meat. If you poke it, it may feel hard (which equals overdone) when in fact the centre, particularly in a larger piece of meat, is not yet cooked. At this point it's best to turn down the heat on the barbecue (I know I just gave myself away: I am a devout convert to gas) and cover it as well, if you can. As it rests after you take it off the heat, it will get a more uniform firmness.

Finally, as I just mentioned, you must let the meat rest after it comes out of the oven or off the barbecue; for a small piece of meat like a steak or a veal loin, 10 minutes is not too long; for a larger piece, such as a roast beef or leg of lamb, 20 minutes is fine. You can loosely cover it with a square of aluminum foil: it helps to keep it warm. Obviously the meat is going to cool off, and there has to be a trade-off between hot meat and juicy meat; but there is a way around this. While the meat is resting, heat the plates in the turned-off oven (or in a low oven). When the meat has rested it will still be warm; the plates will be warm, and the overall effect will be just what you want. No one will notice that the meat is not piping hot – only how juicy it is.

Flank Steak with Red Wine Aioli

A variation on the famous garlic mayonnaise from the south of France. As the garlic is cooked for quite a while, it is not as pungent as you may remember it being in the market in Nice. Serve with boiled new potatoes, as a vehicle for the sauce.

Serves 6 to 8.

	salt and **pepper**
16 cloves	**garlic**, peeled
1 Tbs	**extra virgin olive oil** (see page 133)
1 cup	**dry red wine**
2	**egg yolks**
½ cup	**vegetable oil**
½ cup	**extra virgin olive oil**
½ tsp	**salt**
2 Tbs	**lemon juice**
2 tsp	**garlic, finely chopped**
1	**flank steak**, about 2 lbs

1. Sauté the whole peeled garlic cloves in oil until soft and very pale gold. Transfer the garlic to a small narrow saucepan, leaving the oil behind. Pour in the red wine and reduce over low heat until there is about 2 Tbs left. Remove from heat and allow to cool.

2. Put the cooked garlic, the eggs, and the salt in the work bowl of your food processor; process for a few moments until blended. With the motor running, pour the two oils in a thin stream down the feed tube. Process until a mayonnaise is formed. Then add the lemon juice and the chopped garlic. Process until smooth. Scoop the aioli into a bowl and set aside.

3. Preheat the broiler or barbecue for 15 minutes.

4. Sprinkle the flank steak with salt and pepper; broil or barbecue until done (don't over cook it; flank steak is at its best rare). Let the meat rest for 5 minutes or so before slicing across the grain (see page 109) into thin slices. Serve warm with the red wine aioli and boiled new potatoes.

Pot Roast of Beef with Saffron Noodles

The noodles in this recipe are in fact saffron crêpes rolled and cut into strips, but you could use regular saffron pasta noodles. The meat is served on top of the noodles with a spicy crème fraîche and tomato sauce. It is a delicious combination.

Serves 6 to 8.

FOR THE POT ROAST

3½ to 4 lb	**pot roast** (short-rib roast, or any braising roast, tied)
1 Tbs	**vegetable oil**
2 Tbs	**olive oil**
12 cloves	**garlic**, peeled
½ cup	**thinly sliced carrot**
1 cup	**thinly sliced onion**
1½ cups	**dry red wine**
4 cups	**beef** OR **Chicken Stock** (see page 226)

1. Preheat the oven to 325°F.

2. Heat the vegetable oil in a heavy frying pan over medium-high heat. Brown the roast on all sides. Transfer to a large casserole with a tight-fitting lid.

3. Clean the frying pan; pour in the olive oil and add the whole garlic cloves and sliced carrots and onion. Sauté until lightly browned, then transfer to the pot-roast casserole. Pour on the red wine and stock and bring to a boil. Cover tightly with the lid (put a sheet of foil between the lid and the pot if it's not very tight) and bake in the preheated oven for 2 hours.

FOR THE NOODLES

good
  pinch of **saffron threads**
1 Tbs	**boiling water**
3	**eggs**
½ tsp	**salt**
1 cup	**all-purpose flour**
⅔ cup	**milk**
¼ cup	**water**

FOR THE SAUCE

1 cup	**Crème Fraîche**
	(see page 226)
2 Tbs	**prepared horseradish**
2	**tomatoes**, peeled,
	seeded and diced
¼ tsp	**salt**
½ tsp	**black pepper**

WHY CUT MEAT ACROSS THE GRAIN

Tender cuts of meat are expensive. However, you can make less-expensive cuts seem tender by carving them properly. If you carve meat in the same direction as the grain, the slices will have long fibres running across the slice; when you cut these slices to eat them you have to cut through these fibres. And when you chew, you have to chew through them as well. If the fibres are at all strong, the meat will seem tough. However, if you carve the other way – across the grain – you will cut the fibres into short pieces (they will be just as long as the thickness of the slice). When you cut or chew the meat, you only have to deal with short fibres, and the meat will seem tender. Flank steak responds particularly well to this treatment.

4. Put the saffron threads in a small bowl and pour the boiling water over them. Let sit for half an hour.

5. Beat the eggs in a large bowl; beat in the salt and flour, then gradually beat in the milk and water; add the saffron water.

6. Heat a (non-stick) omelette or crêpe pan over medium-low heat (pour in a little oil if not using a non-stick type). Pour in enough batter to cover the bottom with a thin film; swirl the pan to spread it evenly over the bottom. Cook until the top becomes dry-looking. Flip the crêpe and cook for a few moments on the other side. Pile up the cooked crêpes on a plate. Make crêpes until all the batter is used up.

7. Roll up 3 or 4 crêpes jelly-roll fashion; with a sharp knife cut them into ½″ slices. Repeat with remaining crêpes. Cover and set aside, but don't refrigerate.

8. Combine the crème fraîche, horseradish, diced tomatoes, salt, and pepper in a small bowl. Set aside.

9. Remove the casserole from the oven and transfer the roast to a platter; cover loosely with foil and keep warm in the turned-off oven. Strain the contents of the pan through a sieve, pressing down to get all the juice. Return the sauce to the casserole, skim as much fat as you can from the surface, and bring it to a boil over high heat, stirring occasionally; it will become lightly syrupy, but not really thick. Check the seasoning.

10. To serve: Add the sliced saffron noodles to the sauce and heat them through; Remove the strings from the roast and slice it; Arrange the noodles on a platter, and place the sliced meat over it. Serve and pass the sauce separately.

BEEF WELLINGTON

It may have been around for a long time, but Beef Wellington is still enormously popular.

Serves 8 to 12.

1 medium **onion**, finely chopped
1 lb   **fresh mushrooms**,
1 medium **onion**, finely chopped
2 Tbs   **butter** (see page 23)
2 Tbs   **oil**
               salt and **pepper**
1   **beef tenderloin**, about
               4 pounds completely
               trimmed of fat
2 Tbs   **oil**
2 Tbs   **Dijon mustard**
2 lbs   **Puff Pastry**
               (see page 231), thawed
               if previously frozen

FOR THE SAUCE
4 Tbs   **finely chopped**
               shallots
1 Tbs   **butter**
¼ cup   **dry red wine**
1 tsp   **fresh thyme**
               (½ tsp if dried)
8   **black peppercorns**
3 cups   **brown veal stock**
               (beef in a pinch)
2 Tbs   **Madeira**

1.   Sauté the onion in butter until soft; add the chopped mushrooms and cook until all the liquid has been rendered and has evaporated. Add salt and pepper.

2.   Heat the oil in a large frying pan until almost smoking. Brown the filet quickly on all sides. Set aside.

3.   Divide pastry in two. Roll out each piece to a rectangle about 6″ wide and 3″ longer than the beef (it should be ⅛″ to 3/16″ thick).

4.   Place on piece of pastry in the centre of the baking sheet. Centre filet on it, leaving a border all round. Spread top and sides with mustard; press mushroom filling onto the mustard.

5.   Damp exposed pastry border with water. Drape second pastry sheet on top of beef; press down firmly around sides of filet and seal against the bottom pastry sheet.

6.   Trim excess pastry, leaving a ¾″ border all round. Pull it in at 1″ intervals to create a scalloped effect.

7.   Cut two small round vents in the top; decorate with pastry cut-outs if you wish. Brush with egg glaze and set aside in the fridge until ready to bake.

8.   Make the sauce: Sauté the shallots in butter until lightly browned. Add the red wine and cook down until almost evaporated; add the tarragon, veal stock, and the peppercorns. Boil rapidly over high heat until reduced to 1 cup; strain through a fine sieve, pressing through as much of the liquid as possible. Return the sauce to the pan, add the Madeira, and adjust the seasoning. *(May be prepared up to 24 hours ahead to this point.)*

9.   Preheat the oven to 425° F. Set the rack on the lower centre rung.

10. Brush the Wellington with the egg glaze again; set it in the oven and bake for 15 minutes.

11. Reduce the oven temperature to 350° F. Continue to cook (25 minutes longer for rare; 30 minutes for medium).

12. Remove from the oven. Set aside in a warm place, loosely covered with foil. Slice with a serrated knife about ½″ to ¾″ thick. Serve with Madeira sauce.

WARM BEEF TENDERLOIN WITH CRISP-FRIED ONIONS AND SHAVED PARMESAN

An excellent first course for a formal dinner; or the centrepiece of a summer meal with the beef cooked on the barbecue. As a first course, serve two thin slices of beef per person; follow it with fish as the main course, or you could serve pasta or something adventurous like sweetbreads. In the summer, bruschetta would go very well before; and it only needs a salad to follow.

Serves 8 to 10 as a first course; 4 to 6 as a main course.

FOR THE DRESSING

4 tsp	**finely chopped shallots**
1½ tsp	**chopped fresh thyme**
¼ tsp	**salt**
1 Tbs	**red wine vinegar**
4 Tbs	**extra virgin olive oil** (see page 133)
2	**red peppers**, roasted (see page 47)
1½ lbs	**filet of beef**, in a piece
1 Tbs	**oyster sauce** (see page 114)
½ tsp	**black pepper**
3 cups	**vegetable oil**
1 cup	**finely sliced white onions**
1 cup	**flour**
4 oz	**Parmesan cheese**

1. Preheat the oven to 375°F.

2. Combine the shallots, thyme, and salt in a small bowl; press with the back of a spoon to crush the herbs and shallots. Stir in the vinegar, then slowly beat in the oil. Set aside.

3. Roast the red peppers (see page 47).

4. Rub the beef with the oyster sauce and black pepper; roast it in the centre of the preheated oven (about 23 minutes for rare, 30 for medium). Set aside to rest for at least 10 minutes before slicing.

5. Heat the vegetable oil in a deep heavy pan to 325°F (see page 85).

6. Toss the onions with the flour, shaking off the excess in a colander or sieve.

7. Fry the onions in 4 batches in the hot oil until golden brown. Drain on paper towels.

8. Slice the roasted peppers into thin strips. *(May be done up to 4 hours ahead to this point, but do not refrigerate the beef or the onions.)*

9. Carve the beef into thin (¼″) slices; lay the slices around the edge of a serving platter. Arrange the red-pepper strips around the beef, and mound the onions in the centre. Spoon the shallot vinaigrette over the beef. With a vegetable peeler, shave the Parmesan onto the beef.

WHY MEAT NEEDS TO REST BEFORE SLICING

When meat is roasted, the heat forces the natural juices out of the hot tissue towards the centre. If you slice meat right after it comes out of the oven, you will see that the centre is pink, but that the outer meat is a brown/grey. You will also notice that a lot of juice runs out of the meat and collects in the serving dish. However, if the meat is allowed to cool for at least 10 minutes before carving, the juices that had earlier been forced out by the heat will be reabsorbed by the tissues. This makes the whole roast juicier; it also gives it a uniform colour, so that it will be pink throughout.

THAI BEEF SALAD

A really different and wonderfully tasty salad; excellent for a summer buffet. It makes an excellent lunch when you serve it in the tradtional Thai style, where each guest wraps some salad in a leaf of lettuce to create a lettuce roll.

Serves 4 to 6.

1½ lbs	**flank steak**
1 Tbs	**oyster sauce** (see page 114)
1 tsp	**black pepper**
½ tsp	**finely chopped garlic**
3 Tbs	**lemon grass** (see page 114)
¾ cup	**coriander leaves**
1 cup	**fresh mint**
½ cup	**finely sliced green onions**
4 Tbs	**toasted rice powder**
4 Tbs	**lemon juice**
2 Tbs	**Thai fish sauce** "Squid Brand" (see page 114)
2 tsp	**sugar**
½–1 tsp	**dried chili flakes**
1 cup	**mung bean sprouts** (heads and tails removed if you have the patience)

1. Preheat the broiler or barbecue for 10 minutes.

2. Rub the flank steak with oyster sauce, pepper, and garlic. Broil or barbecue for 3 to 4 minutes on each side, until cooked rare. Set aside to cool.

3. Remove the dry top and fibrous outer covering from the lemon grass. Chop it finely and grind it (in a mortar, coffee grinder, or food processor). Put it in a large bowl and add the coriander, mint, green onions, and toasted rice powder.

4. When the flank steak is cool, cut it into 3 pieces lengthwise: these cuts should be made in the same direction as the grain of the meat. (The grain on flank steak is quite coarse so you should be able to see it.) Then cut each piece across the grain into very thin slices. Add them to the bowl.

5. Add the lemon juice, fish sauce, sugar, and chili flakes to the bowl. Toss well. Add the bean sprouts and toss again.

6. To serve: Western style – Serve on a plate with a knife and fork. Oriental style – serve with a platter of leaf lettuce; each guest wraps the salad in a leaf of lettuce to create a roll.

OXTAIL BRAISED WITH AMARONE

Karen makes these oxtails instead of turkey for holiday dinners. She says it is very comforting and soothing to the anxieties that sometimes attend family gatherings (although certainly not in any of our families…).

Serves 6 to 8.

2 Tbs	**oil**
2	**oxtails**, cut in 2″ pieces
¼ cup	**extra virgin olive oil** (see page 133)
1 cup	**finely chopped onion**
½ cup	**finely diced carrot**
½ cup	**finely diced celery**
1 Tbs	**finely chopped garlic**
2 Tbs	**finely chopped parsley**
1 sprig	**rosemary** OR **thyme**
3 cups	**Amarone** (or other sturdy dry red wine)
2 cups	**beef** OR **Chicken Stock** (see page 226)
⅔ cup	**Italian canned tomatoes**, drained and seeded
	salt and **pepper**

1.   Heat the oil in a large, heavy frying pan over medium-high heat. Put in the oxtails in one layer; (in batches if necessary – do *not* overcrowd them); and brown them well on all sides. Transfer them to a large ovenproof casserole that has a lid.

2.   Preheat the oven to 300° F.

3.   Wipe out the frying pan; add the olive oil and the vegetables and sauté over medium heat until lightly browned. Add them to the oxtails.

4.   Add the tomatoes, red wine, and stock to the casserole; set it over medium heat and bring to a boil. Cover tightly with the lid and transfer to the preheated oven. Bake for 3 hours; check now and again to make sure that the liquid has not evaporated (add more water if it gets low), and that it is cooking neither too fast nor too slow, but is just right (like Baby Bear's porridge).

5.   Remove the casserole from the oven; take out the oxtails and put them in a serving dish in the oven, covered with foil. Skim as much fat as you can from the cooking liquid. Set the casserole over high heat and reduce the sauce until it thickens up a little – it should become slightly syrupy. (If your dish can't go on top of the stove, transfer to a saucepan.) Check the seasoning and pour over the oxtails.

6.   Serve with something delicious to mop up the sauce – mashed potatoes, scalloped potatoes, polenta, or good crusty bread. It is far from proper, but some people (mentioning no names) like to serve a green salad on the same plate afterwards; the dressing and the sauce combine to create a unique gastronomic experience.

LAMB TENDERLOINS AND SPINACH IN PUFF PASTRY

This recipe was inspired by David Nichol of Loblaws and his wife, Terry. While at the Connaught Hotel in London, he ordered lamb in puff pastry off the trolley. It was so good they asked us to make it for them for a party here in Toronto. This is what we came up with.

Makes 4 not very large servings.

2 large	**lamb tenderloins**
1 Tbs	**oil**
1 lb	**fresh spinach**
2 Tbs	**butter**
	(see page 23)
	salt and **pepper**
pinch of	**nutmeg**
1¼ lbs	**Puff Pastry**
	(see page 231)
1	**egg**

OYSTER SAUCE
A thick, dark brown sauce that makes an excellent marinade for beef. It contains water, sugar, salt, oyster extracts, corn starch, vegetable protein, and caramel (for colour). Buy a brand that has no MSG.

LEMON GRASS
A herb that looks a bit like a pale green onion, except that the top and outer leaves are much more tough and fibrous. Use only the more tender bottom part. You can buy it in any Chinese or Vietnamese food store.

FISH SAUCE
A pale brown watery sauce with a pronounced fish flavour, made from anchovy extract, water, and salt. You will find it in Vietnamese stores.

1. Trim all the fat from the tenderloins. Heat the oil in a frying pan until very hot; quickly sear the lamb on all sides. Remove and allow to cool.

2. Wash the spinach well; place in a saucepan with the water that clings to the leaves. Cook covered over medium heat until wilted. Drain and allow to cool.

3. Squeeze all the water out of the spinach; chop it coarsely. Melt the butter in a pan, add the spinach and cook until the butter is absorbed. Season with salt, pepper, and a pinch of nutmeg. Set aside and allow to cool.

4. Divide the puff pastry in two. Roll each piece out on a lightly floured surface to a rectangle about 14" by 8", ⅛" to 3/16" thick.

5. Lay the lamb tenderloins side by side on the smaller of the two pieces of pastry; they should be pointing in opposite directions, so that the thin end of one is beside the thick end of the other; leave a gap about ½" wide between them.

6. Pat the spinach onto the top and sides of the lamb, filling up the space between the tenderloins; the lamb should be completely covered, and the surface should be quite even. Leave a 1" border of uncovered pastry all around.

7. Dampen the exposed pastry edge with water. Place the second sheet of pastry over the lamb, and press down well to seal it against the bottom layer. Trim off the excess pastry, leaving a ½" border all round (use the excess pastry to make pastry cut outs to decorate the top if you wish). Beat the egg, and brush it over the pastry. Refrigerate until ready to proceed. (See page 231 for more detailed instructions about working with puff pastry.) *(May be done up to 24 hours ahead to this point.)*

8. Preheat the oven to 425°F.

9. Bake the lamb in the preheated oven for 15 minutes; then turn the temperature down to 375°F and bake for 15 minutes more. Remove from the oven and allow to stand in a warm place for at least 10 minutes (it will stay hot for up to 30 minutes if loosely covered with foil).

10. Slice with a serrated knife into ½" slices. Serve on warm plates. Scalloped potatoes would go well with it.

RACK OF LAMB WITH TZATZIKI AND GARLIC CHIVES

Garlic chives have a very pungent aroma, but after cooking they loose a lot of their strength. The flavour of garlic is an accent, but not at all dominant.

2	**racks of lamb**, French trimmed
2 Tbs	**oyster sauce** (see page 114)
¼ tsp	**salt**
¼ tsp	**black pepper**

FOR THE TZATZIKI

2 cups	**full-fat plain yoghurt**
½ tsp	**salt**
2 Tbs	**finely chopped fresh mint**
2 Tbs	**Italian parsley**
½ tsp	**finely chopped garlic**
½ lb	**Chinese garlic chives**, stem blossoms only (stems without buds are too strong)
1 Tbs	**olive oil**

1. U.S. lamb is bigger and the meat is very tender; it's worth buying if you can find it. Have the butcher French trim it – trim off the fat and scrape the meat off the chop bones so that they are exposed. Rub the meat with oyster sauce, sprinkle with salt and pepper, and allow to marinate at room temperature for 2 hours, or refrigerate overnight.

2. Spoon the yoghurt into a sieve lined with cheese-cloth or paper towel (or into a cone-shaped coffee filter with a paper liner). Allow to drain for 2 hours.

3. Transfer the drained yoghurt to a bowl; add the salt, mint, parsley, and garlic; mix well and allow to sit at room temperature for the flavours to blend. *(May be done up to 2 hours ahead to this point, or may be refrigerated overnight.)*

4. Preheat the oven to 400°F.

5. Roast the lamb in the preheated oven (20 minutes for rare, 25 minutes for medium).

6. Wash and dry the chives; cut away the hard base of the stems; cut the soft part into 2" lengths.

7. Remove the lamb from the oven and set it aside in a warm place.

8. Heat the oil in a frying pan; sauté the chives until bright green (about 2 to 3 minutes).

9. To serve: Cut the lamb into chops and distribute between 4 warm plates. Put a spoonful of tzatziki on each plate, and surround the chops with the garlic chives.

MARINATED LAMB WITH LIME, MUSTARD, AND BASIL BUTTER

This marinade may also be used with chicken or Cornish game hens.

2	**double lamb chops**; OR
1	**chicken breast**; OR
½	**Cornish game hen** per person

FOR THE MARINADE

juice of 6	**limes**
juice of 2	**lemons**
¼ cup	**extra virgin olive oil** (see page 133)
2 Tbs	**Dijon mustard**
2 Tbs	**grainy mustard**
1 Tbs	**chopped fresh tarragon**
½ Tbs	**chopped chives**
1 Tbs	**chopped basil**
1 clove	**garlic**, crushed
2 tsp	**fresh thyme leaves**
2 tsp	**chopped fresh rosemary**
2 tsp	**salt**
2 tsp	**cracked black peppercorns**
2 tsp	**cracked pink peppercorns**
2 tsp	**cracked green peppercorns**

FOR THE LIME, MUSTARD, AND BASIL BUTTER

½ cup	**butter**, at room temperature (see page 23)
2 Tbs	**chopped fresh basil**
1 Tbs	**finely chopped shallots**
1 tsp	**finely chopped chives**
juice of 1	**lime**
1 clove	**garlic**, crushed
2 tsp	**Dijon mustard**
2 tsp	**grainy mustard**
½ tsp	**salt**
½ tsp	**pepper**

1. Mix all of the marinade ingredients together in a large bowl. Put in the lamb (or chicken or Cornish game hen) and marinate for at least 1 hour, or refrigerate overnight.

2. Cream the butter until light; add all the other ingredients and mix well together. Put the butter on a sheet of plastic wrap, pull one edge of the wrap up over the butter, and form the butter into a roll. Seal completely and refrigerate or freeze until ready to use. *(May be done up to 24 hours ahead to this point.)*

3. Preheat the barbecue on high heat for 15 minutes.

4. Grill the chops, chicken, or Cornish hens until brown on the outside but still tender and juicy in the middle (the time depends very much on your barbecue).

5. Cut the cold butter roll into rounds; place one or two rounds on each piece of meat just as you serve.

MOUSSAKA

Cooking the eggplant in the oven gives much less oil in the finished dish – but still enough to give authentic flavour! Serve with good bread and a green salad.

Serves 4.

1 large	**eggplant**, cut in ⅓″ discs
½ cup	**olive oil**
1 large	**onion**, chopped
½ large	**red pepper**, chopped
2 Tbs	**olive oil**
1 lb	**ground lamb**
1 28-oz can	**Italian plum tomatoes**, drained
1 tsp	**dried oregano**
	salt and **black pepper**
1 recipe	**Béchamel Sauce** (see page 224)
2	**eggs**
pinch of	**cinnamon**

1. Preheat the oven to 400°F.

2. Find a large baking sheet (or two smaller ones) on which all the eggplant slices will fit. Pour half of the oil on the pans. Arrange the eggplant slices on the pans, moving them around to make sure that the under-sides are lightly coated with oil. Pour the rest of the oil on top of the slices. Bake in the preheated oven for 12 minutes. Remove the pans from the oven and turn the eggplant slices over. They should be starting to turn light brown; if not give them a few minutes more. If they look dry, pour on a bit more oil. Cook for 10 minutes on the other side, until very lightly browned. Turn the oven down to 375°F.

3. Sauté the chopped onion and red pepper in 2 Tbs oil over medium heat until softened.

4. Turn up the heat to medium-high and add the ground lamb. Cook, stirring, until it has completely changed colour to brown.

5. Remove the seeds from the drained tomatoes; add the tomatoes to the meat. Add the oregano, salt, and pepper. Reduce the heat to medium low and cook for 20 minutes.

6. Make the béchamel sauce (see page 224). When it is finished, beat in the 2 eggs and the cinnamon.

7. To assemble: Choose a baking dish at least 2″ deep, preferably 3″. Spread one third of the meat mixture over the bottom; cover with slices of eggplant. Spread with another third of the meat, another layer of eggplant, then the rest of the meat and top it with a final layer of eggplant. Pour the béchamel sauce over the top. *(May be done ahead to this point.)*

8. Bake in the preheated oven for 40 minutes. Check it after 25 minutes; if the béchamel sauce is browning too much, cover the dish loosely with aluminum foil. It is done when it is lightly browned on top and well heated.

LAMB LOIN WITH FIGS BAKED IN PORT

An interesting combination of flavours; the figs are cooked separately and served alongside the roast lamb loins.

Serves 4.

2	**lamb loins** (preferably U.S.)
1 tsp	**chopped fresh rosemary**
¼ tsp	**salt**
¼ tsp	**black pepper**
½ tsp	**finely chopped garlic**
2 tsp	**olive oil**
1 Tbs	**balsamic vinegar** (see page 138)
8	**fresh figs**, cut in half
4 Tbs	**port**
2 Tbs	**butter** (see page 23)

1. If you can find it, U.S. lamb is worth buying; the loins are larger and the meat is very tender. Have the butcher bone them out (or do it yourself, if you're feeling adventurous).

2. In a bowl or dish large enough to hold the lamb, mix together the rosemary, salt, pepper, garlic, olive oil, and balsamic vinegar. Roll the lamb loins in the marinade to coat them thoroughly. Set aside to marinate for 2 hours, or refrigerate overnight.

4. Place the figs cut-side down in a baking dish in which they fit comfortably. Pour in the port, and dot with butter. *(May be done up to 12 hours ahead to this point.)*

5. Preheat the oven to 400° F. (If marinated in the refrigerator, allow the lamb to come to room temperature before proceeding.)

6. Bake the lamb in the preheated oven (15 minutes for rare, 20 minutes for medium). Bake the figs at the same time for 15 minutes.

7. Remove both lamb and figs from the oven and allow to rest in a warm place for 10 minutes.

8. To serve: Cut the lamb into ¼" to ½" slices; arrange on warm plates with 4 fig halves.

LEG OF LAMB STUFFED WITH PROVOLONE, SPINACH, AND SUNDRIED TOMATOES

This lamb may also be baked in the oven.

Serves 6 to 8.

1	**leg of lamb**, butterflied **salt** and **pepper**
1 Tbs	**Dijon mustard**
4 cloves	**garlic**, crushed
8 leaves	**fresh basil**
2 Tbs	**chopped chives**
½ bunch	**fresh spinach**, washed and dried

1. Have the butcher trim all the fat and fell from the leg, then remove the bone, open up the leg, and cut it so that it lays flat. Sprinkle with the salt and pepper.

2. Combine the mustard, garlic, basil, and chives in a small bowl; spread this mixture on the inside of the lamb. Trim the stems from the spinach leaves; lay the leaves over the lamb so that it is well covered. Then

6 slices	**provolone cheese**
8	**sundried tomatoes**
1 Tbs	**olive oil**

put on a layer of sundried tomatoes, and finally a layer of provolone cheese.

3. Roll the leg up jelly-roll fashion so that it is quite compact – make sure that the stuffing is tucked inside the roll and does not hang out of the ends. Tie it securely in several places with string. Rub the outside with oil. *(May be done up to 24 hours ahead to this point, if refrigerated.)*

4. Preheat the barbecue on low heat OR preheat the oven to 375°F.

5. Barbecue (with the cover on if you have one) for 45 minutes to 1 hour; watch it carefully so that it does not burn. It is done medium rare when you notice the meat has shrunk noticeably; allow 10 more minutes if you don't like it a bit pink. Let it sit for 15 minutes before carving. It may be baked in the oven for the same length of time.

VITELLO TONNATO

Veal and tuna may seem to be an unlikely combination, but it is an Italian classic; for a summer lunch or buffet, it is hard to beat.

Serves 8 to 12.

1	**provimi veal inside round**, or other lean cut (see page 123)
1 Tbs	**oil**
1 medium	**carrot**, sliced
1 medium	**onion**, sliced
1 tsp	**dried thyme**
1	**bay leaf**

FOR THE SAUCE

1 cup	**Mayonnaise** (see page 227)
1 can	**white tuna**, drained
¼ cup	**lemon juice**
½ cup	**Crème Fraîche** (see page 226) OR **whipping cream**
2	**anchovy filets**

FOR DECORATION

10	**anchovy filets**
3 Tbs	**capers**, drained

1. Preheat the oven to 375°F.

2. Place the carrot, onion, thyme, and bay leaf in a roasting pan with the oil and toss well. Set the veal on top, cover the pan tightly with foil, and roast in the preheated oven for 1 hour. Remove from the oven and allow to cool.

3. Combine the mayonnaise, drained tuna, lemon juice, crème fraîche, and anchovy filets in the work bowl of a food processor. Process until smooth.

4. To serve: Slice the veal very thinly (it should still be slightly pink in the middle). Lay the slices on a serving platter. Spoon the sauce over it. Cut the anchovy filets in half lengthwise, and arrange them in a criss-cross lattice over the veal. Sprinkle with the capers and serve with good Italian bread to mop up the sauce.

VEAL WITH WILD MUSHROOMS IN PUFF PASTRY

Serves 10 to 12.

1 oz	**dried morels** OR **trompettes de la mort** (see page 83)
about 1 cup	**boiling water**
½ lb	**fresh mushrooms**, finely chopped
1 medium	**onion**, finely chopped
2 Tbs	**butter**
2 Tbs	**oil**
	salt and **pepper**
1	**provimi veal loin** completely trimmed of fat (see page 123)
1 Tbs	**oil**
1 Tbs	**oyster sauce** (see page 114)
1½ lbs	**Puff Pasty** (see page 231), thawed in fridge if previously frozen
1	**egg**, beaten

FOR THE SAUCE

2 Tbs	**finely chopped shallots**
1 Tbs	**butter** (see page 23)
¼ cup	**dry red wine**
1 Tbs	**fresh tarragon leaves** (1 tsp if dried)
2 cups	**brown veal stock** (beef in a pinch)
8	**black peppercorns**
¼ tsp	**salt**
⅛ tsp	**black pepper**

1.   Put the dried mushrooms in a small bowl; pour over enough boiling water to cover and allow to steep for 30 minutes. When soft, cut open the morels and rinse out any sand. Finely chop the mushrooms; strain and reserve the soaking liquid.

2.   Sauté the onions in butter and oil until soft; add the finely chopped fresh and dried mushrooms. Cook until the juices have been rendered. Continue to cook, stirring frequently, until all the liquid has evaporated, and the mixture is quite dry (it should be like a chunky paste). Season with salt and pepper; set aside to cool.

3.   Heat the oil in a large frying pan until almost smoking. Brown the veal quickly on both sides. Set aside to cool, then rub the oyster sauce over the top and sides – *not* the bottom.

4.   Divide the pastry in two. Roll out each piece into a rectangle about 6″ wide and 3″ longer than the veal. The pastry should be ⅛″ to 3/16″ thick – no thinner.

5.   Lay one piece of pastry (the smaller if there is a difference) in the centre of a baking sheet. Centre the veal on it, so that there is a border all round. Press the mushroom stuffing onto the top and sides of the veal.

6.   Damp the exposed border of pastry with water; drape the second sheet of pastry on top of the veal. Press the top pastry sheet firmly down around the sides of the filet and seal against the bottom one.

7.   Trim the pastry all around, leaving a ¾″ to 1″ border. With the back of a knife, pull the edge of the pastry in at 1″ intervals to create a scalloped effect all around the edge.

8.   Cut two small round vents in the top to let steam escape during cooking. Decorate with pastry cut-outs if desired. Beat the egg well; brush the pastry with the egg wash and set aside in the fridge until ready to bake. Keep the remaining egg wash.

9.   Make the sauce: Sauté the shallots in butter until lightly browned. Add the red wine and cook down until almost evaporated; add the tarragon, veal stock, re-served mushroom soaking liquid, and the peppercorns.

Boil rapidly over high heat until reduced to ¾ cup; strain through a fine sieve, pressing through as much of the liquid as possible. Return the sauce to the pan and adjust the seasoning. *(May be prepared up to 24 hours ahead to this point.)*

10. Preheat the oven to 425° F. Set the rack on the lower centre rung.

11. Brush the pastry again with egg wash (if any left). Set the veal in the oven and bake for 15 minutes.

12. Reduce the oven temperature to 350° F and bake for 20 minutes longer.

13. Remove from the oven and set aside in a warm place, loosely covered with foil. Reheat the sauce.

14. Slice with a serrated knife into ½" slices. Serve on warm plates with a little of the mushroom sauce.

VEAL SHOULDER WITH WARM NEW POTATO SALAD

Serves 6 to 8.

1	**provimi veal shoulder**, boned, rolled and tied; 3½ to 4 pounds (see page 123)
1 tsp	**finely chopped garlic**
½ tsp	**salt**
¼ tsp	**black pepper**
1 Tbs	**olive oil**

FOR THE POTATO SALAD

4 Tbs	**red wine vinegar**
1 Tbs	**minced fresh tarragon**
4 Tbs	**finely chopped shallots**
½ tsp	**salt**
3 pounds	**small new potatoes**, washed
2 tsp	**salt**
4	**egg yolks**
¾ cup	**Crème Fraîche** (see page 226)
1 Tbs	**Dijon mustard**
1 head	**leaf** OR **Boston lettuce**

1. Preheat the oven to 350° F.

2. Mix together the oil, salt, pepper, and garlic; rub this mixture over the veal and set it in a roasting pan. Roast in the preheated oven for 1½ hours, basting occasionally with any juices that run out.

3. Make the dressing: Combine the vinegar, tarragon, shallots, and salt together in a large bowl.

4. When the veal has been in for 1 hour, cut the potatoes in half, place them in a large saucepan and cover with cold water. Add the salt and bring to a boil and cook until the potatoes are just tender. Drain them and place while still hot in the bowl with the wine vinegar; toss well.

5. Remove the veal from the oven; let it rest in a warm place for 10 minutes before slicing.

6. Combine the egg yolks with the crème fraîche and mustard in a small saucepan; heat over low heat until the mixture thickens – be careful not to boil it. (You can do this in a double boiler, but it takes longer.) Toss with the potatoes, which should still be warm.

7. Slice the veal and arrange it around the edges of a serving platter; spread out the lettuce leaves in the centre, then mound the potato salad on top.

VEAL TENDERLOIN WITH TARRAGON CREAM SAUCE

Tenderloin (the filet) or loin (the sirloin) work equally well with this sauce.

Serves 4 (loin, 8).

1	**provimi veal tenderloin** OR **loin** (see page 123)
2 Tbs	**olive oil**

FOR THE SAUCE

1 Tbs	**butter** (see page 23)
1 Tbs	**finely chopped shallot**
1 clove	**garlic**
¼ cup	**vermouth** OR **dry white wine**
1¾ cups	**whipping cream**
2 Tbs	**lemon juice**
1 Tbs	**lemon zest**
2 Tbs	**fresh tarragon leaves**
¼ tsp	**salt**
⅛ tsp	**black pepper**
¼ cup	**whipping cream**

1.   Heat the oil in a large frying pan until almost smoking. Put in the meat and sear it on all sides (it should be medium brown, but it won't be even, so don't worry). Remove from the pan and set on a baking sheet. Pour off the excess oil from the pan, but do not wash the pan.

2.   In the same pan melt the butter; sauté the garlic and shallot until soft. Turn up the heat and pour in the wine. Scrape all the brown bits off the bottom of the pan. Cook until the wine is reduced to a couple of tablespoons. Pour in 1¾ cups of cream and bring to a boil.

3.   Add the lemon juice, lemon zest, and tarragon to the sauce. Boil until the sauce reduced to about 1 cup and is lightly thickened. Season with salt and pepper. *(May be prepared up to 24 hours ahead to this point; if refrigerated, let the veal come to room temperature before proceeding.)*

4.   Preheat the oven to 400° F.

5.   Roast the veal in the preheated oven (18 minutes for rare, 23 minutes for medium). Remove from the oven and allow to rest in a warm place for 10 minutes.

6.   Whip the ¼ cup of cream to soft peaks. Reheat the sauce to almost boiling. Stir and fold the whipped cream into the sauce.

7.   Slice the veal into ½" slices; spoon the sauce onto warm plates and arrange the veal over it.

LOIN OF VEAL WITH MUSTARD AND SAGE

A very simple way to prepare veal – but with veal simplicity is best because you must be careful not to overpower the flavour of the meat. (This recipe may also be used with veal tenderloin.)

Serves 8 (tenderloin, 4).

1	**provimi veal loin,** 3 to 4 lbs, OR **tenderloin**, about 2 lbs (see below)
2 Tbs	**olive oil**
2 Tbs	**Dijon mustard**
1 Tbs	**chopped fresh sage**
1½ Tbs	**butter** (see page 23)
1 tsp	**finely chopped shallots**
2 Tbs	**Madeira**
¾ cup	**Veal Demi-Glace** (see page 225) OR
1½ cups	**brown veal stock** (use beef stock in a pinch)

PROVIMI VEAL
Provimi is not a breed of cow. It stands for PROtein VItamin MIneral, and refers to the diet fed to calves to give the best balance of colour, texture, and taste to their meat. Provimi veal has the whitest colour, the mildest flavour and tenderest texture.

The next grade down is called CHOICE; it is darker in colour. It is really too dark to use in recipes where the meat is grilled or sautéed; you could use it for braising. It also has a more pronounced flavour.

1. Tie the tenderloin at 3″ intervals. Tuck the tail under to make it an even thickness, and secure with string. You don't need to tie a loin – it will lie quite flat.

2. Heat the oil in a large frying pan until almost smoking. Sear the veal quickly on all sides until brown (don't worry if it is not even). Remove from the pan and set aside to cool. Do not wash out the pan.

3. Spread the cooled veal with the mustard, and sprinkle with the chopped sage. *(May be prepared 4 to 6 hours ahead to this point.)*

4. Preheat the oven to 375°F.

5. Bake the veal in the preheated oven (20 minutes for rare, 25 minutes for medium).

6. Set the (unwashed) frying pan over medium heat; melt the butter and sauté the shallots until softened. Add the Madeira and scrape up all the brown bits from the bottom of the pan.

7. Pour in the demi-glace or stock and reduce until just slightly thickened (just enough to coat the back of a spoon). This will take longer if using stock rather than demi-glace.

8. Remove the veal from the oven and allow to rest in a warm place for 10 minutes. Cut into ½″ slices.

9. Spoon the sauce onto warm plates; lay the veal slices on top and serve immediately.

VEAL AND BLACK BEAN CHILI

A delicious informal supper if you serve it with flour tortillas, grated cheese, chopped tomatoes, sour cream, and shredded lettuce. The distinctive taste of chili comes from the cumin, coriander seeds, and fresh coriander leaves. Start the beans soaking the night before.

Serves 6 to 8.

2 cups	**dried black beans**
½ cup	**vegetable oil**
2 lbs	**stewing veal**, cut in 1″ cubes
1½ cups	**finely chopped onions**
1 Tbs	**finely chopped garlic**
2 tsp	**ground cumin**
¼ tsp	**ground allspice**
2 tsp	**ground coriander seeds**
10 cups	**Chicken Stock** (see page 226) OR **veal stock**
4 Tbs	**butter**
6 Tbs	**all-purpose flour**
1 tsp	**hot chili flakes**
½	**orange**
1½ tsp	**dried oregano**
	salt
1 cup	**chopped coriander leaves**

1. *THE DAY BEFORE SERVING:* Soak the beans in a large bowl of cold water overnight.

2. *THE NEXT DAY:* Drain the beans, transfer to a large pot, cover with fresh water, and cook until tender (1 to 2 hours, depending on how fresh the beans are).

3. Heat the oil in a large heavy-bottom pan; dry the veal well and brown it on all sides in the oil (do it in several batches so that you don't crowd the meat).

4. Pour off most of the oil from the pan; put in the onion and garlic and cook over medium heat until lightly browned. Add the cumin, allspice, and ground coriander. Stir for a few moments and set aside.

5. Heat the stock to almost boiling and have it ready on the back of the stove. In a large saucepan, melt the butter and stir in the flour and cook over medium heat for 3 minutes without browning. Ladle in about 3 cups of stock, and whisk until smooth and boiling. Add the rest and bring to a boil, whisking to make sure it is smooth.

6. Add the browned veal and the onions; then the chili flakes, the half orange, and dried oregano. Reduce the heat to a simmer and cook for 1½ hours, stirring occasionally.

7. Add the black beans and cook for 1 more hour (2½ hours total); add more water as necessary to keep the chili soupy, but on the thick side. Stir occasionally, mashing some of the beans against the side of the pot to thicken it up.

8. Remove the half orange; stir in the fresh chopped coriander. Check the seasoning and serve.

VEAL KIDNEYS WITH ROSEMARY AND BALSAMIC VINEGAR

These are kidneys for people who think they don't like kidneys. Soaking them gives them a very mild flavour; the sauce is a delicious combination of veal stock, balsamic vinegar, and rosemary.

Serves 4.

2	**veal kidneys**, about ¾ lb each
	cold water
2 Tbs	**salt**
2 Tbs	**finely chopped shallots**
2 Tbs	**balsamic vinegar**, good quality (see page 138)
1 tsp	**fresh rosemary leaves**, chopped
¼ tsp	**salt**
¼ tsp	**black pepper**
2 tsp	**butter** (see page 23)
3 Tbs	**finely chopped shallots**
2 Tbs	**dry red wine**
1 Tbs	**fresh rosemary leaves**
8	**black peppercorns**
3 cups	**brown veal stock**
1 Tbs	**balsamic vinegar**, good quality
1 Tbs	**vegetable oil**
2 Tbs	**cold butter**, cut in small pieces

1. *THE DAY BEFORE SERVING:* Mix salt and water in a bowl large enough to hold the kidneys. Soak the kidneys overnight in the fridge.

2. *UP TO 4 HOURS BEFORE SERVING:* Remove the kidneys from the water. Rinse and dry.

3. Stir shallots, balsamic vinegar, rosemary, salt, and pepper together in a bowl. Push the marinade between the lobes of the kidneys. Let marinate for at least 1 hour (up to 4 hours).

4. Sauté shallots in butter over low heat until lightly browned. Add the red wine and cook down until almost evaporated. Add the rosemary, peppercorns, and veal stock.

5. Boil rapidly over high heat until reduced to 1 cup. Strain through a fine sieve, pressing as much of the liquids through as possible.

6. Return the sauce to the pan; add the balsamic vinegar and adjust the seasoning if necessary. Keep warm. *(May be done up to 4 hours ahead to this point.)*

7. Preheat the oven to 350° F.

8. Heat a heavy, oven-proof frying pan over medium-high heat until hot; add 1 Tbs of the vegetable oil. Put in the kidneys and sear on all sides (about 4 minutes). If the juices start to run out, they have been seared enough.

9. Put the pan with the kidneys in the oven. Bake in the preheated oven for 12 minutes. Remove kidneys to a warm plate while you finish the sauce.

10. Bring the sauce to a boil over high heat. Rapidly whisk in the butter, a few pieces at a time. As soon as all the butter is whisked in, remove the sauce from the heat.

11. Slice the kidneys thinly. Arrange the slices on four warm plates, pour the sauce around and serve immediately.

Osso Bucco

One of the great dishes of Italian cooking; the classic example of long, slow cooking producing almost perfect texture and flavour.

Serves 6.

6 pieces	**centre-cut veal shank,** 1″ thick
½ cup	**all-purpose flour**
½ cup	**vegetable oil**
¼ cup	**olive oil**
1 cup	**finely sliced onion**
½ cup	**finely sliced celery**
½ cup	**finely sliced carrot**
1 tsp	**finely chopped garlic**
1 Tbs	**finely chopped parsley**
2 cups	**dry white wine**
2	**bay leaves**
1 cup	**veal** OR **Chicken Stock** (see page 226)
14 oz can	**Italian plum tomatoes,** drained
2 strips	**lemon peel**
1 sprig	**fresh thyme** (or ½ tsp dried)
8	**fresh basil leaves** **salt** and **pepper**

FOR THE GREMOLATA

2 Tbs	**finely chopped parsley**
1 tsp	**finely chopped garlic**
2 tsp	**finely chopped lemon rind**

1.   Heat the oil in a large frying pan; dip the veal shanks in flour, shake off the excess, and brown on both sides in the oil. Remove and set aside.

2.   Pour off the oil from the pan; pour in the fresh olive oil and sauté the onions, celery, carrots, garlic, and parsley until lightly browned. Set aside.

3.   Preheat the oven to 350° F.

4.   Choose a large casserole that will hold the veal in one layer (this may be hard to find; if so, choose the biggest one that you have). Lay the veal in the bottom (in two layers if necessary). Spread the onions and carrots over the veal (and between the layers.)

5.   Pour the white wine into the casserole; add the bay leaves and chicken stock. Remove the seeds from the drained tomatoes and chop them up (the tomatoes; throw away the seeds) and add them to the veal. Put in the lemon strips, thyme, and basil.

6.   Bake in the preheated oven for 1 hour, then remove and turn the veal over (move the top layer to the bottom if necessary). Bake for another hour – 2 hours in total.

7.   Make the gremolata by mixing together the finely chopped parsley, garlic, and lemon rind.

8.   Remove casserole from the oven, spoon off the fat from the surface, check for salt, and add the pepper.

9.   The classic accompaniment is Risotto Milanese (see page 60); pass the gremolata for each person to sprinkle on top.

CORNMEAL-FRIED SWEETBREADS WITH SPICY TOMATO SALSA

Sweetbreads are not everybody's cup of tea. But if you like them enough to be thinking about this recipe, consider preparing some extra at the same time, and make the canelloni recipe that follows on page 128. It is a quite different (and much more traditional) way of preparing them, but none the worse for that; as far as I am concerned sweetbreads, mushrooms, and cream are a "menage à trois" made in heaven.

Serves 4.

1 lb	**provimi veal sweetbreads** (see page 123)
2 Tbs	**vinegar**
1 tsp	**salt**
2	**bay leaves**
1	**egg**
2 tsp	**Dijon mustard**
1 Tbs	**water**
1 cup	**all-purpose flour**
1 cup	**cornmeal** **oil**, for frying

FOR THE SALSA

2 cups	**Tomato Concassé** (see page 228)
½ cup	**cucumber**, peeled, seeded and diced
¼ cup	**finely chopped red onion**
1 Tbs	**finely chopped coriander**
1 tsp	**salt**
½ cup	**finely chopped roasted red pepper** (see page 47)
4 Tbs	**extra virgin olive oil** (see page 133)
¼ tsp	**red pepper flakes**
1 tsp	**red wine vinegar**

1. Cover the sweetbreads with cold water; add the vinegar and let them soak for at least 4 hours in the fridge.

2. Bring a large pot of water to a boil; add the salt. Rinse the sweetbreads under cold water, put them into the boiling water, then reduce the heat to a bare simmer and cook for 20 minutes. Drain and allow to cool.

3. Peel as much of the covering membrane off the sweetbreads as you can. Cut them into ½" slices.

4. Beat the eggs, mustard, and water in a small bowl. Spread out the flour and cornmeal on separate plates.

5. Dip the sweetbreads first in flour, then the egg. Let most of it drip off, then roll in cornmeal. Set aside on a tray sprinkled with cornmeal; allow to dry for half an hour at room temperature.

6. Prepare the salsa: Combine the tomato, cucumber, red onion, coriander, salt, red pepper, olive oil, hot pepper flakes, and vinegar. Chop them all by hand if you like a chunkier salsa; or process briefly if you like it smooth.

7. Pour 1½" of oil into a heavy pan; heat to 325° F. Cook the sweetbreads a few at a time until lightly browned. Do not overcrowd them or they will become greasy. Drain on paper towels and keep warm.

8. To serve: Arrange the sweetbreads in a ring on the serving plate; spoon the salsa in the middle. Garnish with coriander.

CANELLONI WITH
SWEETBREADS AND MUSHROOMS

Serves 6 to 8

1½ lbs	**provimi veal sweetbreads** (see page 123)
4 sheets	**fresh pasta**
½ ounce	**dried mushrooms**, morels or trompettes (see page 83)
1 Tbs	**butter** (see page 23)
4 Tbs	**finely chopped shallots**
2 cloves	**finely chopped garlic**
½ lb	**sliced oyster mushrooms**
¼ cup	**dry white wine**
2 Tbs	**demi-glace** (optional: see page 225)
3 cups	**whipping cream**
1 Tbs	**fresh tarragon** (or 1 tsp dried)
¼ cup	**grated Parmesan cheese**

1.   Prepare the sweetbreads following steps 1 to 3 in the recipe on page 127.

2.   Bring a large pot of water to a boil. Cut each sheet of pasta into half lengthwise, then across into 3 equal pieces. Add salt to the boiling water and cook the pasta for 3 minutes. Drain, transfer to a bowl of cold water, and then dry on towels when cool.

3.   Place the dried mushrooms in a small bowl; pour over just enough boiling water to cover. Let steep for 20 minutes, then remove the mushrooms and slice them. Strain the liquid through cheesecloth or a coffee filter and reserve.

4.   Heat the butter in a large frying pan or saucepan. Sauté the shallots and garlic until soft; add the sliced oyster and dried mushrooms and cook over medium-high heat for 3 minutes, until the mushrooms are done. Pour in the wine and reduce to 2 Tbs.

5.   Add the demi-glace (if using), cream, and tarragon; reduce to 1½ cups; add the sliced sweetbreads and cook until the sauce thickens up a little more. Remove from the heat and cool slightly.

6.   Preheat the oven to 375°F. Butter a shallow baking dish generously.

7.   Lay a piece of pasta on the work surface; place a good spoonful of sweetbread filling on it and roll it up to form a canelloni. Place in the buttered baking dish and continue with the rest of the pasta squares.

8.   Sprinkle the Parmesan cheese over the top; cover with foil and bake in the preheated oven for 20 minutes. (*May be made 24 hours ahead, or frozen.*)

TOURTIÈRE

Traditional at Christmas and very easy to make. This recipe uses pork; you may use a mixture of beef and pork, or all veal if you prefer. It is the spices that make the difference.

Serves 6.

2 lbs	**lean ground pork**
1½ cups	**finely chopped onions**
1 tsp	**ground ginger**
¼ tsp	**ground cloves**
¼ tsp	**ground allspice**
½ tsp	**black pepper**
1 tsp	**salt**
½ cup	**water**
1 cup	**fine dry breadcrumbs**
	9″ round pie dish
1 recipe	**Shortcrust Pastry** (see page 233)
1	**egg**, beaten with 1 tsp water

1.   Combine the ground meat, onions, ginger, cloves, allspice, pepper, and salt in a large heavy pot. Cook over medium heat, stirring to break up the meat, until the pork looses its raw colour. Add the water, bring to a boil, and simmer for ½ hour, stirring occasionally.

2.   Stir in the breadcrumbs; remove the pot from the heat and allow to cool.

3.   Lightly flour your work surface; divide the pastry in two; roll out each half into a circle about 11″ in diameter (large enough to fit the dish with a bit over). Roll one circle up around your rolling pin, and unroll it on top of the dish.

4.   Spoon the cooled meat into the pastry; dampen the edges of the pastry with water and lay the second sheet on top, pressing the edges together well. Trim off the excess with a sharp knife. Cut a couple of slashes for steam to escape. Make cut-outs from the excess pastry and decorate the top if your like. Brush with the beaten egg. (*May be prepared up to 2 days ahead to this point. Keep refrigerated, or you may freeze.*)

5.   Preheat the oven to 425°F.

6.   Bake the tourtière in the preheated oven for 15 minutes; then reduce the heat to 350°F and bake for 40 minutes longer, until the pastry is golden brown. Remove from the oven and allow to cool for 20 minutes before cutting.

CASHEW-BREADED PORK ON MUSTARD SHERRY GREENS

Serves 4.

1 large	**boneless pork loin**, about 1–1½ lbs
1	**egg white**
3 Tbs	**cornstarch**
¼ tsp	**salt**
⅛ tsp	**black pepper**
1 Tbs	**oyster sauce** (see page 114)
2 lbs	**Oriental greens**
2 cups	**cashew pieces**
3 cups	**vegetable oil** for frying
2 cups	**fresh white breadcrumbs**
2 Tbs	**dry** OR **medium sherry**
2 Tbs	**oyster sauce**
1 Tbs	**Dijon mustard**
¼ cup	**Chicken Stock** (see page 226) OR **water**
2 tsp	**cornstarch**
5 thin slices	**ginger**, crushed
3 cloves	**garlic**, crushed
1 Tbs	**oil**

1.   Cut the pork loin into 1″ slices; place each slice between sheets of waxed (or parchment) paper and pound to ¼″ thickness.

2.   Combine the egg white, cornstarch, salt, pepper, and oyster sauce in a bowl large enough to hold the pork slices. Stir well and add the pork, turning to coat each piece thoroughly. Cover and set aside for 1 hour, or refrigerate overnight.

3.   Wash and dry the Oriental greens; remove the leaves and slice the stalks diagonally into ½″ slices. Bring a large pot of water to a boil, salt it, and then add all the greens (leaves included). Cook for 1 minute. Drain, refresh under cold water, and allow to cool. Squeeze out as much water as you can with your hands.

4.   Blanch the cashew pieces (if you don't they will burn when you deep-fry them). Bring a pot of water to a boil, add the cashew pieces, bring back to a boil, and cook for 1 minute. Drain and chop into pea-size pieces.

5.   Heat the vegetable oil in a heavy deep pan or skillet to 325° F. (see page 85).

6.   Mix the breadcrumbs with the cashews. Remove the pork from the marinade, let most of the liquid drain off, then coat them with the breadcrumb mixture, pressing it on with your hands.

7.   Check the oil temperature (see page 85); fry the pork 2 or 3 pieces at a time, turning once until golden. Drain on paper towel.

8.   Combine the sherry, oyster sauce, and mustard in a small bowl or cup. Dissolve the cornstarch in the chicken stock or water in another bowl. Set aside. *(May be done ahead to this point; but don't refrigerate the pork.)*

9.   Heat the oven to 275° F; put in the pork uncovered, to rewarm it.

10. Heat a large wok or heavy frying pan until very hot. Add the oil, ginger, and garlic, and stir-fry until brown. Scrape them out of the pan and discard.

11. Add the greens to the pan; stir fry for 2 or 3 minutes. Pour in the sherry mixture; cook for 1 minute, then add the cornstarch. Cook until thickened, then transfer to a warm serving platter.

12. Slice each piece of pork into 4 strips; arrange on top of the greens. Serve.

GREEK PORK KEBAB

This method makes the pork very succulent. Serve with tzatziki (see page 115), pita bread, and a tomato, cucumber, and onion salad.

Serves 4 to 6.

1	**boneless pork butt,** about 2 lbs
1½ tsp	**salt**
1 tsp	**pepper**
2 Tbs	**lemon juice**
2 tsp	**dried oregano**
2 tsp	**finely chopped garlic**

1. Preheat the oven to 350°F.

2. Cut the pork butt into long thin strips (about 2" by 2" by 8" long).

3. Mix together the salt, pepper, lemon juice, oregano, and garlic in a large bowl. Put in the pork and toss it around to coat with the marinade.

4. Lay the pork strips on a baking sheet or roasting pan. Roast in the preheated oven for 2 hours. Remove from the oven and cut into 1" pieces. Serve.

SALADS & VEGETABLES

We have become used to thinking of vegetables as playing second fiddle to the meat, as an afterthought that provides the balance of colour and texture that a well put-together plate requires. And in fact vegetables are very important in this respect: it is much easier to produce a dinner plate, or a buffet table, that is vibrant, interesting, and well-balanced when you have the whole vegetable kingdom at your disposal.

The danger, of course, is that vegetables and salads become second-class citizens, always the bridesmaid but never the bride. There are two ways around this: one is to take a leaf from the French book, and serve vegetables and salads as a separate course; with salads we have already come a long way, since they are very often served separately anyway – either before the main course, in the North American style (which is just fine), or afterwards, in the European. But with vegetables it is another story. The other solution is to serve a vegetable that is a distinctive part of the main course, not simply an accent. This works best when there is a strong affinity between the meat (or poultry or fish) and the vegetable – such as Risotto Milanese with Osso Bucco, Belgian endive with beef (or, especially, with ham, which has a bit of sweetness to offset the bitterness of the endive). The vegetable is as much a part of the dish as the meat.

The way we eat has a lot to do with habit; and the practice of serving vegetables with the meat is so ingrained that it will be hard to change. However, many of our vegetable recipes would do very well on their own, if you want to experiment a little. For example, if you serve a starchy vegetable that has a good affinity with the main course – such as Scalloped Potatoes with Lamb Tenderloins and Spinach in Puff Pastry – you could serve a green vegetable afterwards, as a separate course instead of a salad. It makes a pleasant change; and it puts a bit more focus on the vegetables, which can be just as delicious as the main course – often, even more so.

EXTRA VIRGIN OLIVE OIL

Olive oil is made by pressing ripe olives in a press to extract the oil. A batch of olives may be pressed two or three times, then finally heated and pressed to get all the oil out. At each pressing, the quality of the oil produced declines.

What makes olive oil extra virgin? In a word: acidity. To be classed as "extra virgin" an oil must have less than 1 per cent acidity. At each pressing the acidity level of the oil increases. Generally, only the oil from the first cold pressings has a low enough acidity to qualify as extra virgin. Most extra virgin oils are labelled "first cold-pressed extra virgin oil" or, if it is not from the first pressing, simply "Cold Pressed Extra Virgin Oil". Oil that does not qualify as extra virgin is labelled "Pure Olive Oil" or "Refined Olive Oil".

Extra virgin oil has a deeper colour and more intense flavour than other oils. Italian extra virgin oils in particular have quite a pronounced "peppery" bite. California oils are known for being fruity, as are oils from the South of France. Greek oil is generally heavy and strongly flavoured; and Spanish oil is also quite strong. These are generalizations: you will always find exceptions to prove the rule.

We are often asked why extra virgin olive oil is better. The answer is: Better for what? It depends entirely on what you want to use the oil for. There are many cases where an extra virgin oil is not the right choice: mayonnaise made entirely from extra virgin oil would have such a strong flavour that it would dominate whatever you served with it. Use an extra virgin oil where you want the pronounced flavour of the oil to come through; with sliced tomatoes and bocconcini cheese, on grilled fish or vegetables, on focaccia and thin pizza, and in salads where you have a strongly flavoured lettuce like arugula. On other salads you might want to use extra virgin oil in half-and-half combination with pure oil, or pure oil entirely for a lighter dressing. Extra virgin oil is very good for sautéeing fish or meat, because it can go to a higher temperature than regular oil without burning.

Even more often we are asked how one extra virgin oil can cost so much more than another. Olive oil is like wine; you get what you pay for and then you pay a bit extra for the label. There are extra virgin oils produced in large factories using olives from a number of different olive groves, although generally from the same region. The oil is often blended to produce a consistent flavour from one year to the next; these oils are like "vin de table". Next up the scale is the oil equivalent of "Appellation Contrôlée" wine – oil produced from trees in a specific area, not blended, but mechanically harvested and produced in a factory environment on quite a large scale. At the top of the scale are the "Grands Châteaux" of olive oils – made from olives from a single estate, often picked by hand and pressed on traditional presses. This is the "crème de la crème" of olive oil – and it is expensive.

In recipes where it matters whether you use extra virgin, or just plain old olive oil, we have specified what we think works better. In cases where it is not specified, you may suit yourself – generally the quantity is so small that it will not make a difference. In recipes that simply call for "oil", any mild-flavoured vegetable oil will be fine.

CAESAR SALAD

2½ cups	**Italian** OR **French bread**, cut into ½″ cubes
2 Tbs	**olive oil**
1½ tsp	**finely chopped garlic**
¼ tsp	**salt**
1 large	**anchovy filet**
1 Tbs	**Dijon mustard**
2 Tbs	**lemon juice**
6 drops	**Tabasco Sauce**
8 drops	**Worcestershire Sauce**
5 Tbs	**extra virgin olive oil** (see page 133)
1	**egg**
1 slice	**prosciutto**, not too thin, cut into strips (see page 53)
2 tsp	**oil**
2 heads	**romaine lettuce**, washed, dried and torn into pieces
½ cup	**freshly grated Parmesan cheese**

1. Preheat the oven to 350°F.

2. Spread the bread cubes on a large baking sheet and toss with 2 Tbs oil. Bake in preheated oven, tossing every 5 minutes to brown them evenly. It will take 10 to 20 minutes, depending on how fresh the bread is. Remove from the oven and allow to cool.

3. Make the dressing: Crush the garlic and salt together in a small bowl, using the back of a spoon. Stir in the anchovy and mustard, then the lemon juice, Tabasco, and Worcestershire; gradually beat in the olive oil. Crack the egg into the dressing and beat vigorously to form a smooth emulsion.

4. Sauté the prosciutto in 2 tsp oil until crisp. Set aside.

5. Put the lettuce, torn into strips, in your salad bowl; pour on the dressing and toss it. Add the croutons, the prosciutto, and the Parmesan, and toss it again.

MUSHROOM SALAD WITH RED PEPPER VINAIGRETTE

Serves 8.

3 lbs	**fresh white mushrooms**, quite small
2 tsp	**salt**
2	**lemons**

FOR THE DRESSING

3 cloves	**garlic**, crushed
3	**red peppers**, cored & seeded
¼ cup	**red wine vinegar**
1 tsp	**salt**
½ tsp	**pepper**
3 tsp	**Dijon mustard**
¾ cup	**olive oil**
2 Tbs	**black sesame seeds** (optional)

1. Wash the mushrooms and trim off any hard or black parts on the stems.

2. Bring a large pot of water to a boil; add salt and cut the lemons in half and squeeze the juice into the water. Put in the lemon halves; add the mushrooms and cook for 3 minutes. Drain in a colander.

3. Make the dressing: Place the garlic, peppers, vinegar, olive oil, salt, pepper, and mustard in the work bowl of a food processor. Process until reduced to a purée. With the motor running, pour the oil through the feed tube. Stir in the black sesame seeds.

4. Transfer the mushrooms to a bowl, pour the dressing over them, and refrigerate until ready to serve.

DIET SALAD

An unusual salad with an unusual name. Not many salad recipes tell you to squeeze the leaves to make them look wilted, but here it allows the complex flavours to blend and mingle. In Laos, where it comes from, it is served as a less-filling alternative to meat – hence the name.

Serves 6.

FOR THE SALAD

½ cup	**thinly sliced celery hearts**
2	**green onions**, cut in half lengthwise then cut into 1″ pieces.
16 sprigs	**fresh coriander**, top leaves only
½ cup	**fresh mint leaves**, washed and dried
1 medium	**tomato**, cut in half, then thinly sliced crosswise.
½ cup	**thinly sliced English cucumber**
1 head	**romaine lettuce**, inner leaves
1 head	**Boston lettuce**, inner leaves
1 bunch	**watercress**, large stems removed
3	**hard-boiled eggs**, whites only, thinly sliced

FOR THE DRESSING

6 Tbs	**oil**
3 tsp	**finely chopped garlic**
3	**hard-boiled eggs**, yolks only
1 tsp	**sugar**
5 Tbs	**lemon juice**
1 Tbs	**Thai fish sauce** "Squid Brand" (see page 114)

1. Prepare all the salad ingredients as described, and combine them in a large bowl.

2. Sauté the garlic in oil until very pale gold. Remove from the heat and allow to cool.

3. Mash the egg yolks to a paste; stir in the sugar, lemon juice, and fish sauce. Slowly beat in the oil and garlic mixture.

4. Pour the dressing over the salad. Toss well, gently pressing the ingredients together, for 2 minutes. Allow to sit for 5 minutes to allow the flavours to develop and blend.

WARM NEW POTATO SALAD

See Veal Shoulder with Warm New Potato Salad, page 121. This salad is delicious with grilled fish, especially salmon; it is also good cold.

EGGPLANT SALAD

Serves 6 to 8.

4 small	**eggplants** (about 3 lbs)
1 Tbs	**salt**
3 cups	**vegetable oil**
1 large	**tomato**, peeled, seeded, and diced
1 Tbs	**finely chopped parsley**
2 Tbs	**fresh basil leaves**, cut in strips

FOR THE DRESSING

½ lb	**cream cheese**
1 cup	**plain yoghurt**
½ tsp	**salt**
¼ tsp	**ground pepper**
1½ tsp	**chopped fresh thyme leaves**
1 tsp	**finely chopped garlic**

1.   Cut the stem off the eggplant and cut it in half lengthwise. Cut each half lengthwise again into 4 long wedges, then cut each wedge in half crosswise. Sprinkle with the salt and allow to drain in a colander for at least 2 hours (may be left overnight).

2.   Wash the eggplant under cold water and pat dry with paper towels.

3.   Heat the vegetable oil in a large heavy pan to 350°F (see page 85). Add some of the eggplant pieces; do not overcrowd the pan (crowding reduces the temperature too much and the eggplant becomes greasy). Cook until the eggplant is golden brown. Remove with a slotted spoon and drain on paper towel. Repeat until all the eggplant is done.

4.   Make the dressing: Place the cream cheese in a bowl and whisk it until it becomes smooth; gradually whisk in the yoghurt; add the salt, pepper, thyme, and garlic.

5.   Arrange the eggplant on a serving dish. Spoon the dressing over it, and sprinkle on the diced tomato, parsley, and basil.

SNOW PEA AND RED PEPPER SALAD

Serves 4 to 6.

1 lb	**snow peas**, trimmed and strings removed
1 cup	**red pepper julienne strips**

FOR THE DRESSING

1 Tbs	**soya sauce**
1 tsp	**sugar**
1 tsp	**red wine vinegar**
2 Tbs	**vegetable oil**
1 tsp	**sesame oil**
2 tsp	**black sesame seeds**

1.   Bring a large pot of water to a boil; add the snow peas and drain as soon as they turn bright green. Refresh under cold water and drain well.

2.   Make the dressing: Stir the soya sauce, sugar, and vinegar together. Slowly beat in the vegetable oil and sesame oil.

3.   Just before serving toss the snow peas and peppers with the dressing; sprinkle with the sesame seeds. (If you add the dressing too early the snow peas will start to turn yellow.)

FRENCH GREEN BEAN AND CARROT SALAD

In the store we make this salad with very small French green beans, bought at the huge Rungis market near Charles de Gaulle airport. In the winter they are not grown in France at all but in more tropical countries, often former colonies of France. In our experience, the very best come from Kenya. This salad goes very well with cold poached salmon, and with roast beef, veal, or chicken.

Serves 6.

1 lb	**fine French beans** OR **young local green beans**, topped and tailed
1 tsp	**salt**
1 medium	**carrot**, cut in julienne strips

FOR THE DRESSING

2 Tbs	**red wine vinegar**
1 clove	**finely chopped garlic**
1	**finely chopped shallot**
2	**anchovy filets,** chopped
2 tsp	**Dijon mustard**
dash of	**Worcestershire Sauce**
¼ tsp	**salt**
¼ tsp	**ground black pepper**
1	**egg**
½ cup	**olive oil**
10	**capers**
1 tsp	**tarragon leaves,** fresh or dried

1. Bring a large pot of water to a boil; add the salt, then the beans and the carrots. Bring back to a boil and cook for 4 minutes. Drain and refresh under cold water to set the colour and stop the cooking. Dry on paper towel.

2. Make the dressing: Combine the vinegar, garlic, shallots, anchovy filets, mustard, Worcestershire, salt, and pepper in a small bowl. Mix and press against the side of the bowl until the anchovies dissolve. Slowly beat in the oil; add the egg and beat well to blend; stir in the capers and tarragon.

3. Pour the dressing over the beans. Allow to stand for 30 minutes or so, until the flavour of the dressing permeates the beans.

FENNEL, ORANGE, AND CAPER SALAD

Serves 4.

2 bulbs	**fennel**
1 Tbs	**capers**, drained
1 Tbs	**chopped fresh dill**

FOR THE DRESSING

¼	**orange**, seeded
2 tsp	**red wine vinegar**
1 Tbs	**Dijon mustard**
2 tsp	**sugar**
½ tsp	**salt**
4 Tbs	**olive oil**

1. Trim the stalks from the fennel; cut the bulb in half lengthwise, then cut crosswise into very thin slices. Place in a large bowl with the capers and the dill.

2. Make the dressing: Cut the quarter orange in small pieces and place in the work bowl of a food processor or blender with the vinegar, mustard, sugar, and salt. Process until smooth. With the motor running, slowly pour in the olive oil. Pour over the fennel, toss well, and serve.

GRILLED CHAYOTE WITH MINT AND BALSAMIC VINEGAR

A good salad if you are having a barbecue; the chayote is finished off on the grill.

2 tsp	**olive oil**
2	**chayote**

FOR THE DRESSING

2 tsp	**balsamic vinegar** (see below)
½ tsp	**salt**
¼ tsp	**black pepper**
¼ tsp	**finely chopped garlic**
3 Tbs	**extra virgin olive oil** (see page 133)
½ cup	**coarsely chopped mint leaves**

1. Preheat the oven to 350°F. Spread the oil on a baking sheet.

2. Cut the chayote lengthwise into ⅜" slices. Lay them on the baking sheet, cover tightly with foil, and bake in the preheated oven for 15 minutes. Remove from the oven, uncover, and allow to cool.

3. Make the dressing: Stir the vinegar, salt, pepper, and garlic together. Slowly beat in the oil. Set aside.

4. Grill the chayote on both sides over hot coals; try to get nice grill marks.

5. Arrange the chayote on a platter; pour the dressing over and scatter with the chopped mint.

BALSAMIC VINEGAR

A wine vinegar produced in Modena and the surrounding area, in Northern Italy. The vinegar is aged in a succession of barrels of different wood and acquires a deep reddish-brown colour. Older vinegar is blended with the newer to produce a slightly sweet, very aromatic, and intensely flavoured vinegar. It is excellent in a salad dressing, and has a particular affinity with tomatoes. In Modena it is believed to have powerful healing properties, which may explain its unusual name (from "balm") as it does not derive from being aged in balsam-wood barrels, since this wood is not used in its production.

In Modena, vintages of balsamic vinegar as old as 150 years can be found. In Canada, the oldest you will find is 80 years.

SPINACH WITH BALSAMIC VINEGAR

1 lb	**spinach**, washed, stems removed
4 Tbs	**butter** (see page 23)
1 Tbs	**finely chopped shallot**
1 clove	**garlic**, finely chopped
2 Tbs	**chopped sundried tomatoes**
2 Tbs	**balsamic vinegar** (see above)
½ tsp	**salt**
¼ tsp	**black pepper**

1. Chop the washed spinach coarsely and set aside to drain.

2. Melt the butter in a pan large enough to hold the spinach; sauté the garlic and shallot until soft but not brown. Add the spinach to the pan; cook, stirring gently, for 3 or 4 minutes, until almost wilted. Add the chopped sundried tomatoes and stir into the spinach. *(May be prepared ahead to this point.)*

3. Heat the spinach over medium heat until hot; add the balsamic vinegar and stir to mix well in. Add salt and pepper and serve.

MEDITERRANEAN SALAD

A very attractive salad that adds colour to a buffet. It gets its name from the Middle Eastern spices in the dressing.

2 cups	**French** OR **Italian bread**, preferably day-old, cut into 2" cubes
1 Tbs	**olive oil**
1 cup	**English cucumber**, in ½" cubes
⅓ cup	**green pepper**, in ½" pieces
⅓ cup	**red pepper**, in ½" pieces
½ cup	**thinly sliced green onion**
4 cups	**parsley leaves**, coarsely chopped
2 medium	**tomatoes**, cut into ½" cubes

FOR THE DRESSING

2 Tbs	**lemon juice**
¾ tsp	**salt**
1 large	**garlic clove**, finely chopped
½ tsp	**ground black pepper**
1 tsp	**ground cinnamon**
¼ tsp	**ground allspice**
9 Tbs	**extra virgin olive oil** (see page 133)

1. Preheat the oven to 350°F.

2. Spread the bread cubes on a large baking sheet and toss with the oil. Bake in the preheated oven until golden brown, turning them every few minutes. They will take 10 to 20 minutes, depending on how fresh the bread is.

3. Assemble the cucumber, peppers, green onion, and parsley in a large bowl; leave out the tomatoes for now.

4. Prepare the dressing: Stir the lemon juice, salt, and garlic together until the salt dissolves. Add the pepper, cinnamon, and allspice, then slowly beat in the olive oil. *(May be prepared up to 12 hours ahead to this point.)*

5. Place the cut-up tomatoes on top of the other vegetables. Pour on the dressing and toss well; add the croutons and toss again. NOTE: After a couple of hours, the croutons will start to absorb the dressing. Some people like this; others (including the reviewer for *Toronto Life*!) do not. Time the addition of the croutons to suit your taste.

SMOTHERED PEAS AND FENNEL

½ cup	**finely diced onion**
2 cups	**fresh shelled peas** OR **frozen**
½ cup	**finely diced fennel**
4 Tbs	**butter** (see page 23)
1 small sprig	**fresh thyme**
1 Tbs	**finely chopped mint leaves**
¼ tsp	**salt**

1. Melt the butter in a heavy pot with a well-fitting lid. Sauté the diced onions until translucent. Add the fennel until it also becomes translucent.

2. *If using fresh peas:* Add them now, along with the thyme sprig. Stir well, cover with a lid, and cook over a low heat for 10 minutes, stirring occasionally.
If using frozen peas: add them now with the thyme sprig. Cover with the lid again and cook until the peas are hot (about 5 minutes). Serve immediately.

Spaghetti Squash Salad with Sundried Tomato Vinaigrette

Serves 4 to 6.

1 small	**spaghetti squash**, about 2 lbs
½ cup	**water**
2 large	**tomatoes**, peeled and seeded
½ cup	**chopped parsley**
¼ cup	**basil leaves**, cut in thin strips
½ cup	**pitted black olives** (optional)

FOR THE DRESSING

1½ Tbs	**red wine vinegar**
½ tsp	**salt**
½ cup	**extra virgin olive oil** (see page 133)
3	**sundried tomatoes**, chopped
1 tsp	**finely chopped garlic**
¼ tsp	**ground black pepper**

1.   Preheat the oven to 350° F.

2.   Place the squash cut-side down in a baking dish; pour ½ cup of water around it. Cover tightly with foil and bake for 1 hour.

3.   Remove the squash from the oven; turn it cut-side up and allow to cool. Scrape the shreds out of the squash with a fork into a bowl. Let cool completely, then add the tomatoes, basil, and parsley.

4.   Place salt and vinegar in the work bowl of a food processor (provided that it is small; there is not enough liquid to work in a large one). Process briefly; with the motor running pour the olive oil down the feed tube in a slow steady stream. Add the sundried tomatoes, process until puréed, then add the garlic and black pepper.

5.   Pour the dressing over the squash and toss well. Let sit for 30 minutes at room temperature to allow the flavours to blend.

Fried Eggplant with Gremolata

Makes an excellent cold eggplant salad; also very good hot.

Serves 4.

3 small	**eggplant**, sliced in ⅜" rounds
2 tsp	**salt**

FOR THE GREMOLATA

2 tsp	**Grated Lemon Zest** (see page 237)
1 tsp	**finely chopped garlic**
2 Tbs	**Italian parsley**, chopped coarsely
2 Tbs	**basil leaves** cut in strips
½ cup	**Tomato Concassé**, (optional – see page 228)
¾ cup	**olive oil**, for frying

1.   Toss the eggplant slices with the salt. Place in a colander and allow to drain for 1 hour. Rinse well and pat dry.

2.   Make the gremolata. Mix the lemon rind, garlic, parsley, and basil together. Set aside.

3.   In a shallow frying pan heat the olive oil to 350° F (see page 85). Put in a few slices of eggplant and fry until golden brown on one side; turn and brown on the other side. Remove to a plate covered with paper towels set in a low oven while you brown the rest.

4.   Arrange the eggplant slices on a warm platter; sprinkle with the herb mixture, and the tomato concassé, if you are using it. Serve immediately.

EGGPLANT WITH TOMATO AND MOZZARELLA

Substantial enough, and good enough, to serve alone; or an excellent accompaniment to meat or chicken that does not have a sauce of its own.

Serves 4 to 6.

1 large	**eggplant**, cut in ⅓″ discs.
½ cup	**olive oil**
1 large	**onion**, chopped
½ large	**red pepper**, seeded and chopped
2 Tbs	**olive oil**
1 28-oz can	**Italian plum tomatoes** drained
1½ lbs	**mozzarella** OR **scamorza cheese** (see page 66)
	salt and **black pepper**

1. Preheat the oven to 400° F.

2. Find a large baking sheet (or two smaller ones) on which all the eggplant slices will fit. Pour half of the oil onto the pan(s). Arrange the eggplant slices on the pans; move them around to make sure that their undersides are lightly coated with oil. Pour the rest of the oil over the slices. Bake in the preheated oven for 12 minutes. Remove from the oven and turn them over with a spatula. The bottoms should just be starting to turn golden brown; if not, give them a few more minutes. If they look dry, pour over a bit more oil. Cook for 10 minutes on the other side, until very lightly browned. Turn the oven down to 350° F.

3. Sauté the chopped onion and red pepper in 2 Tbs oil over medium heat until softened but not browned.

4. Remove as many seeds as you can from the drained tomatoes; add the tomatoes to the onions and peppers, and cook over medium heat for 10 minutes. Season with salt and pepper and set aside.

5. Slice the cheese into rounds ⅛″ to ¼″ thick. Set aside.

6. When the eggplant is ready, assemble the casserole. Choose a baking dish at least 2″ deep, preferably 3″. Put one third of the tomato sauce on the bottom, cover with a layer of eggplant slices, then a layer of cheese slices. Repeat twice more, ending with the cheese on top.

7. Bake in the preheated oven just long enough to heat through; if it cooks too long the cheese will get tough. If the sauce is hot when you assemble it, and you bake it immediately, it will take only 20 minutes to heat, and the cheese will be deliciously soft. If you have preassembled it, baking will take about 40 minutes. The cheese will be stringier, but the taste will still be good.

THE BEST TABOULEH

Is this excessive? Yes it is. Is it worth it? Definitely!

Serves 6.

1 cup	**pine nuts**
2 Tbs	**oil**
1 cup	**chopped mint leaves**
2 cups	**finely chopped parsley**
⅓ cup	**tomato,** seeds and core removed; cut into thin strips, then across into ⅛″ pieces
¼ cup	**English cucumber,** peeled, halved, and seeded; cut into thin strips, then cut across into ⅛″ pieces
¼ cup	**finely chopped green onion**
2 Tbs	**lemon juice**
½ tsp	**salt**
½ tsp	**finely chopped garlic**
5 Tbs	**extra virgin olive oil** (see page 133)
¼ tsp	**freshly ground black pepper**
¼ tsp	**ground cinnamon**
¼ tsp	**ground allspice**

1. Sauté the pine nuts in the oil over low heat until they start to turn golden. Remove from the heat immediately and allow to cool.

2. Put the mint, parsley, tomato, cucumber, and green onion into a large bowl.

3. Prepare the dressing: Stir the lemon juice, salt, and garlic together. Slowly beat in the oil; then stir in the pepper, cinnamon, and allspice. *(May be prepared up to 4 hours ahead to this point.)*

4. Drain the pine nuts of oil; add them to the salad ingredients. Pour on the dressing and toss well together.

VARIATION: Soak ¼ cup bulgar in 1 cup cold water for 20 minutes. Squeeze dry and use in place of the sautéed pine nuts.

DIJON-GLAZED CARROTS WITH NIÇOISE OLIVES

1 lb	**tender young carrots,** scrubbed
1 Tbs	**unsalted butter** (see page 23)
1 Tbs	**brown sugar**
1 Tbs	**Dijon mustard**
12	**Niçoise olives**

1. Cut the carrots into ½″ slices, on the diagonal.

2. Bring a pot of water to a boil. Add the carrots and cook until barely tender (about 5 minutes). Drain and set aside.

3. Melt the butter in a heavy saucepan over medium heat. Stir in the brown sugar, and let it dissolve. Add the mustard, olives, and carrots. Stir constantly until heated and to coat the carrots thoroughly with the glaze. Serve immediately.

TOMATO, ARTICHOKE AND FETA SALAD

Serves 8 to 12.

2 14 oz cans	**artichoke hearts**
½ lb	**feta cheese**, cut in ½" cubes
1 cup	**finely sliced red onion**
2 large	**tomatoes**, cut in ½" cubes

FOR THE DRESSING

1 Tbs	**red wine vinegar**
¼ tsp	**salt**
½ tsp	**finely chopped garlic**
1½ tsp	**dried oregano**
½ tsp	**black pepper**
½ cup	**basil leaves**, finely sliced
1 cup	**coarsely chopped parsley**
½ cup	**olive oil**

1. Cut the artichoke hearts in quarters; place on paper towel to drain for ½ hour.

2. Cut the feta into ½" cubes; slice the onion. Put them in a large bowl and set aside.

3. Make the dressing: Stir the vinegar, salt, and garlic together. Add the oregano, pepper, basil, and parsley; then slowly beat in the oil. Pour the dressing over the feta and onions, and toss well.

4. Add the drained artichokes to the feta and toss. *(May be prepared ahead to this point. Will keep refrigerated for a few days.)*

5. When ready to serve, add the tomato cubes and toss everything together.

BITTER GREENS WITH HOT PANCETTA DRESSING

Serves 6.

1 head	**chicory** OR **curly endive** OR
1 bunch	**dandelion greens;** OR any mixture of bitter and sweet greens
2 Tbs	**red wine vinegar**
½ tsp	**salt**
¼ tsp	**black pepper**
2	**eggs**
1 cup	**grated Romano cheese** (use Parmesan if you can't find Romano)
¼ lb	**pancetta**, cut as thick as bacon, chopped (see page 53)
8 Tbs	**extra virgin olive oil** (see page 133)

1. Wash the greens and dry thoroughly; tear them into bite-sized pieces and place in a large bowl.

2. Mix the vinegar, salt, and pepper in a small bowl; pour over the greens and let them sit for at least 15 minutes (up to 1 hour).

3. Beat the eggs with the cheese and set aside.

4. Heat the olive oil over medium heat and fry the pancetta, but do not let it brown very much.

5. Just as the pancetta is ready, toss the salad with the eggs and cheese; then pour on the hot oil and pancetta, toss it all again and serve it up.

SAUTÉED SWISS CHARD WITH PROSCIUTTO AND PARMESAN CHEESE

Serves 6.

4 Tbs	**finely diced prosciutto** (see page 53)
1 tsp	**finely chopped garlic**
1½ to 2 lbs	**fresh Swiss chard**, washed
¼ tsp	**black pepper**
½ cup	**freshly grated Parmesan cheese**

1. Remove the leaves from the Swiss chard stems; cut the stems into ¼″ thick slices on the diagonal. Coarsely chop the leaves.

2. In a large frying pan heat the olive oil over medium heat. Add the diced prosciutto and garlic; sauté until the garlic turns pale gold. Add the chard stalks and sauté until they start to wilt.

3. Turn the heat up to high and add the chopped leaves. Sauté, stirring constantly, until the greens are completely wilted. Stir in the pepper and Parmesan cheese, and serve immediately.

BELGIAN ENDIVE BRAISED WITH PROSCIUTTO AND CREAM

This is a delicious combination that works particularly well with roasted or grilled meats that have no sauce of their own.

Serves 4.

2 slices	**prosciutto**, not too thin (see page 53)
1 Tbs	**butter** (see page 23)
4 large	**Belgian endives**
¼ cup	**stock** (beef, chicken, or veal)
⅔ cup	**whipping cream**

1. Cut the prosciutto into small dice; melt the butter in a heavy saucepan that will hold the endives comfortably lying down. Sauté the prosciutto until quite crispy. Remove to a dish and reserve.

2. Pour all but 2 Tbs of fat out of the pan; set the pan over medium heat, put in the endives and let them brown, turning them two or three times so that they are well browned on all sides. They will not be evenly coloured; but they should be quite dark.

3. Turn the heat down to low, pour in the stock, cover the pan tightly, and let the endives braise for 30 to 40 minutes (bigger ones take longer; this is one vegetable where undercooking is a greater sin than overcooking). *(May be prepared up to 24 hours ahead to this point.)*

4. Reheat the endives (if necessary) over medium heat; pour in the cream and let it boil to reduce it slightly. Sprinkle the prosciutto over them and season with salt and pepper. Serve.

BROCCOLI WITH GARLIC, ANCHOVIES, AND HOT PEPPERS

This can be served hot or at room temperature.

Serves 4 to 6.

2	**anchovy filets**
1 tsp	**finely chopped garlic**
2 tsp	**balsamic vinegar**
4 Tbs	**extra virgin olive oil** (see page 133)
½ tsp	**hot pepper flakes**
1 large head	**broccoli**
1 tsp	**salt**

1.   Put a large pot of water on to boil.

2.   Make the dressing: Mash the anchovies with the garlic. Stir in the balsamic vinegar, then slowly beat in the olive oil and hot pepper flakes.

3.   Cut the broccoli into florets; peel the stems and cut them into ¼″ diagonal slices. Salt the water and put in the broccoli. Cook for 5 to 6 minutes (it should still be slightly crunchy). Drain.

4.   To serve hot: Toss the drained broccoli with the dressing. To serve at room temperature: Refresh the drained broccoli under cold water to set the colour. Drain again, then toss with the dressing.

BAKED RED ONIONS WITH BALSAMIC VINEGAR AND SAGE

Serves 4 to 6 as a vegetable.

6 medium	**red onions**, about 1½ lbs
1 Tbs	**extra virgin olive oil** (see page 133)
1½ tsp	**balsamic vinegar** (see page 138)
¼ tsp	**salt**
4 tsp	**olive oil** OR **butter**
8	**sage leaves**, chopped
⅛ tsp	**black pepper**, ground

1.   Preheat the oven to 300° F.

2.   Cut off the top of the onions and peel off the papery skin: leave the root end intact. Set in a baking pan, cut-end down. Cover with aluminum foil and bake in the preheated oven for 2 hours.

3.   Remove the onions from the oven and transfer to a plate. Mix the vinegar, salt, olive oil or butter, chopped sage, and pepper into the pan juices, and set aside in the pan. Turn the oven up to 400° F.

4.   Cut the root end off the onions, cut them into quarters and remove the leathery outer layer. Set them in a sieve to drain for 30 minutes.

5.   Stir the onions into the vinegar mixture. Bake uncovered in the preheated oven for 20 minutes.

SWEET POTATO AND GORGONZOLA PURÉE

The sweet potato elevated to the aristocracy. Serve with veal or chicken – or go all out at Christmas or Thanksgiving and serve it with your traditional bird.

Serves 8.

3 large	**sweet potatoes**, peeled and cubed
4 Tbs	**Crème Fraîche** (see page 226)
1 Tbs	**butter** (see page 23)
½ tsp	**salt**
¼ tsp	**black pepper**
4 oz	**Gorgonzola cheese**, cut in cubes
1 Tbs	**finely chopped fresh sage**

1. Cover the sweet potatoes with cold water, bring to a boil, and cook over medium-high heat until tender (15 to 20 minutes). Drain.

2. Purée the sweet potatoes in a food processor, or in a food mill fitted with the fine disk. With a food processor, add the crème fraîche, butter, salt, and pepper; process to incorporate, then return to the pot. If using a food mill, purée it back into the pot, then add the crème fraîche, butter, salt, and pepper.

3. Add the Gorgonzola to the purée and stir over low heat until the cheese has almost melted. Stir in the finely chopped sage. *(May be prepared ahead up to 4 hours to this point; but do not refrigerate.)*

4. Reheat gently over low heat.

WINTER VEGETABLE CASSEROLE

This vegetable dish goes very well with calves' liver, kidneys, or a not-too-elaborate lamb or beef dish, for example, like a braised lamb shoulder or pot roast of beef.

Serves 4 to 6.

¾ lb	**potatoes**, peeled and cut into 1″ cubes
¾ lb	**rutabaga** OR **turnip** peeled and cut into 1″ cubes
¼ lb	**carrots**, peeled and sliced into rounds
1 small	**savoy cabbage**, cored and cut in ½″ slices
1½ tsp	**salt**
¼ tsp	**ground pepper**
½ lb	**cream cheese**
½ cup	**grated Parmesan cheese**
1 Tbs	**butter** (see page 23)

1. Place all the vegetables in a large pot, cover with cold water, and bring to a boil. Cook until all the vegetables are done. Drain well and put them back into the pot; mash them coarsely with a potato masher.

2. Preheat the oven to 350° F.

3. Stir the salt, pepper, cream cheese, and Parmesan into the vegetables. Transfer to a baking dish, dot the top with butter, and bake for 45 minutes, until the top is lightly browned.

SCALLOPED POTATOES

A very simple recipe that works.

Serves 6.

1½ cups	**finely sliced onions**
1½ lbs	**potatoes**, peeled and finely sliced
4 Tbs	**flour**
1½ tsp	**salt**
½ tsp	**black pepper**
1½ cups	**milk**
1½ cups	**whipping cream**

1.   Preheat the oven to 350° F.

2.   Select a baking dish that has 2″ to spare once the potatoes and onions are in it – the cream bubbles up and may spill over.

3.   Mix together the flour, salt, and pepper in a small bowl.

4.   Layer the sliced potatoes and onions in the dish, sprinkling the flour mixture between the layers. Mix the milk and cream together, pour over the potatoes. Cover the dish tightly with aluminum foil.

5.   Bake in the preheated oven for 1 hour; remove the foil and bake for 1 hour more.

PERFECT ROAST POTATOES

1 med.	**potato** per person
2 Tbs	**oil**
	salt, pepper, and **paprika**

1.   Preheat the oven to 350° F.

2.   Peel the potatoes (or just scrub them if you prefer). Cut in half lengthwise, then cut each half in 4 long wedges, and dry them quite well.

3.   You will need a heavy baking sheet with a rim for baking the potatoes (a thin one will buckle and the potatoes are more likely to burn). Spread the oil on the sheet; roll the potatoes around in it so that they are well covered. Set them one flat side down on the pan, taking care not to crowd them.

4.   If your stove is gas, set the pan right on the bottom of the oven; if electric, set the rack on the lowest rung. Bake the potatoes for 15 to 20 minutes, until golden brown on the bottom. Turn them with an egg lifter, and bake for another 15 to 20 minutes until brown on the other side.

5.   Drain off the oil and toss the potatoes with salt, pepper, and paprika if you like it. They are best eaten straightaway.

SAUTÉ OF FRESH CORN WITH ZUCCHINI AND RED ONIONS

Serves 4 to 6.

2 cups	**fresh corn kernels**
1 cup	**diced zucchini**
1 cup	**finely chopped red onion**
4 Tbs	**unsalted butter** (see page 23)
½ tsp	**salt**
½ tsp	**black pepper**

1.   Melt the butter in a heavy saucepan. Add the chopped red onions and sauté over medium heat for a few minutes, without browning, until translucent.

2.   Add the diced zucchini and sauté until it starts to become translucent – *don't* overcook it.

3.   Add the corn; continue to cook for 4 or 5 minutes until everything is piping hot.

ARTICHOKES WITH AVGOLEMONO

The artichokes are trimmed completely so that the whole thing can be eaten.

Serves 4.

4 very large	**artichokes**, trimmed
½ cup	**Chicken Stock** (see page 226)
2	**egg yolks**
¼ cup	**lemon juice**
½ tsp	**salt**
1 Tbs	**Italian parsley**, coarsely chopped
1 Tbs	**mint leaves**, coarsely chopped

1.   Trim the artichokes completely (see below, the second method).

2.   Bring a large pot of water to a boil. Put in the trimmed artichokes and cook in rapidly boiling water for about 40 minutes, until just tender. Drain and set aside. *(May be prepared a few hours ahead to this point.)*

3.   Bring the chicken stock to a boil in a large pot (the one you cooked the artichokes in). Put in the artichokes, cover with the lid, and steam until they are hot (about 10 minutes). Remove the pan from the heat and set aside.

4.   Beat the egg yolks and lemon juice together. Pour this mixture over the artichokes. Stir rapidly to coat the artichokes with the mixture: the heat will cause the yolks to thicken and form strands. Stir in the chopped parsley and mint. Serve immediately.

TRIMMING ARTICHOKES

To prepare artichokes to be eaten by pulling off the leaves and dipping them in a sauce or butter, cut the points off all the outside leaves with scissors, so that the artichoke is still the same shape but now has a flat top. Trim the base so that is will stand upright on a plate. Immerse in water acidulated with the juice of a lemon, or plain white vinegar to prevent the artichoke from turning brown.

To prepare artichokes to be eaten with a knife and fork, or used as a vegetable or salad, trim the artichoke of all inedible parts: Pull off all the outside leaves, until the bottom of the heart is exposed. Now cut all the tough parts off the remaining leaves, so that only the edible part is left. Now open up the centre, and and spread it. With a small spoon, scoop out all the fibrous core (the choke). Trim off some of the stalk. Everything that you have left should be edible – if in doubt, trim some more off. Immerse in acidulated water until ready to cook.

DESSERTS

A couple of years ago I read a magazine interview with a fashionable Italian caterer. He said that in his experience the guests at the dinner parties he catered generally did not remember the main course; what stood out in their memory was always the first course and the dessert. Exactly the same thing could be said about Toronto. Not, of course, that there is anything wrong with the main courses that we make. But desserts are very important in this city; and while the first impression of your dinner, made by what you start it with, is important, it is that last taste that will linger with your friends as they leave.

With all food, presentation is very important. When it comes to desserts the opportunities for a wonderful presentation are greater than at any other stage in the meal. To begin with there are the colours, shapes, and textures of all the different varieties of fruit. You will notice that we often suggest using a raspberry purée. Not only does it add the fresh, sweet-sharp flavour of raspberry, but its vibrant colour makes a dramatic contrast with whatever you put on top – even if it is red berries again (fresh strawberries look wonderful on raspberry purée).

Then there is chocolate, white and dark, which can be shaved, moulded, melted, and drizzled to make an endless arrangement of form and substance – from the dense, solid heaviness of a sour cream chocolate cake to the fresh and light-hearted feel of shaved white chocolate flakes.

Surprisingly, the use of contrasting textures can add a very interesting dimension to soufflés. A cold sauce served with a hot soufflé provides an unexpected but very welcome contrast; in fact, serving any sauce with a soufflé adds a whole new interest. Soufflés sound delicious and look even better; but I often find myself a bit disappointed when it comes to eating them. Adding a sauce moves them back into the realm of exceptional desserts – and of exceptional first courses, too.

You can take the same approach with ice cream; almost any ice cream or sorbet can be made into a dramatic dessert by adding a sauce of contrasting texture and colour (imagine a mango sorbet on a blackcurrant sauce). You can also create contrasts of colour and texture within the ice cream itself – for example, one of our recipes has tiny rum truffles folded into an espresso chocolate ice cream: when they are frozen the truffles become hard and you get a crunch of intense chocolate rum flavour against the background of smooth and creamy chocolate-coffee.

With all these materials at your disposal, it is easy to give in to the temptation to make your desserts as extravagant and splashy as possible. There are certainly occasions when this style is what is called for – when you are making a dessert table, or when the dessert is the most important course of the dinner. Here for example is a chocolate extravaganza that we did for a particularly important dinner:

Pistachio studded chocolate pâté
Quenelles of white and dark chocolate mousse
Chocolate majorlaine
Fresh raspberries
Chocolate-dipped strawberries
Chocolate orange truffles

They were all served on the same (large) plate! But they could just as well have been the components of a chocolate dessert buffet.

There will be other occasions when extravagance is not the right note for the dessert course. It is true that there are people who feel that a party is not complete without something chocolate for dessert; but it will do them no harm to discover that there are other ways to end a dinner that are just as good, and in many ways even more appropriate. If the other courses of the dinner have been heavy or rich (or where the mood or the setting calls for something simpler – such as, a summer dinner in the garden or on the patio), think about serving something supremely simple. What could be better than a perfectly ripe white peach, served whole in all its glory on a white plate? It will have far more dramatic impact and be much more appropriate than any more complex dessert could ever be.

Success in dessert-making requires certain skills and disciplines that are not necessary for most other branches of cooking. To make good pastries and desserts – for baking in general – you need to be more precise, more careful, and generally more attentive to detail than in other cooking. You do not (necessarily) have to be a nit-picking personality type to turn out a good dessert (some of my best friends are good dessert cooks!). This is not to say that you cannot be creative; but there is a discipline that must be mastered before you let your creativity loose. When I first started cooking, I used to get a lot of friendly criticism for the way that I would religiously follow recipes; this always came from people who said that they "just cooked what they felt like". With desserts you cannot cook what you feel like and hope to get a result that you will be proud to serve to your friends – at least not until you have mastered the basic skills and understand some of the principles behind what you are doing. As an example, if you are making the apple crêpes, do not change the proportions in the crêpe batter until you have made it a few times and understand what effect the changes are likely to have; but you should feel free the second time you make it (follow the recipe the first!) to change the filling, or the sauce, or the presentation.

Apple Crêpes with Cider Beurre Blanc

These crêpes are filled with apples and caramel, folded into triangles, and served with a delicious cider-based sauce. Most of the work can be done ahead and it would be a fitting dessert for a formal dinner party.

Makes 16 crêpes.

FOR THE CRÊPES

1 cup	**all-purpose flour**
1⅓ cups	**milk**
¼ cup	**water**
¼ cup	**Calvados**
3 large	**eggs**
2	**egg yolks**
2 Tbs	**sugar**
½ tsp	**ground nutmeg**
⅛ tsp	**ground cinnamon**

FOR THE FILLING

6 large	**Granny Smith apples**
2 Tbs	**lemon juice**
1½ cups	**granulated sugar**
½ cup	**water**
2 Tbs	**unsalted butter**
	(see page 23)

FOR THE CIDER BEURRE BLANC

1 cup	**cider**
¼ cup	**cider vinegar**
1 tsp	**vanilla extract**
pinch of	**ground cinnamon**
2 Tbs	**granulated sugar**
6 oz	**unsalted butter,** chilled

1. Make the crêpe batter first: Sift the flour into a bowl; whisk in ⅔ cup of the milk to make a smooth paste. Gradually whisk in the rest of the milk, the water, Calvados, eggs, and egg yolks. Stir in the sugar, cinnamon, and nutmeg. Whisk the batter well until large bubbles form on the surface. Cover with plastic wrap and let stand at room temperature for 1 hour.

2. While the crêpe batter is sitting, prepare the filling. Peel, core, and slice the apples into ¼″ slices. Toss in a bowl with 2 Tbs lemon juice. Set aside.

3. Have ready an oven-proof baking dish, preferably glass or ceramic, large enough to hold the apples. In a small heavy saucepan bring the sugar and water to a boil over medium heat (see page 187). When it boils, turn up the heat to high and cook to a light caramel colour. Immediately pour the caramel into the baking dish, and rotate it so that all of the bottom is covered. Pour the apples over the caramel and dot with 2 Tbs butter. Cover the dish with a piece of foil or buttered parchment, and bake in the preheated oven for about 15 minutes. Take it out of the oven and stir well. Bake 15 minutes more, until the apples are soft (the mixture should be quite smooth and spreadable. Bake another 10 to 15 minutes if necessary.)

4. Make the crêpes: Heat a 6″ or 7″ crêpe or omelette pan over medium-high heat. Add a dot of butter and swirl it around the pan; ladle in 2 to 3 Tbs of the batter, rotating the pan so that it covers the bottom completely. Cook for about 2 minutes, until air bubbles appear around the edges. Flip it over (how you do it is up to you) and cook about 1 minute on the other side. Stack them up as they are ready (make 16, to serve 6 to 8).

5. Assemble the crêpes: Butter a large shallow baking dish. Spread one side of each crêpe with apples and some of their juice; fold in half, then in half again to form a triangle. Lay the crêpes in one layer in the dish (use more than one dish if necessary). Cover with foil.

6. Start to make the beurre blanc: Combine the cider, vinegar, vanilla, and cinnamon in a small saucepan. Bring to a boil over medium-high heat and reduce to about 3 Tbs (will take 15 to 20 minutes). *(May be done up to 4 hours ahead to this point, but do not refrigerate.)*

7. Preheat the oven to 400°F.

8. To finish the beurre blanc: Place the reduced cider over low heat, add 2 Tbs sugar and cook gently until the sugar is dissolved. Cut the cold butter into small cubes (they must be cold). Put two butter cubes into the cider and whisk until they dissolve. Add 2 more and whisk again; repeat until all the butter has been added and the sauce is lightly thickened. Don't add more butter until the previous batch has been completely incorporated. Keep the heat low. Keep the finished sauce warm on the edge of the stove, but not on the element.

9. Bake the covered crêpes in the preheated oven for 6 to 8 minutes, until heated through.

10. To serve: Arrange 2 crêpes with their tips towards the centre on a plate; spoon the beurre blanc over and serve warm.

APPLE FEUILLETÉES WITH CARAMEL SAUCE

Serves 6 to 8.

1¼ lbs	**Puff Pastry** (see page 231) thawed
4 med.	**green apples**
4 Tbs	**unsalted butter** (see page 23)
8 Tbs	**granulated sugar**
1½ cups	**whipping cream**

FOR THE PASTRY CREAM

4 Tbs	**all-purpose flour**
6 Tbs	**granulated sugar**
2 cups	**milk**
6 large	**egg yolks**
1½ Tbs	**Calvados**
2	**eggs**

1. Preheat the oven to 425°F.

2. The puff pastry should be cold but not frozen. Lightly flour your work surface and roll out the pastry to a rectangle 10″ by 12″, about ¼″ thick. Trim the edges square with a sharp knife, then cut into 8 smaller pieces, each 3″ by 5″. Lay on a baking sheet and freeze for 1 hour.

3. Peel, core, and slice the apples. Sauté them in a large frying pan (in two batches if necessary) in the butter and half the sugar. Set the sautéed apples aside on a plate.

4. When all the apples are done, put in the other 4 Tbs of sugar and cook over medium-high heat until it caramelizes to a medium brown. Immediately pour in the cream, covering your hand with a cloth and averting your face – *it will sputter up*. Cook until the sauce is smooth and lightly thickened. Set aside and keep warm.

5. Make the pastry cream: Rinse out a pan with water and pour in the milk; heat over medium heat until almost boiling, then set aside. In a bowl, whisk together the egg yolks, flour, and sugar; pour in ¼ of the hot milk, whisking constantly; gradually pour in the rest of the milk and stir well. Clean the pan (or find a new one), pour in the pastry cream, and cook over medium-high heat, stirring all the time, until it comes to a boil. Let it cook for 1 minute, then pour into a bowl, cover with plastic wrap, and allow to cool to room temperature.

6. Beat the eggs well; remove the puff pastry from the freezer, brush with the egg and bake in the preheated oven for 10 minutes; then reduce the oven temperature to 350° F and bake for 20 minutes longer. Remove from the oven and allow to cool a little. Leave the oven on.

7. With a serrated knife, cut the tops of the puffs, quite close to the top; reserve them. Use a fork to scoop out the soft, uncooked interior of the bottom. Set aside until nearly ready to serve.

8. To serve: Stir the Calvados into the pastry cream. Reheat the puff-pastry bottoms in the oven for 2 minutes. Spoon some pastry cream into each puff; then spoon some of the sautéed apples on top. Pour some caramel sauce onto each serving plate; place a filled puff on each plate, set the pastry lids on top, and serve.

APPLE FEUILLETÉES WITH RASPBERRY PURÉE

1 recipe **Apple Feuilletées with Caramel Sauce** (see pages 152-53)	**1.** Follow the recipe for Apple Feuilletées with Caramel Sauce, leaving out Step 4.
2 cups **Raspberry Purée** (see page 237)	**2.** To serve: Spoon raspberry purée onto plate; set the filled puffs on top and serve.

CRÈME BRÛLÉE WITH CANDIED ORANGE

An elegant dessert that can be made on short notice, with ingredients that you may just have on hand.

Serves 2 or 3.

2 large	**navel oranges**
¼ cup	**sugar**
¼ cup	**water**
3 large	**egg yolks**
¼ cup	**sugar**
1½ Tbs	**Grand Marnier** OR **orange liqueur**
1 cup	**whipping cream**

"COATING THE BACK OF A SPOON"
This is a common phrase in cooking, particularly when making egg-thickened sauces. It is important to remember that these sauces will never get really thick. People who have not made this kind of sauce before often expect it to thicken up like canned soup. It won't (only canned soup has that property!).

When egg yolks are cooked to 165°F their protein combines with the protein in the milk to make a slightly thickened sauce; if the cooking goes on past 185°F the custard will curdle. If you don't have a thermometer, dip a spoon into the custard and lift it out upright. Draw your finger across the back of the spoon horizontally to make a line in the custard. If this line persists for more than a few seconds, the custard is as ready as it's going to be; there is very little additional thickening between 165°F and 185°F, so take it off the heat and stir for a minute or two, then cover and let cool.

1. Use a vegetable peeler to remove the zest from the oranges in long strips; try not to take off any of the white pith – it is very bitter. Cut the strips lengthwise into julienne (long thin strips).

2. Combine sugar and water in a small heavy saucepan; bring to a boil over medium-high heat; boil for 1 minute. Add the orange strips, and cook for 5 minutes more. Remove from the heat, pour into a small bowl, cover, and refrigerate.

3. With a sharp knife, peel the pith and the outer membrane of the oranges as you would peel an apple; cut into sections, cutting the flesh away from the membranes. Set the sections aside on a plate.

4. Bring the cream to a boil over medium heat. Set aside and keep warm.

5. While the cream is coming to a boil, beat the egg yolks and sugar in a bowl that can go over hot water (or in the top of a double boiler). Set the bowl over simmering water and whisk in the orange liqueur; continue to whisk until the yolks start to thicken. Now gradually add the scalded cream. Cook, stirring, until the custard thickens enough to coat the back of a spoon.

6. Turn on the broiler and let it get hot.

7. Divide the orange sections between 2 or 3 ovenproof serving plates: arrange them in a star or flower pattern. Pour the sauce around the oranges, but not over them. Sprinkle the orange zest over the top.

8. Pass the plates under the broiler for about 90 seconds, just long enough to glaze the surface of the cream. Serve straight away.

CRÈME CARAMEL

Serves 6.

½ cup	**granulated sugar**
2 tbs	**water**
1 drop	**lemon juice**
2 cups	**milk**
1½	**vanilla beans**, split
½ cup	**half and half cream**
2 large	**eggs**
2	**egg yolks**
½ cup	**granulated sugar**

1. Preheat the oven to 350°F. Find a straight-sided, 4-cup or 6-cup soufflé dish; or 6 individual ramekins. Have them ready for the caramel.

2. Make the caramel: Put the sugar, water, and lemon juice in a heavy-bottom saucepan. Melt the sugar over medium heat. Once it has dissolved, increase the heat to high and cook without stirring until the sugar boils; brush down the sides of the pan with a pastry brush dipped in water from time to time. When the syrup has turned a rich caramel colour, remove from the heat and pour into the dish. Rotate the dish in your hands to make sure that the caramel covers the bottom.

3. Heat the milk, cream, and vanilla bean over medium heat until almost boiling. Remove from heat and let stand for 5 minutes.

4. Whisk the eggs, egg yolks, and sugar until very well mixed. Pour in the hot milk in a thin stream, whisking all the time. Strain through a sieve into the caramel-lined mould.

5. Set the dish in a roasting pan half-filled with boiling water; it should come about 1″ up the side of the dish. Set the pan in the preheated oven; immediately reduce the heat to 325°F. Bake for 50 to 60 minutes, until a tester comes out almost clean. (If using individual ramekins, they will be done in 20 minutes.) Chill until ready to serve.

6. Run a knife around the edge of the dish to loosen the custard. Invert onto a serving plate; some of the caramel will have melted during cooking and provides a very good sauce for the custard.

LEMON MOUSSE

A fresh and attractive ending to a rich meal.

Serves 6.

4 tsp	**gelatin**
8 Tbs	**water**
¾ cup	**lemon juice**
½ cup	**granulated sugar**
3	**egg yolks**
3	**egg whites**
½ cup	**granulated sugar**
1 cup	**whipping cream**

BEATING EGG WHITES

Recipes generally call for egg whites to be beaten to "soft" or "stiff" peaks. Cooks use 4 stages to describe how eggs are to be beaten:

Stage 1: Does not apply to whites, only to whole eggs. Whole eggs at this stage are called "well-beaten eggs"; they are used for omelettes, scrambled eggs, etc.

Stage 2: Whites have coarse bubbles, a more or less even consistency, and begin to look white. The recipes call this stage "frothy". Add cream of tartare at this stage; and start to add the sugar, if it is used.

Stage 3: Dip your whisk into the beaten whites and pull it out with some of the whites on it. Turn it so that the peaks of the whites point up. At the lower end of this stage the peaks will bend over, and be very soft – it is called "soft peaks". Keep beating, testing the peaks frequently; soon they will stand straight up – this is "stiff peaks".

Stage 4: If you keep beating, the whites will become dry, stiff, and brittle. They have gone past the point where they are of any use.

If you add sugar at Stage 2, the beaten whites will become smooth and glossy as you continuue to beat. It will take longer to reach stiff peaks, and it will be very hard to overbeat them to Stage 4.

---

1. Pour the water into a small bowl; sprinkle the gelatin over the surface and allow it to dissolve (about 5 minutes).

2. Combine the lemon juice, sugar, and egg yolks in a bowl that can go over water (or in the top of a double boiler); whisk well together. Set over simmering but not boiling water and heat until warm but not hot to the touch (about 115°F). Remove from the heat. Set gelatin in bowl over hot water until melted, then whisk it into the lemon. Refrigerate in the bowl until cool but not at all set.

3. When the lemon mixture is cool, beat the egg whites to firm peaks; start adding the ½ cup of sugar 2 Tbs at a time as soon as the whites become foamy. Gently fold into the lemon and eggs (make sure that you fold in all the lemon juice that has sunk to the bottom). Chill again for 15 to 20 minutes, until it starts to set around the edges.

4. Whip the cream to soft peaks. Gently fold into the lemon, again making sure to incorporate all the juice. The mousse should be a uniform pale yellow, with no white streaks. Pour into a glass bowl or into 6 wine goblets. Refrigerate until ready to serve. The mousse may be garnished with rosettes of whipped cream; lightly candied lemon peel; fresh raspberries or blueberries.

WARM BERRY COMPOTE WITH ORANGE CUSTARD

Serves 8.

FOR THE CUSTARD

2½ cups	**half and half cream**
½ cup	**granulated sugar**
2	**egg yolks**
2 large	**eggs**
2 Tbs	**grated orange zest** (see page 237)
2 Tbs	**Grand Marnier** OR **orange liqueur**

FOR THE SAUCE

1 bunch	**grapes**, about 1 lb
1 pint	**strawberries**, hulled and sliced
1 pint	**raspberries**
1 Tbs	**grated orange zest**
¼ cup	**orange juice**
1 Tbs	**lemon juice**
½ cup	**granulated sugar**
1 pint	**strawberries**, hulled and sliced
1 pint	**raspberries**

1. Preheat oven to 350° F. Lightly butter 8 small ramekins.

2. Heat the cream and sugar in a saucepan over medium heat; stir until the sugar has dissolved. When hot but not boiling, remove from the heat.

3. Lightly beat the yolks, whole eggs, and orange zest together in a bowl. Gradually pour in ¼ of the hot cream, beating all the time. Pour in the rest of the cream in a thin stream, and mix well. Add the orange liqueur. Strain through a fine sieve.

4. Pour the custard into the prepared ramekins. Place ramekins in a roasting pan half full of hot water, cover with aluminum foil, and bake in preheated oven for 45 to 60 minutes, or until a tester comes out fairly clean – it does not matter if there are a few bits of custard clinging to it.

5. Combine grapes, strawberries, raspberries (1 pint of each), orange zest and juice, lemon juice, and sugar in a saucepan. Cook over medium heat for 5 to 8 minutes, stirring constantly. Push the mixture through a food mill (or process in a food processor and push through a sieve); return to the pan and keep warm.

6. To serve: Spoon a bit of warm sauce into a dessert plate; unmould the custard on top of the sauce, drizzle more sauce over the custard, and arrange the remaining strawberries and raspberries around it.

PAVLOVA

This is Australia's national dessert, and it truly is a spectacular confection – a mountain of whipped cream with fresh fruit scattered all over it. Underneath there is a delicate meringue filled with more fruit.

Serves 6 to 8

4	**egg whites**, at room temperature
¼ tsp	**salt**
¼ tsp	**cream of tartar** (see page 233)
1 cup less	
1 Tbs	**granulated sugar**
1 Tbs	**cornstarch**
1 tsp	**white wine vinegar**
½ tsp	**vanilla extract**
1½ cups	**whipping cream**
about 3	
cups	**fresh fruit** – kiwi (of course), strawberries, raspberries, passion fruit, mangoes, pineapple, all sliced

1.   Preheat the oven to 275°F. Line a baking sheet (at least 12" square) with a piece of parchment. Using a cake pan, bowl, or plate as a guide, draw a circle about 9" in diameter on the paper. Now turn the paper over: you will be able to see the line through the paper, but it won't be picked up by the meringue as it bakes.

2.   Beat the egg whites with the salt and cream of tartar until they hold a stiff peak. Add the sugar, 2 Tbs at a time, beating well between additions. The meringue should be thick and glossy. Then gently beat in the cornstarch, vinegar, and vanilla.

3.   With a large spoon or spatula, scoop the meringue onto the parchment, using the circle as a guide; it should be mounded up to a high dome in the middle. Bake in the preheated oven for 1½ to 2 hours, until very lightly browned, and crisp on the outside (it should still be soft in the middle). Check it after 1 hour of baking; if it is getting brown already, turn the oven down to 225°F. Remove from the oven and cool completely. As it cools, it may collapse in the middle so that it looks like a volcano; this is just fine.

4.   Whip the cream to soft peaks. If your meringue does not yet look like a volcano, take a sharp knife and cut off the top of the dome so that is does. Fill the crater with almost ½ of the fruit. Then spread the whipped cream all over the top of the fruit and the outside of the meringue (it should look like a mountain after a very heavy snowfall). Arrange the rest of the fruit in an abstract (but meaningful to you) pattern. Refrigerate until ready to serve.

Pears with Mascarpone

Serves 4 to 8, depending on whether you serve a whole or half pear per person

4	**comice** OR **Anjou pears**
1½ cups	**dry white wine** (Italian for the authentic flavour)
½ cup	**granulated sugar**
1	**cinnamon stick**
2	**whole cloves**
1 strip	**lemon rind**
½ cup	**mascarpone cheese**
5 Tbs	**granulated sugar**
2 Tbs	**brandy**
¾ cup	**whipping cream**
⅔ cup	**granulated sugar**
1 package	**amaretti cookies**

1.   Peel the pears; it's best done with a vegetable peeler, working from top to bottom in parallel strips. Cut them in half lengthwise and scoop out the cores.

2.   Combine the wine, sugar, cinnamon, lemon rind, and cloves in a heavy non-corrodable saucepan large enough to hold the pears in one layer. Put in the pears cut-side down and warm over a medium heat until the sugar has dissolved. Increase the heat so that the liquid barely bubbles. Poach until the pears are soft when pierced with a fork (about 30 minutes). Turn the pears half-way through the cooking if the wine does not completely cover them, so that they cook evenly.

3.   In a medium bowl, combine mascarpone, sugar, and brandy. Beat together with a wooden spoon until fluffy. *EITHER* fit a pastry bag with a star tip and spoon the mascarpone into the bag *OR* set aside in the bowl and fill the pears by hand later.

4.   Warm ¾ cup of cream in a small saucepan (it should be hot but not boiling). Set aside.

5.   Remove the pears to a platter. Return the poaching liquid to a high heat and reduce to ½ cup. Lower the heat and add ⅔ cup sugar, stirring until it is dissolved. Increase the heat to medium high and cook the syrup to a light caramel. Be careful that it does not get too dark. As soon as it has reached the colour that you want, remove from the heat and slowly add the warm cream. *Be careful* when doing this: It may bubble up and spit at you. Return the pan to a medium heat and cook, stirring, until the sauce is smooth.

6.   To serve: Put a ladleful of sauce onto each plate; place half a pear on top, cut-side up; then pipe the mascarpone filling into the cavity. Crush the amaretti cookies and sprinkle the crumbs over the filling. If you are filling the pears with a spoon, it is better to do it before you set them on the sauce.

FRESH STRAWBERRIES WITH CHAMPAGNE SABAYON

Strawberries with fresh cream are very hard to beat, but sometimes you may want to dress them up a bit more. Champagne sabayon will do the trick – and you can make it ahead of time.

Serves 6.

7 large	**egg yolks**
½ cup	**granulated sugar**
pinch of	**salt**
1 cup	**dry champagne** (if it's flat, so much the better – you couldn't drink it anyway!)
3 Tbs	**Kirsch**
⅔ cup	**whipping cream**
2 pints	**fresh strawberries**

1. In a stainless-steel bowl, or the top half of a double boiler, beat the egg yolks well. Gradually add the sugar, beating until the eggs are pale yellow and very thick. Do not set it over hot water yet.

2. Pour in the champagne. Set the bowl over simmering but not boiling water, and whisk until the eggs have increased in volume and have the consistency of very lightly whipped cream. They should feel very hot to the touch, but far from boiling. The eggs must be properly cooked or they may separate later on. Remove from the heat and cool completely.

3. Whip the cream and the Kirsch to soft peaks; fold into the cooled sabayon.

4. To serve: Spoon the sabayon onto one half of a dessert plate; arrange the sliced strawberries over the other half. *Or* spoon sabayon into wide-mouthed wine glasses; top with the sliced strawberries.

SUMMER PUDDING

This is one of the great treats of summer. It brings back memories of summers the way I wish that they had been but probably never really were. You can make it only for a few weeks at the height of summer, because red currants and raspberries are only available together for a very short time. We are giving two recipes, one for what I consider to be the pure essence of summer pudding; the second uses more kinds of fruit and some people prefer it. Whatever happened to all the purists?

SUMMER PUDDING #1

Serves 8.

1 loaf	**day-old white bread,** crusts removed
3 cups	**raspberries**
1½ cups	**red currants**, stems removed
1 cup	**granulated sugar**

1. Cut the bread into slices and remove the crusts. (Actually it's probably easier to remove the crusts then slice.) Line a medium-size bowl with the bread, cutting the slices into the right shape to fit the bowl; leave enough to cover the filling.

2.   Put the red currants and the sugar in a saucepan; cook over medium heat, stirring gently, until the sugar starts to melt and the juice just begins to run from the red currants. Now add the raspberries, and cook until the juice runs a little. Try to stir as little as possible, so the fruit does not get crushed. Remove from heat and pour into the bread-lined bowl.

3.   Cut more bread to completely cover the filling. Spread a sheet of plastic wrap over the bread, set a plate on top and weight it with about 2 pounds (a couple of cans will do). Refrigerate overnight (or up to 2 days). The juice from the fruit will stain most of the bread a deep and delicious purple.

4.   To serve: Turn out onto a plate; cut into wedges like a cake. Serve with thick cream (English Devon cream is pretty good) if you like; but this is the only fruit dessert I can think of that just may be better on its own.

SUMMER PUDDING #2

¾ cup	**raspberries**
¾ cup	**red currants**
¾ cup	**loganberries**
1½ cups	**blackcurrants** OR **blackberries**
¾ cup	**sliced strawberries** OR **fresh cherries**
¾ cup	**granulated sugar**
1 loaf	**day-old white bread,** crusts removed

1.   Remove the crusts and slice the bread. Line a medium-sized bowl or pudding basin with the bread; leave enough to make a lid.

2.   Remove the stems from all the fruit. Wash gently if necessary. Combine all the fruit except the strawberries in a heavy-bottom saucepan with the sugar. Cook over medium heat until the juice starts to run from the red currants (about 6 to 8 minutes). Remove from the heat and add the sliced strawberries.

3.   Pour into the bread-lined bowl with all the juice. Cut lid pieces out of the bread and cover the top. Lay a sheet of plastic wrap over the top, set a plate on top and weight it with about 2 pounds (a couple of cans work well). Refrigerate for 24 hours (or up to 2 days).

4.   Turn out onto a plate and cut into wedges. Serve with thick cream.

Pears in Pastry with Caramel Sauce

Serves 6.

1 recipe	**Sweet Flaky Pastry** (see page 235)
6 ripe	**pears**
1½ cups	**granulated sugar**
1½ tsp	**ground cinnamon**
3 large	**eggs**
6 Tbs	**whipping cream**

FOR THE SAUCE

1½ cups	**granulated sugar**
9 Tbs	**water**
1½ cups	**whipping cream**

1. Prepare the pastry; set it aside to chill while you prepare the pears.

2. Peel the pears carefully. With a paring knife or vegetable peeler remove as much of the core of the pear as you can from the bottom: leave the stem of the pear intact.

3. Combine sugar and cinnamon on a plate; roll the pears in it so they are well coated.

4. Divide the dough in two to make it easier to work with. Roll each piece out to a rectangle about ⅛" to ³⁄₁₆" thick, then cut into 6 squares, about 6" by 6". With a sharp knife (or cookie cutter) cut a 1" hole in the centre of each pastry square.

5. Slip a pastry square over each pear, so that the stem sticks out through the hole. As neatly as you can, gather the pastry and tuck it under the pear, pressing up into the cavity.

6. Roll out the trimmings to ⅛" thick and cut them into leaf shapes; score them with the back of a knife to look like the veins on a leaf. Beat the eggs with the cream to make a glaze; brush it onto the pears and press the leaves on to make them look as attractive as possible (pretty is what we are after here). Brush the whole thing with glaze again, then chill for 20 minutes.

7. Preheat the oven to 375° F.

8. Brush the pears with glaze again, then bake in the preheated oven for 40 minutes, until golden brown.

9. While the pears are baking, prepare the sauce: Warm the cream in a small saucepan until hot but not boiling; set aside. Combine sugar and water in a heavy-bottom saucepan. Cook over medium heat until the sugar has dissolved, brushing down the sides of the pan with a wet pastry brush (see page 187) until the sugar has dissolved. Increase the heat to high and boil until the syrup turns a light caramel colour (be careful not to let it burn). As soon as it is golden, remove from the heat and pour in the warm cream in a thin stream (it may bubble up and spit, so cover your hand with a cloth and avert your face when you do this). Return to the heat and cook until the sauce is smooth. Allow to cool for 30 minutes before using.

10. Serve the pears warm, sitting in a pool of caramel sauce.

TIRAMISU

Daphna learned this recipe, via sign language, in a village in Tuscany from a lady called Romola; she in turn had learned it from her mother (the instructions probably also accompanied by sign language, in the Italian manner). While Romola made the tiramisu, Daphna measured the ingredients and wrote down the method. The result is an especially creamy tiramisu, with an intense mascarpone flavour. This dessert looks best presented in a straight-sided glass bowl.

Serves 6 to 8.

1 recipe	**Lady Fingers** (see page 233)
5 large	**egg yolks**
5 Tbs	**granulated sugar**
1 carton	**mascarpone** (preferably imported), 500 gr
5 Tbs	**dark rum**
5	**egg whites**
1 cup	**strong black coffee**
1 cup	**unsweetened cocoa powder**

1. Prepare lady fingers according to recipe; allow to cool completely.

2. In an electric mixer (you can do it by hand if you wish) whisk the yolks and the sugar until pale yellow and thick.

3. Fold the mascarpone into the yolks; add the rum, and transfer to a clean bowl.

4. Whisk the egg whites to stiff but not dry peaks (see page 158); stir ⅓ of the whites into the yolks and mascarpone, then gently fold in the rest.

5. With a pastry brush, brush coffee onto enough lady fingers to line the bottom of the serving bowl. Gently pour a layer about 1″ thick of mascarpone mixture over the lady fingers; spread it evenly with a spatula. Place ¼ of the cocoa powder in a fine mesh sieve and sift over the mascarpone. This completes one layer.

6. Repeat the process 2 or 3 times (so that you have 3 or 4 layers altogether). It's probably best to brush the lady fingers with coffee on a separate plate and then transfer them to the bowl, so that you don't have coffee everywhere. Finish with a layer of cocoa. Cover with plasic wrap and refrigerate overnight.

7. For a more elaborate presentation, decorate the edge with a border of grated semi-sweet chocolate.

STRAWBERRIES IN CHOCOLATE TULIPES

Serves 8 to 12.

3 pints	**fresh strawberries**, hulled and sliced
½ cup	**Grand Marnier** OR **Kirsch** (or another liqueur)

FOR THE CHOCOLATE TULIPES

⅔ cup	**cake** OR **all-purpose flour** (see page 233)
3 Tbs	**unsweetened cocoa powder**
⅛ tsp	**salt**
¼ cup	**unsalted butter**, at room temperature (see page 23)
⅔ cup	**granulated sugar**
½ tsp	**vanilla extract**
1 large	**egg white**
½ cup	**blanched sliced almonds**
1 recipe	**Raspberry Purée** (see page 237) OR
4 oz	**semi-sweet chocolate**, melted

1.   Preheat the oven to 400° F. Cover one large or two smaller baking sheets with parchment or butter and flour them.

2.   Sift together the flour, cocoa, and salt.

3.   In an electric mixer with the paddle attachment, cream the butter and sugar until light and fluffy. Add the vanilla. Turn the mixer speed to low and add the egg white and then the flour. Beat until well blended, then fold in the almonds.

4.   Cut a 7″ circle out of the centre of a piece of card; trim the surround so that it is only about 1″ wide (you will have a flat ring). Lay this in one corner of the baking sheet and drop a spoonful of the batter in the middle. With a spatula, or the back of a spoon dipped in water, spread the batter out to cover the inside of the ring. Lift off the ring and repeat as many times as you have room for on the baking sheet.

5.   Have a muffin pan or two at hand, they will be the moulds in which to form the tulipes once they are baked.

6.   Bake one sheet at a time in the preheated oven for 5 minutes, or just until the outside edges start to brown.

7.   This is the good part. Open the oven door and set the baking sheet on the door, so that the tulipes stay hot but don't cook any more. Lift one off with a spatula and drape it into a muffin cup; pinch the outside edge gently together to encourage it into the muffin tin to form a cup. Practice is the key. As quickly as you can, form all the cooked circles into tulipes.

8.   When you have recovered sufficiently, repeat steps 4 to 7 (you don't need a new ring – the old one will keep for quite a long time), until all the batter is used up.

9.   Place the sliced strawberries in a bowl, pour in the liqueur and leave to macerate for several hours.

10.   To serve: *EITHER* spoon some raspberry purée onto a plate, set a tulipe on top, and fill with the macerated strawberries *OR* set the tulipe on the plate, fill with strawberries, and drizzle melted chocolate over the top.

STRAWBERRY PROFITEROLES

An attractive presentation of simple ingredients: you could even use bought ice cream!

Serves 6 to 8.

1 recipe	**Choux Pastry** (see page 231)
1	**egg**
1 recipe	**strawberry ice cream** (see page 183)
1 pint	**strawberries**
2 Tbs	**powdered sugar**
1 Tbs	**Kirsch**
	fresh mint leaves

1.   Preheat the oven to 400° F. Lightly butter two baking sheets or line them with parchment.

2.   Prepare the choux pastry, following the recipe. Spoon the pastry (you can use it while it is still warm) into a piping bag fitted with a ⅜" plain tip. Pipe out little mounds about 1½" across and 1½" high onto the prepared baking sheets. Lightly beat the egg and brush the little mounds (don't put so much on that it drips onto the baking sheet).

3.   Bake in the preheated oven for 20 minutes. After 20 minutes, remove them from the oven and, with a sharp knife, make a little incision in the side of each puff. Return them to the oven to allow the insides to dry out. (It's important that they dry out enough that they don't collapse after they come out of the oven.) Remove to a rack and allow to cool.

4.   Make the ice cream following the recipe; keep frozen until ready to assemble.

5.   Prepare the sauce: Hull the strawberries and purée in a food processor. Strain into a bowl and stir in the sugar and Kirsch.

6.   To assemble: Slice the puffs in half, fill with ice cream, and put the tops back on. Spoon some of the sauce onto each plate; arrange 3 puffs on the sauce and spoon some more sauce over each. Garnish the plate with sliced strawberries and fresh mint leaves.

CHOCOLATE MOUSSE

Chocolate mousse can never be what you might call light. But this recipe has no butter and whipped cream, so it is not quite as rich as some others.

Serves 6.

4 oz	**unsweetened chocolate**
¾ cup	**granulated sugar**
¼ cup	**strong black coffee**
5	**egg yolks**
1 to 2 Tbs	**Brandy** OR **rum** OR **Grand Marnier**
5	**egg whites**
2 Tbs	**granulated sugar**

FOR DECORATION
whipped cream OR **toasted sliced almonds**
(see page 185)

1. Melt the chocolate, sugar, and coffee in a stainless-steel bowl or double boiler set over simmering but not boiling water. Stir to ensure that it melts smoothly.

2. Remove from the heat; beat in the egg yolks one at a time, beating well after each one. Stir in the liquor and allow to cool to room temperature.

3. Beat the egg whites until frothy (see page 156); add the sugar and continue to beat to stiff peaks. Stir ⅓ of the beaten whites into the chocolate to lighten it, then gently fold in the rest.

4. Pour into 6 wine goblets or individual soufflé dishes. *Cover with plastic wrap and refrigerate for 4 hours or overnight.* Garnish with rosettes of whipped cream or sprinkle on toasted sliced almonds before serving.

CHOCOLATE FONDUE

A few hints when making fondue: Make sure that the pieces of fruit are bite-size – your guests may not want to dip half-eaten pieces back in the chocolate. If you are using a juicy fruit, such as pineapple, make sure that it is well drained and dried before dipping; extra liquid in the chocolate will change its consistency. This recipe calls for both semi-sweet and unsweetened chocolate; the unsweetened chocolate gives a very intense flavour. However, you may use all semi-sweet chocolate if you do not mind a sweeter flavour.

Serves 8 to 10.

10 oz	**semi-sweet chocolate**, in pieces
2 oz	**unsweetened chocolate**, in pieces
¾ cup	**whipping cream**
3 to 4 Tbs	**liqueur** (Cognac, Grand Marnier, Kirsch, Framboise, etc.)

1. Melt both chocolate with the cream in a bowl set over simmering water. Stir occasionally until fully melted and smooth. Remove the pan from the heat and add the liqueur. Keep warm over hot water. If it cools and becomes too sticky, simply reheat over simmering water.

CHOCOLATE BRANDY TRUFFLES

Makes about 50 truffles.

1⅔ cups	**whipping cream**
3½ oz	**unsalted butter** (see page 23)
1 lb	**semi-sweet chocolate**, chopped
3 Tbs	**brandy**
about ½ cup	**unsweetened cocoa powder**

1. Heat butter and cream in a saucepan until butter is melted and cream is almost boiling.

2. Place chocolate pieces in a bowl; pour in the hot cream and butter; whisk until all the chocolate is melted. Pour in the brandy. Cover with plastic wrap and chill. Stir 2 or 3 times as it is cooling, then allow it to set completely.

3. Sift the cocoa powder onto a plate. With a teaspoon, scoop out small amounts of the chocolate, then roll them into a ball between the palms of your hands. Roll them in cocoa until completely coated. Put on a plate, or in small paper cups, and refrigerate until ready to serve.

TARTS & PIES

APPLE CRANBERRY TART

A very festive dessert for Thanksgiving.

Serves 8.

1 recipe	**Sweet Flaky Pastry** (see page 235)
¾ cup	**raw cranberries**, halved
⅓ cup	**granulated sugar**
¼ cup	**currants**
¼ cup	**dark rum**
8 large	**green apples**, peeled, cored, and sliced
⅔ cup	**sugar**
1 Tbs	**lemon juice**
1 Tbs	**Grated Lemon Zest** (see page 237)
1 Tbs	**cornstarch**
½ tsp	**ground cinnamon**
1	**egg**
2 Tbs	**milk**

1. Preheat the oven to 425°F.

2. Combine the cranberries with ⅓ cup of sugar and let stand for 1 hour.

3. Combine currants and rum in a small saucepan; heat until hot to the touch; remove from heat and let stand for 30 minutes.

4. Roll out ⅔ of the dough on a lightly floured work surface to ⅛" to ³⁄₁₆" thick and large enough to line a 9" or 10" pie plate. Lay it in the pie plate and trim the edge; refrigerate until ready to bake.

5. Roll out the remaining ⅓ of the dough into a rectangle about 10" long; with fluted pastry cutter (or pizza wheel) cut into strips about ¾" wide. Refrigerate these until you need them.

6. In a large bowl, combine the sliced, peeled, and cored apples, the cranberries, ⅔ cup of sugar, the currants, and any rum that hasn't been soaked up. Add the lemon juice, grated lemon rind, cornstarch, and cinnamon, and toss together.

7. Spoon the filling into the pie shell, mounding it up slightly in the middle.

8. Arrange the pastry strips over the top of the filling in a lattice pattern, pressing down carefully where it joins the bottom crust to seal together.

9. Beat together the egg and milk to make a glaze; brush it onto the pastry.

10. Bake in preheated oven for 20 minutes; then turn the oven temperature down to 350°F and bake for a further 40 minutes, until the pastry is golden and the filling is bubbling nicely. Serve warm, with lightly whipped cream or with vanilla ice cream.

BLUEBERRY AND PEPPERMINT CREAM TARTLETS

Serves 4.

½ recipe	**Sweet Pastry** (see page 232)
½ tsp	**peppermint extract**
1 cup	**milk**
¼ cup	**granulated sugar**
1 Tbs	**flour**
2 tsp	**cornstarch**
1 large	**egg**
2 Tbs	**unsalted butter** (see page 23)
⅓ cup	**whipping cream**
1½ pints	**fresh blueberries**
	icing sugar (optional)

1. Make the pastry following the recipe on page 232. Preheat the oven to 375°F.

2. Roll the pastry out in a circle ⅛" to ³⁄₁₆" thick. Roll onto rolling pin and unroll onto a 9" tart tin, or into four 4" tins. Trim the edge. Line the tart(s) with parchment or foil, fill with weights or dried beans and bake in the preheated oven for 15 minutes. Remove the weights and paper; bake for 10 to 15 minutes more, until pale golden and completely cooked. Remove from the oven and allow to cool.

3. Combine the peppermint extract and the milk in a small saucepan; bring to a boil over high heat. Set aside.

4. Combine the sugar, flour and cornstarch in a bowl; whisk in the egg. Pour in the boiling milk in a steady stream, whisking constantly. Wash the pan (or find a clean one) and return the custard to the heat. Cook, whisking steadily, until it is very thick and bubbling up. It should boil for at least 1 minute to remove the raw taste of flour and starch.

5. Remove from the heat and stir in the butter. Cover with plastic wrap and cool completely.

6. Whip the cream to quite firm peaks; fold it into the cooled pastry-cream mixture. Spoon into the tart shell(s) and smooth the surface. Cover with fresh blueberries. (Blueberries look better unglazed, but you can sift some icing sugar onto them if you like).

CHOCOLATE TRUFFLE TART WITH RASPBERRIES

Raspberries and chocolate are naturals together; this tart has nothing else in it to spoil the marriage – even the pastry is chocolate.

Serves 6.

1 cup	**all-purpose flour**
½ cup	**granulated sugar**
½ cup	**cocoa powder**
3 oz	**unsalted butter**, chilled (see page 23)
1	**egg**
6 oz	**semi-sweet chocolate**, chopped
1 cup	**whipping cream**
2 boxes	**raspberries**

1. Combine flour, sugar, and cocoa in the work bowl of a food processor. Pulse 2 or 3 times to aerate. Chop the butter into pieces and distribute over the flour. Process just until the mixture resembles coarse meal – do *not* over process.

2. With the motor running, drop the whole egg (no, we do not mean the shell too) through the feed tube. Process very briefly – do *not* let the dough come together into a ball or your pastry will be tough. Remove the dough from the work bowl and set aside at room temperature until the filling is made.

3. Place the chopped chocolate in a medium-sized bowl; bring the cream to a boil over medium-high heat. Pour it over the chocolate, and whisk until all the chocolate is melted. Cover with plastic wrap and re-frigerate until set.

4. Preheat the oven to 375°F.

5. Work the chocolate pastry with your hands and press it into an 8″ or 9″ tart pan with removable bottom; try to get it to an even thickness. Chill for 20 minutes.

6. Prick the bottom of the pastry with a fork. Bake in preheated oven for 20 to 25 minutes. Cool completely.

7. To assemble: Remove the tart gently from the pan and set it on a platter. Spoon or pipe the truffle filling into the shell, and smooth the surface. Arrange the raspberries over the top in concentric circles.

8. Serve at room temperature for the fullest flavour.

FRESH RASPBERRY AND STRAWBERRY TART

If you avoid recipes like this because you can't make good pastry, try this one before you give up completely. It's hard to believe that such a light and short pastry could be so easy.

Serve 6.

1 recipe	**Shortcrust Pastry** (see page 233)
1 recipe	**Pastry Cream** (see pages 152-53)
½ pint	**fresh raspberries**
½ pint	**fresh strawberries**
2 Tbs	**apricot jam**
2 Tbs	**water**

WHAT TO GLAZE
We glaze everything EXCEPT raspberries and blackberries and, generally, blueberries; they look better in their natural state. But we find that all other fruit looks more appetizing with a good shiny glaze. If using raspberries alone, they look very good with a dusting of icing sugar.

---

1. Prepare the pastry following the recipe. When the dough has rested, take small pieces of dough and press them into a 9″ to 11″ tart pan with a removable bottom. Try to make the thickness even but, don't worry – smoothness is not really important. Refrigerate until firm (about 30 minutes – you can put it in the freezer if you are in a hurry).

2. Preheat oven to 375° F.

3. Bake pastry just as it is in preheated oven for 20 to 30 minutes, until pale golden brown and cooked the way you like it. Remove from oven and cool completely.

4. Prepare the pastry cream following the recipe. Allow to cool.

5. To assemble: Pipe or spoon the pastry cream into tart shell (you should have about ½″ depth of cream). Arrange the fruit on top – alternating concentric circles would look good, but it's your tart, so do what you want.

6. To glaze the tart: Melt the apricot jam and water in a small saucepan. Pour through a sieve to remove the lumps, then return to the pan and bring to a boil. Cook until most of the water has evaporated and the glaze falls from the brush in discrete sticky drops rather than in a thin stream (it must be thick enough to stick to the fruit). Try it out if you are not sure; if it gets too thick to brush on, add more water and cook it down again.

FRUIT TART VARIATIONS

Almost anything that looks good will taste good; here are some that are popular in the store:

strawberry and kiwi
mango (peeled and cut into slices) and blackberry
peach and raspberry
kiwi and mandarin orange
peach and blueberry

BRANDY AND GINGER PEACH TART

Serves 8.

1 recipe	**Shortcrust Pastry** (see page 233)
½ tsp	**ground ginger**
1 recipe	**Pastry Cream** (see pages 152-53)
3 Tbs	**brandy**
7 to 8	**ripe peaches**
⅓ cup	**brandy**
½ tsp	**Grated Lemon Zest** (see page 237)
¼ tsp	**ground ginger**
10 oz	**red currant jelly**
2 Tbs plus	
2 tsp	**cornstarch**
¼ cup	**water**

1. Prepare the shortcrust pastry, following the recipe, but add ½ tsp ground ginger to the flour. Let rest at room temperature for 30 minutes.

2. Prepare the pastry cream, following the recipe, but add the brandy at the same time as the final butter. Allow to cool.

3. Place the peaches in a large bowl and pour boiling water over them. Prick the skins in a few places; remove one after 15 seconds to see if the skin comes off. If not put it back and leave them a bit longer. Peel and slice all the peaches; toss them in a bowl with the brandy, lemon peel, and ginger. Let shand at room temperature for 30 minutes.

4. Preheat the oven to 375°F.

5. Work together small pieces of the dough with your fingers and press them into an 11″ tart pan with a removable bottom; try to make it an even thickness. Chill for 30 minutes.

6. Pour the peach liquid into a measuring cup; add enough water to make 1 cup. Transfer to a small saucepan and add the currant jelly. Cook over medium heat until jelly melts. Mix cornstarch with water and stir into the jelly. Increase heat to medium high and cook, stirring constantly, until mixture thickens and starts to boil. Boil for 1 minute; remove from heat, transfer to a bowl and cool slightly.

7. Bake tart shell until golden brown (25 to 30 minutes). Remove from oven and allow to cool.

8. To assemble: Remove cool tart shell from pan and set on plate. Pipe or spoon cooled pastry cream into shell. Arrange the peach slices in concentric circles on top of the cream. Spoon or brush the glaze over the top. Refrigerate until set.

MANGO TART

1 recipe **Pastry Cream**
(see pages 152-53)

FOR THE PASTRY

1 cup less
2 Tbs | **all-purpose flour**
2 Tbs | **finely ground almonds**
1 Tbs | **granulated sugar**
4 oz | **unsalted butter**, chilled (see page 23)
½ tsp | **vanilla extract**
3 tiny drops | **almond extract**
1 | **egg yolk**
2 | **ripe mangoes**
½ cup | **apricot jam**
2 Tbs | **water**
½ cup | **pistachios**, chopped

1. Prepare pastry cream according to recipe; allow to cool while you make the pastry.

2. Place flour, almonds, and sugar in the work bowl of a food processor fitted with the steel blade. Pulse twice to aerate. Cut the butter into pieces and distribute them over the flour. Process briefly until the mixture resembles coarsely ground meal.

3. Beat the yolk with the vanilla and almond extracts. With the motor running, pour the egg down the feed tube of the processor. Process just until the mixture starts to come together, but not so much that it forms a ball, or your pastry will be tough.

4. Turn the dough out onto a lightly floured work surface; knead it gently until it gathers into a cohesive dough. With your fingers press the dough into a 8" or 9" tart pan with a removable bottom; try to make the thickness as even as possible. Refrigerate for 1 hour.

5. Preheat the oven to 350° F.

6. Prick the bottom of the tart shell with a fork; bake in preheated oven for 20 to 25 minutes, until golden brown. Remove from oven and cool.

7. Heat the jam with the water in a small saucepan; when melted, strain through a sieve to remove large pieces of fruit. Return to heat and cook until the glaze falls from the spoon in discrete drops, not in a steady stream (it must be quite sticky to adhere to the mangoes). Keep warm.

8. Peel the mangoes; remove the flesh of each one in two large pieces. Cut them crosswise into thin slices.

9. To assemble: Pipe or spoon the pastry cream into the cooled tart shell. Arrange the mango slices decoratively on top of the pastry cream. Brush with the apricot glaze. Sprinkle the chopped pistachios around the edge.

10. Refrigerate up to 30 minutes before serving, then allow it to come to room temperature.

PEACH BLUEBERRY PIE

You can't go wrong with peaches and blueberries; the streusel topping makes them even better.

Serves 6.

½ recipe	**Sweet Pastry** (see page 232)

FOR THE STREUSEL TOPPING

¼ cup	**granulated sugar**
¼ cup	**light brown sugar**, firmly packed
½ cup	**all-purpose flour**
¼ cup	**unsalted butter** (see page 23)
6 cups	**fresh peaches**, peeled and sliced (see below)
1½ cups	**blueberries**, fresh or frozen
1 cup	**granulated sugar**
6 Tbs	**cornstarch**
2 Tbs	**lemon juice**
pinch of	**ground cinnamon**

PEELING PEACHES
Place the peaches in a bowl, pour boiling water over them, and leave for 15 seconds. Remove one and see if the skin comes off easily; if not put it back for a bit longer. Sometimes the skin simply will not come off and you will have to cut it away with a knife.

---

1. Preheat the oven to 375°F.

2. Roll out the pastry to ⅛" to ³/₁₆" thick; roll it up around the rolling pin and unroll onto a 9" pie dish. Trim the edges and refrigerate.

3. Make the topping: Put the sugars and flour in the work bowl of the food processor; pulse once or twice to combine. Cut the cold butter into ½" cubes and distribute over the flour. Process only until the mixture resembles fine crumbs – do *not* let it form large clumps. If working by hand, cut the cutter in with two knives or a pastry cutter. Set aside.

4. Peel and slice the peaches; put them in a bowl and add the blueberries, sugar, cornstarch, lemon juice, and cinnamon and toss well. Turn this filling into the pie shell, mounded up in the centre. Cover with the streusel topping.

5. Bake in the preheated oven for 40 to 45 minutes, until the topping and crust are golden, and the filling is bubbling up. Remove from the oven and allow to cool slightly.

6. Serve warm with lightly whipped cream.

STRAWBERRY RHUBARB TART

Strawberry and rhubarb is a time-honoured combination. Most of the pies that feature it don't look half as good as they taste. This one is the exception (no, it doesn't taste awful; it looks fantastic).

Serves 6.

½ recipe	**Sweet Pastry** (see page 232)
1 lb	**rhubarb,** fresh or frozen, in small pieces
¾ cup	**granulated sugar**
3 Tbs	**cornstarch**
1 Tbs	**Kirsch**
½ cup	**red currant jam**
¼ cup	**water**
1 – 1½ pints	**fresh strawberries,** sliced
1 large	**whole strawberry mint leaves**

1.   Make the pastry following the recipe on page 232.

2.   Roll out the pastry on a lightly floured work surface to an 11″ circle. Roll up around your rolling pin, and unroll over an 8″ or 9″ tart pan with a removable bottom. Press the dough lightly into the pan, and trim the edge so that the pastry is flush with the top of the pan. Chill for at least 30 minutes.

3.   Prepare the filling while the pastry is chilling. Combine the rhubarb, sugar, cornstarch, and Kirsch in a stainless steel or enamel saucepan. Bring to a boil, stirring constantly. Continue to boil until the mixture starts to thicken. Reduce the heat to a simmer and cook uncovered until the fruit softens and the mixture is thick (about 8 to 10 minutes). Remove from the heat and cool without stirring.

4.   Preheat the oven to 375° F.

5.   Line the chilled tart shell with parchment or waxed paper and fill with weights (such as dried beans). Bake in the preheated oven for 20 minutes. Then remove the weights and paper and prick the bottom of the tart all over with a fork. Return to the oven and bake for 20 minutes more, until golden brown and fully cooked. Remove from the oven and allow to cool completely in the pan.

6.   Heat the jam and water in a small saucepan until the jam is completely dissolved. Allow to boil until the glaze falls from the spoon in drops rather than a steady stream. (The glaze must be thick enough to stick to a strawberry, not run off the surface).

7.   Carefully remove the pastry shell from the tart pan; set it on a serving plate. Brush all over the bottom of the shell with the glaze (this prevents the pastry from becoming soggy from the fruit).

8.   Fill the shell with rhubarb and smooth the surface with the back of a spoon. Arrange the strawberry slices in concentric circles on top of the rhubarb. Brush them with the glaze. Set the whole strawberry in the middle; arrange the mint leaves around it as decoration.

COBBLERS & PUDDINGS

ORANGE STEAMED PUDDING

Serves 8.

FOR THE PUDDING

½ cup	**unsalted butter**, at room temperature
1 cup	**granulated sugar**
4 large	**eggs**
2 cups	**all-purpose flour**
2 tsp	**baking powder**
½ cup	**orange juice**
2 Tbs	**grated orange zest**
2 Tbs	**Grated Lemon Zest** (see page 237)

FOR THE HARD SAUCE

9 Tbs	**unsalted butter**, at room temperature (see page 23)
1½ cups	**icing sugar**, sifted
3 Tbs	**grated orange zest**
2 Tbs	**orange juice**
1 tsp	**lemon juice**

1. Butter a 1-quart steamed-pudding mould.

2. Cream the butter and sugar until light and fluffy (the easiest way is in an electric mixer with the paddle attachment). Add the eggs, one at a time, beating well after each addition.

3. Reduce speed to low, add the flour and baking powder and the orange juice; then stir in the grated zests.

4. Transfer the batter to the prepared mould. Cover tightly with the lid, or with a double layer of foil tied securely with string. Sit the mould on a rack in a large pot (which has a lid); fill with water to about halfway up the mould (or less if it starts to float). Cover with the lid, bring to a boil, then reduce the heat to a simmer and steam for 2 hours.

5. While the pudding is steaming, prepare the hard sauce. Cream together the butter and sugar; beat in the orange juice and orange rind; beat until fluffy and smooth (again an electric mixer is the way to go). Refrigerate until 30 minutes before serving.

6. Remove the pudding from the steamer. Let it stand for 15 minutes. Invert onto a serving platter; serve with the hard sauce.

NOTE: If you need to keep the pudding warm, do not un-mould it. Leave it, still covered, in the steamer, until ready to serve. It will stay hot for an hour or so like this.

FRUIT CRUMBLE

This is a good and simple dessert that can be put together at the last moment – it can be ready in an hour, and the actual preparation time is only about 25 minutes. It can be made a day or two ahead, and will be just as good when warmed up. A word on the fruit selection: Try to include some berries in your mixture; the juice they give off as they cook makes a big contribution to the final product.

Serves 4 to 6.

3 cups	**mixed fruit**, in small chunks
1 Tbs	**lemon juice**

FOR THE CRUMBLE TOPPING

3 oz	**melted unsalted butter** (see page 23)
1 cup	**rolled oats**
½ cup	**all-purpose flour**
½ cup	**light brown sugar**, firmly packed
¼ cup	**granulated sugar**
2 Tbs	**ground cinnamon**
2 Tbs	**granulated sugar**

1.   Preheat the oven to 375°F.

2.   Cut all the fruit into bite-sized pieces (remember, it is important to use *some* berries); place in a large bowl and toss with the lemon juice.

3.   Melt the butter. Combine the oats, flour, and two sugars in a large bowl; pour on the butter and stir until the mixture is crumbly.

4.   Transfer the fruit into an ungreased baking dish. With your hands, loosely mound the crumble topping over the fruit. Mix the cinnamon and sugar together and sprinkle over the top of the crumble.

5.   Bake in the preheated oven for 30 to 40 minutes, until the topping is golden and the fruit bubbles up around the edges.

6.   Serve warm, with vanilla ice cream or lightly whipped cream.

RHUBARB PEACH COBBLER

Serves 6.

6 to 8	**ripe peaches**
3 or 4 stalks	**fresh rhubarb** OR
2½ cups	**frozen rhubarb**
1¼ cups	**granulated sugar**
1 large	**egg**
⅓ cup	**all-purpose flour**
2 tsp	**Grated Lemon Zest** (see page 237)
1 Tbs	**lemon juice**
1 tsp	**ground cinnamon**
3 Tbs	**unsalted butter** (see page 23)

1.   Preheat oven to 375°F. Butter a 4-cup oval gratin dish or an 11" by 7" ovenproof glass baking dish.

2.   Place peaches in a large bowl and pour boiling water over them. Prick the skins in a few places. Remove one after 15 seconds and see if the skin comes off easily. If not, leave them a bit longer. Peel and slice into ½" slices.

3.   Wash rhubarb and cut into ½" pieces.

4.   Combine peach slices, rhubarb slices, sugar, the egg, flour, lemon juice and rind, and cinnamon in a large bowl and toss well to mix. Pour into prepared baking dish and dot the surface with the 3 Tbs butter.

FOR THE TOPPING

½ cup	**all-purpose flour**
6 Tbs	**granulated sugar**
½ tsp	**baking powder**
2 Tbs	**unsalted butter**
¼ tsp	**salt**
½ tsp	**vanilla**
3 Tbs	**whipping cream**
1	**egg yolk**
2	**egg whites**
2 tsp	**Grated Lemon Zest**

5. Combine flour, sugar, and baking powder in a medium-sized bowl (or in the work bowl of a food processor). Cut in the butter with a pastry cutter or two knives (or by processing briefly) until the mixture resembles coarse meal.

6. Combine vanilla, cream, and egg yolk in a small bowl and mix. Add to the flour-butter mixture; mix until just blended.

7. Beat egg whites to firm peaks; gently fold into the topping mixture.

8. Spread batter evenly over the fruit. Bake in pre-heated oven for 20 to 25 minutes, until golden brown. Remove from the oven and allow to cool for 10 minutes or so. Serve warm, with lightly whipped cream or ice cream.

APPLE AND RASPBERRY BREAD PUDDING

Blackberries, strawberries, or cranberries can be substituted for the raspberries.

Serves 6.

1 loaf	**Brioche** OR **egg bread**
4 large	**eggs,** at room temperature
3 Tbs	**all-purpose flour**
½ cup	**granulated sugar**
3 cups	**whipping cream**
½ tsp	**ground cinnamon**
⅛ tsp	**ground nutmeg**
2 medium	**tart green apples**
½ pint	**fresh raspberries**

1. Preheat the oven to 375° F. Lightly butter a 2½ quart soufflé mould (or similiar).

2. Trim the crust off the loaf of bread; slice into ½" thick slices; cut each slice diagonally into two equal triangles.

3. Peel, quarter, and core the apples; cut into ½" slices. Place in a bowl and toss with the cinnamon and nutmeg.

4. Beat the eggs, sugar, and flour until well combined (with an electric mixer if you have one). Reduce the speed to low and pour in the cream; mix until just combined.

5. Arrange 6 to 8 bread triangles to cover the bottom of the soufflé dish; lay half the apple slices on top; scatter the raspberries over the apples, then top with the rest of the apples. Pour in half of the custard; then completely cover with more bread triangles, overlapping them slightly so that the layer of bread is quite thick; arrange them so that there is an open hole in the centre. Pour the rest of the custard over the top.

6. Bake in the preheated oven for 30 minutes; then cover with aluminum foil, turn down the oven to 325° F and bake for an additional 30 minutes, until the custard is set. Remove from the oven and serve warm.

ICE CREAMS

COFFEE ICE CREAM

Serves 6 to 8.

1 cup	**half and half cream**
2 cups	**whipping cream**
¾ cup	**granulated sugar**
7 Tbs	**whole coffee beans**
6 large	**egg yolks**
1 tsp	**vanilla extract**

1. Combine half and half, whipping cream, sugar, and coffee beans in a saucepan. Heat to very hot but still a bit below boiling, stirring to make sure that the sugar does not stick to the bottom. Remove from heat and allow to steep for 45 minutes, to develop a good coffee flavour.

2. Beat egg yolks and sugar until pale yellow and thick. Pour in ¼ of the warm cream, whisking constantly. Whisk in the rest.

3. Return custard to a clean pan and cook over medium heat until a light custard has formed (about 175°F): Do *not* overcook.

4. Remove from heat, strain into a clean bowl, cover with plastic wrap, and cool.

5. Transfer to ice-cream machine, following manufacturer's directions.

NOTE: For more-detailed instructions on steps 2 to 4, see Vanilla Ice Cream, page 179, steps 3 to 5.

CARAMEL ICE CREAM

Serves 10 to 12.

2 cups	**whipping cream**
1 cup	**half and half cream**
1 cup	**milk**
1 cup	**granulated sugar**
1 tsp	**vanilla extract**
3 Tbs	**water**
8	**egg yolks**

1. Combine whipping cream, half and half, and milk in a large saucepan. Heat to scalding (just below boiling) and remove from heat.

2. Combine sugar, vanilla, and water in a small heavy-bottom saucepan. Place over high heat; swirl the pan to dissolve the sugar. Cook until the sugar caramelizes and turns dark brown. Have a large pan (or sink) of cold water ready. As soon as the caramel starts to smoke, remove it from the heat immediately, and lower the pan briefly into the cold water. This will prevent it from continuing to cook.

HOW TO PREVENT SUGAR SYRUP CRYSTALLIZING

Do not stir the syrup once the sugar has melted: shake the pan if you need to mix it around. It also helps to keep a pastry brush in a bowl of cold water close by. As the syrup is cooking, especially after it has boiled and the water is being evaporated, brush down the inside of the pan just above the surface of the syrup. This prevents sugar crystals from forming, and keeps the syrup liquid.

3. Quickly pour the warm cream into the caramel, whisking the cream as you do so. Return to the heat and stir until all the caramel is dissolved. Remove from heat.

4. Beat the egg yolks until well blended. Slowly pour the caramel cream into the yolks, whisking all the time. Pour the mixture into a clean pan and return to the heat. Cook over medium heat stirring constantly until a light custard has formed (about 175°F).

5. Remove from heat and strain into a clean bowl. Cover with plastic wrap and allow to cool.

6. Transfer to an ice-cream machine, following manufacturer's directions.

NOTE: For more-detailed instructions on Step 4, see below, steps 3 to 5.

Vanilla Ice Cream

Serves 10 to 12.

2 cups	**whipping cream**
2 cups	**half and half cream**
1 cup	**milk**
2	**vanilla beans**, halved lengthwise
10 large	**egg yolks**
1 cup	**granulated sugar**

HEATING MILK

To prevent milk from scorching on the bottom of the saucepan, rinse the pan out with water before you pour in the milk.

Do *not* boil milk; most recipes call for you to scald it (heat it to just below boiling point, when a line of bubbles appears round the sides). Then remove from the heat and proceed with the recipe.

1. In a large saucepan heat the whipping cream, half and half, milk, and the split vanilla beans to almost boiling, then remove from the heat.

2. In a large bowl, beat the egg yolks with the sugar until the mixture is pale yellow and quite thick.

3. Whisking the eggs all the time, slowly pour in about ¼ of the hot cream (the purpose is to "temper" the eggs, to increase the temperature gradually so that they do not overcook). Whisk in the rest more quickly. Pour this custard into a clean pan (or wash out the one you used) and return to the heat.

4. Cook the custard, stirring all the time, to about 175°F. Do *not* boil or you will scramble the eggs. When it is ready the custard should coat the back of a spoon very lightly (dip the spoon in the custard, bring it out, and draw a line with your finger across the back of the spoon. The custard should be thick enough that the line is still quite visible after 5 seconds).

5. Strain the custard into a mixing bowl to remove any bits of egg that have cooked on the bottom of the pan. Cover with plastic wrap and cool completely.

6. Use custard in an ice-cream machine, following the manufacturer's instructions.

CHOCOLATE BURNT ALMOND ICE CREAM

Serves 8 to 10.

1 cup	**blanched almonds**
½ cup	**granulated sugar**
3 Tbs	**water**
½ cup	**sugar**
3 Tbs	**water**
2 Tbs	**instant espresso powder**
2 oz	**unsweetened chocolate**
2 cups	**whipping cream**

1. Preheat oven to 350° F. Lightly grease a cookie sheet.

2. Spread almonds on prepared cookie sheet; toast in the oven for 10 to 15 minutes, until light golden brown. Remove and allow to cool.

3. Combine ½ cup of sugar and 3 Tbs water in a small heavy-bottom saucepan. Heat gently to dissolve the sugar, then increase heat to high, and cook till caramelized to a dark golden brown. Have a large pan or sink of cold water ready. As soon as the caramel starts to smoke, remove the pan from the heat and cool its bottom briefly in cold water.

4. After cooling for 5 seconds or so, remove from water and scoop the toasted almonds into the caramel. Stir to mix well, then pour the mixture onto the greased cookie sheet. Allow to cool completely.

5. Break the cold almond caramel into chunks; grind to a powder in a food processor or blender. (May also be done by wrapping caramel in a clean tea towel, placing it on a hard surface and pulverizing it with a rolling pin or cleaver.)

6. In another saucepan, combine second ½ cup of sugar with water; heat gently to dissolve. Remove from heat and stir in espresso powder and the unsweetened chocolate. Stir until melted. Set aside to cool.

7. Combine pulverized caramel, the coffee/chocolate mixture, and the 2 cups of whipping cream, and mix well. Transfer to an ice-cream machine. Follow manufacturer's directions.

ESPRESSO CHOCOLATE RUM TRUFFLE ICE CREAM

Serves 6 to 8.

2 cups	**half and half cream**
6	**egg yolks**
¾ cup	**granulated sugar**
1 cup	**whipping cream**

FOR THE TRUFFLES

3½ oz	**semi-sweet chocolate**
½ oz	**unsweetened chocolate**
2 Tbs	**unsalted butter** (see page 23)
2 Tbs	**water**
⅓ cup	**powdered sugar,** sifted
4 Tbs	**dark rum**
3 to 4 Tbs	**instant espresso powder**
pinch of	**salt**
1½ tsp	**vanilla extract**

1. In a large saucepan, scald the cream (heat to just below boiling), then remove from the heat.

2. In a bowl, whisk together eggs and sugar until pale yellow and thick. Slowly pour ¼ of the hot cream into the eggs, whisking all the time. Pour in the rest of the cream, stirring well.

3. Wash out the saucepan or find a clean one; pour the custard into it. Heat over a medium heat, stirring constantly, until a light custard has formed (about 175°F). Strain the custard into a bowl, cover with plastic wrap, and allow to cool. (For more detailed instructions, see Vanilla Ice Cream, page 179, steps 3 to 5.)

4. Combine the two chocolates, the butter, and water in a bowl that can go over hot water, or in the top of a double boiler. Set over hot water and melt chocolate. When melted add the powdered sugar and rum, and stir well.

5. Pour out onto a cookie sheet; spread it to an even thickness (about ⅛″). Put in freezer and freeze, then cut into small pieces (about the size of large chocolate chips). Keep frozen until ready to use.

6. Remove the cooled custard from the refrigerator. Stir in the instant espresso powder, salt, and vanilla. Freeze in an ice-cream machine according to manufacturer's instructions. When the ice cream is partly frozen but still soft, add the frozen rum truffles. Continue to freeze in the machine until ready to serve.

ITALIAN CHOCOLATE HAZELNUT GELATO

Serves 10 or so.

2 cups	**hazelnuts**, skins removed (see below)
2 cups	**milk**
1 cup	**whipping cream**
3 oz	**semi-sweet chocolate**
1½ oz	**unsweetened chocolate**
3 large	**egg yolks**
6 Tbs	**granulated sugar**

TO REMOVE SKINS FROM HAZELNUTS
You may not be able to find hazelnuts without the skins on. If not, spread the nuts on a baking sheet and roast for about 6 minutes in a 350°F oven. Remove and wrap them loosely in a clean tea towel; roll them in the towel on your work surface so that the nuts rub against each other. You won't get all of the skins off, but perfection doesn't matter in this case.

1. Preheat the oven to 350° F.

2. Spread the skinned hazelnuts on a baking sheet; bake in preheated oven for 10 to 15 minutes. Remove from the oven and transfer to the work bowl of a food processor. Process only until coarsely chopped.

3. Combine milk and whipping cream in a medium saucepan. Heat to scalding (about 180° F). Remove from heat and add the chopped hazelnuts; allow to steep for 30 minutes so that the milk can absorb the hazelnut flavour.

4. Strain the milk into a large bowl; discard the hazelnuts.

5. In a bowl set over hot water, melt both chocolates.

6. In a large bowl, whisk egg yolks and sugar together until the mixture is pale yellow and thick. Slowly pour in the warm hazelnut milk, whisking all the time.

7. Return the custard to a clean pan. Add the melted chocolate; and cook over medium heat, stirring all the time, until a light custard has formed (about 175° F). Strain into a clean bowl, cover with plastic wrap and chill completely. (For more detailed instructions, see Vanilla Ice Cream, page 179, steps 3 to 5.)

8. Transfer the custard to an ice-cream machine and follow the manufacturer's directions.

PEACH ICE CREAM

Serves 6.

1½ cups	**whipping cream**
½ cup plus	
2 Tbs	**granulated sugar**
3 large	**egg yolks**
1 tsp	**vanilla extract**
1 lb	**very ripe peaches**
¼ cup	**granulated sugar**

1. Combine cream and the ½ cup plus 2 Tbs of sugar in a saucepan. Heat, stirring constantly until the sugar is completely dissolved and the cream is very hot; remove from the heat.

2. Whisk the egg yolks. Slowly pour in ¼ of the hot cream, whisking constantly. Pour in the rest and mix well. Add the vanilla extract.

3. Return the custard to a clean saucepan and cook over medium heat until a light custard has formed (about 175° F). Strain into a clean bowl, cover with plastic wrap, and cool completely. (For more-detailed instructions, see Vanilla Ice Cream, page 179, steps 3 to 5.)

instructions, see Vanilla Ice Cream page 179, steps 3 to 5).

4.   Blanch the peaches: Place them in a bowl, pour boiling water over them and prick the skins in a few places. Remove one after 15 seconds; see if the skin peels off easily. If not, return to the water and give them a bit longer. Peel and stone all the peaches.

5.   Cut the peaches into thin slices and toss with the ¼ cup of sugar. Allow to stand for about 1 hour.

6.   Mash the peaches with a potato masher (do *not* purée, there should be some chunks of peach). Add all the peach pulp and juice to the custard.

7.   Transfer to an ice-cream machine and freeze, following the manufacturer's directions.

VARIATION: STRAWBERRY ICE CREAM

Substitute an equal quantity of strawberries for the peaches.

FIG ICE CREAM

Serves 6.

1 lb	**very ripe figs**
3 Tbs	**water**
1 cup	**whipping cream**
½ cup plus	
2 Tbs	**granulated sugar**
3 large	**egg yolks**
½ cup	**whipping cream**
1 tsp	**vanilla extract**
1 to 2 Tbs	**brandy**

1.   Wash the figs. Remove the stems and cut the figs into quarters. Place in non-corrodable saucepan with the water. Cook over low heat, stirring frequently, for 20 to 30 minutes.

2.   Pour figs and water into the work bowl of a food processor; pulse until coarsely chopped. Measure out 1½ cups and reserve; you may eat the rest.

3.   Combine 1 cup cream and the sugar in a saucepan; heat, stirring to prevent the sugar from sticking, until very hot but not boiling.

4.   Whisk the egg yolks; slowly pour in ¼ of the hot cream, whisking all the time. Gradually pour in the rest and mix well. Pour the custard into a clean pan and cook, stirring constantly, over medium heat until a light custard has formed (about 175° F). Strain into a clean bowl, cover with plastic wrap and cool completely. (For more-detailed instructions, see Vanilla Ice Cream, page 179, steps 3 to 5.)

5.   Mix together ½ cup of whipping cream, vanilla, brandy, the cooled custard, and 1½ cups of fig purée. Transfer to the bowl of an ice-cream machine and freeze, following the manufacturer's instructions.

TANGERINE SORBET

Serves 6.

4½ lbs   **tangerines**
1 cup
  plus
  1 Tbs   **granulated sugar**
1 to 2 Tbs **brandy**

1.   Wash 2 tangerines; grate the rinds and reserve.

2.   Juice all of the tangerines; strain out the pips and the pulp. Measure out 1 cup of the juice; reserve the rest for another use.

3.   Combine 1 cup of the tangerine juice with the sugar in a saucepan; heat over medium heat, stirring constantly until the sugar has dissolved. Remove from the heat and add the rest of the tangerine juice (there should be 4 cups altogether).

4.   Stir the brandy into the tangerine juice. Allow to cool completely. Transfer to the bowl of an ice-cream machine and freeze, following the manufacturer's directions.

CASSIS SORBET

This is a really delicious sorbet, and very easy to make. The sugar syrup keeps indefinitely in the refrigerator, and may also be used to poach fruit or to soak cakes.

Serves 8.

3 cups   **water**
2¼ cups   **granulated sugar**
8 cups   **blackcurrants**, fresh or
          frozen

1.   Place water and sugar in a saucepan; whisk to combine. Set over medium heat and bring to a boil; boil until the sugar has completely dissolved and the syrup is clear (about 30 seconds). Remove from heat and cool completely.

2.   Stem the currants. Combine the currants and 2 cups of sugar syrup in a saucepan; bring to a boil. Then remove from the heat and allow to stand for 15 minutes, until the currants are very tender.

3.   Purée in a food processor in batches; strain through a fine sieve, and chill completely.

4.   Transfer to the bowl of an ice-cream machine and freeze, following the manufacturer's directions. Taste the sorbet as it freezes; blackcurrants vary greatly in sweetness and acidity, and you may have to add either sugar or lemon juice to adjust to your taste.

VARIATION: LEMON SORBET

Add 3 to 4 cups of lemon juice to 2 cups syrup (depending on how tart you like it) and freeze in an ice-cream machine.

PARFAITS

A parfait is a frozen dessert made with whipped cream and, generally, eggs. It is usually presented in a glass; it looks its best when made up of alternate layers of parfait mixture and whipped cream. Parfaits are simple to prepare and have the great advantage that they can be made ahead.

HONEY PARFAIT WITH BRANDIED CHOCOLATE SAUCE

Serves 4 to 6.

2	**eggs**
pinch of	**salt**
½ cup	**honey**
1 cup	**whipping cream**
1 tsp	**vanilla extract**
½ tsp	**lemon juice**

FOR THE BRANDIED CHOCOLATE SAUCE

¾ cup	**granulated sugar**
½ cup	**whipping cream**
1½ Tbs	**unsalted butter**
2 oz	**unsweetened chocolate**
3 Tbs	**brandy**
½ tsp	**vanilla extract**
¾ cup	**sliced toasted almonds** (see below)

TOASTING ALMONDS
Sliced almonds are thin wafers of almond; slivered almonds are the little almond sticks. Both can be used for decoration, but both are better toasted. Heat the oven to 350° F; spread the almonds on a baking sheet and toast until golden (it will take 5 to 10 minutes, the slices less time than the slivers). It's all but impossible to get them to brown evenly, but tossing them every 2 or 3 minutes certainly helps. Watch out towards the end – they burn easily, especially the sliced almonds.

---

1. Beat the eggs with a pinch of salt until pale yellow.

2. Place the honey in a small saucepan and bring to the boil over medium-high heat. Pour the hot honey in a thin stream into the eggs, whisking all the time. Return the mixture to the saucepan and cook over medium heat for 5 to 8 minutes, whisking constantly (it will get quite thick). If there is any sign that the eggs are starting to scramble, remove the pan from the heat immediately and place in a shallow bowl or sink of cold water to stop the cooking. Allow to cool.

3. Whip the cream to soft peaks; add the vanilla and lemon juice. Fold the cream into the honey mixture. Turn into a 1½ quart glass bowl, cover with foil or plastic wrap and freeze for 5 hours, until firm.

4. Combine sugar, cream, butter, and chocolate in a saucepan. Cook over low heat, stirring until melted and smooth. Increase the heat to medium and bring to a simmer, still stirring. Allow it to simmer *without stirring* for 5 minutes, then remove from the heat and stir in the brandy and vanilla. Cool for 5 minutes.

5. Scoop or slice the frozen parfait onto chilled dessert plates. Top each serving with a sprinkling of toasted almonds and surround with the sauce.

APRICOT AND COGNAC PARFAIT

Serves 4 to 6.

2½ cups	**dried apricots**
dash of	**vanilla extract**
4 Tbs	**cognac**
4 large	**egg whites**
pinch of	**salt**
½ cup	**granulated sugar**
1 cup	**whipping cream**

1. Place apricots in a stainless-steel or other non-corrodable saucepan; add water just to cover, and cook over low heat until apricots are soft (20 to 30 minutes). Remove from heat and allow to cool slightly. Transfer to the work bowl of a food processor fitted with the steel blade; reduce to a purée. (You will need 1½ cups of purée.) Add a dash of vanilla and the cognac.

2. In a bowl set over simmering water, whisk the egg whites to soft peaks. Gradually add the sugar, 2 Tbs at a time; keep whisking until the mixture is thick, smooth, and quite warm (about 130° F, which feels hot to the touch). Remove from the heat and let cool to room temperature.

3. Stir ⅓ of the egg whites into the apricot purée; then fold in the rest. Beat the whipping cream to soft peaks and fold into the apricot mixture. Spoon into serving glasses and freeze until serving time. You can alternate layers of parfait and whipped cream to make a more colourful presentation.

RUM AMARETTI PARFAIT

Serves 8.

1 cup	**granulated sugar**
½ cup	**water**
4	**large eggs**
pinch of	**salt**
⅓ cup	**dark rum**
¾ tsp	**lemon juice**
½ tsp	**vanilla extract**
2 cups	**whipping cream**
3 cups	**hard amaretti cookies**

COOKING SUGAR SYRUP
When a sugar syrup boils, it will hold its temperature at 212°F (the boiling point of water) until almost all the water has evaporated; this can take a few minutes. (This is a good point at which to calibrate your thermometer; by noting the temperature it reads when the syrup first boils, you can check its accuracy; it should read 212°F.) Then the temperature will start to rise, and eventually the syrup will turn colour and form a caramel, which is very hard and brittle when cooled. Along the way it will pass through three major stages that are important to pastry chefs – the soft ball (235°F), the hard ball (252°F), and the hard crack (295°F). To test what stage you are at, take a bit of the syrup and drop it in a glass of cold water then take it out once it has cooled; at the soft-ball stage the ball will flatten slightly under its own weight; at the hard-ball stage it will hold its shape, but will yield a bit when squeezed; at the hard-crack stage it will not form a ball at all but a long brittle thread.

1. Combine sugar and water in a saucepan; cook over low heat until all the sugar is dissolved. Increase the heat to medium high; boil until all the syrup reaches the soft-ball stage (235°F on a candy thermometer).

2. While the sugar is cooking, beat the eggs with the salt until they are light coloured. When the syrup reaches 235°F, pour it into the eggs in a thin stream, whisking constantly.

3. Return the mixture to the pan and cook over medium heat, whisking all the time, until thick (about 5 minutes). Do not let it boil or you will have very sweet scrambled eggs. When it is thick, place the pan in a shallow bowl or sink of cold water to stop the cooking. Stir occasionally until cool. Add the rum, lemon juice, and vanilla.

4. Whip the cream to soft peaks; fold it into the cooled custard.

5. In a blender or food processor reduce the amaretti cookies to crumbs (you will need 2¼ cups). (May also be done by rolling the cookies between sheets of parchment paper.)

6. Fold 2 cups of crumbs into the parfait mixture. Turn into a 9″ by 5″ by 3″ loaf pan, cover with foil, and freeze until firm (at least 4 hours).

7. To unmould: Dip pan briefly into hot water, then turn out parfait onto serving platter. Slice thickly and sprinkle with the rest of the amaretti crumbs.

CAKES

Cakes are for special occasions. I make a cake three times a year for the children's birthdays (two of them on the same day). Daphna makes cakes just about every day; most of the time they are for birthdays too. All of the cakes here would be fine for birthday or special celebrations (except perhaps the Apple Apricot Strudel). They would also work for a buffet dessert table, where it's a good idea to have a combination of large desserts and individual items.

APPLE APRICOT STRUDEL

Serves 8 to 12.

6 oz	**dried apricots**, chopped
1 cup	**apricot nectar** (available in Italian grocery stores)
⅔ cup	**granulated sugar**
½ cup	**chopped walnuts**
1 Tbs	**lemon juice**
1	**green apple**, peeled, cored, and grated
⅓ cup	**raisins**
1 lb	**Puff Pastry** (see page 231), thawed if previously frozen
1	**egg**
1 Tbs	**milk**

1. Preheat the oven to 425° F. Line a cookie sheet with a piece of parchment paper; or lightly grease it.

2. Combine apricots, nectar, and sugar in a small saucepan; it is not necessary for the nectar to cover the apricots. Bring to a boil, then reduce heat and simmer, covered, until the apricots are tender and most of the liquid has been absorbed (about 15 minutes). Remove from heat and cool to room temperature.

3. When cool, add the walnuts, lemon juice, grated apple, and raisins; set aside.

4. Divide the puff pastry into two equal pieces. Roll out one piece into a 10" by 15" rectangle. Lay it on your work surface with the long side facing you. Spread half of the cooled filling on the lower half of the pastry, leaving a ½" border all round.

5. Beat the egg and the milk well together; brush it on all the exposed pastry surfaces. Fold the top half of the pastry over the filling, and press all the edges firmly together to seal. Chill for 30 minutes.

6. Repeat steps 4 and 5 with the other half of the puff pastry and the rest of the filling.

7. Bake in preheated oven for 20 to 30 minutes, until golden brown. Serve warm.

BUTTERMILK LEMON POUND CAKE

1½ cups	**all-purpose flour**
¼ tsp	**baking soda**
¼ tsp	**baking powder**
⅛ tsp	**salt**
½ cup	**unsalted butter**, softened
1 cup	**granulated sugar**
2 large	**eggs**
½ cup	**buttermilk**
½ Tbs	**finely grated orange rind** (see page 237)
1 Tbs	**finely grated lemon rind**

1. Preheat the oven to 350° F. Lightly grease and flour a loaf pan about 8½″ by 4½″ by 2″.

2. Sift together the flour, soda, baking powder, and salt. Set aside.

3. Cream the butter until fluffy; it's best done in an electric mixer, but can be done by hand. Add the sugar and mix until well blended. Add the eggs one at a time, beating well after each addition.

4. With the mixer on low speed, add ¼ of the flour, then ⅓ of the buttermilk; repeat until all the flour and buttermilk have been added, ending with the last of the flour. Beat in the orange and lemon rinds.

5. Pour the batter into the prepared pan. Bake in preheated oven for 35 to 45 minutes, until a tester comes out clean. Remove from the oven; allow to cool in the pan for 5 minutes; then remove and cool completely on a rack.

CHOCOLATE BUNDT CAKE

This is a very dense and very chocolatey Bundt cake – just make sure that you don't overcook it. It only needs some fresh fruit to go with it.

Serves 10 or more.

3 cups	**all-purpose flour**
3 cups	**granulated sugar**
1 cup	**unsweetened cocoa**
1 Tbs	**baking powder**
1 tsp	**salt**
1 cup	**unsalted butter**, softened (see page 23)
1½ cups	**milk**
1 Tbs	**vanilla extract**
3 large	**eggs**
¼ cup	**light cream (18%)**

1. Preheat the oven to 325° F. Grease a 10″ tube or Bundt pan thoroughly.

2. Sift together the flour, sugar, cocoa, baking powder, and salt; place in the bowl of an electric mixer (or a mixing bowl if using a hand mixer).

3. Make a well in the centre of the flour; put in the butter, milk, and vanilla. Using the mixer's paddle attachment, mix on medium speed for 5 minutes.

4. Add the eggs one at a time, beating well after each addition. Add the cream and beat until smooth.

5. Pour the batter into the prepared pan, and bake in the preheated oven for about 1½ hours. Check the cake after 1 hour, and every 10 minutes after that. It is done when a tester (a skewer or toothpick) comes out almost clean, with just a few crumbs sticking to it. Do *not* overcook.

CARROT CAKE

This cake is very easy to make, and the result is delicious.

Serves 8.

FOR THE CAKE

2 cups	**carrots**, cut into 2" pieces
2 cups	**granulated sugar**
1½ cups	**flavourless vegetable oil**
3 large	**eggs**
1 tsp	**vanilla extract**
2 cups	**all-purpose flour**
2 tsp	**baking soda**
2 tsp	**ground cinnamon**
½ cup	**crushed pineapple**

FOR THE FROSTING

1 lb	**unsalted butter**, softened (see page 23)
1 generous cup	**powdered sugar**, sifted
1 lb	**cream cheese**, at room temperature

Optional:

½ cup	**ground pecans**
8	**pecan halves**

1. Preheat the oven to 325° F. Lightly butter and flour a 8½" springform pan.

2. Drop the carrots through the feed tube of a food processor fitted with the steel blade and chop finely. Scrape out of the work bowl and set aside.

3. Combine the sugar, oil, eggs, and vanilla in the work bowl; process with the steel blade for 30 seconds. Add the carrots, flour, soda, cinnamon, and pineapple; process for 30 seconds more.

4. Scrape the batter into the prepared springform pan; bake in preheated oven for 50 to 60 minutes, until a tester comes out clean. Remove from oven and cool completely.

5. In an electric mixer, cream butter until fluffy. Add the sugar and beat until smooth. Add the cream cheese and beat until incorporated.

6. To assemble: With a serrated knife, cut the carrot cake into two equal layers. Spread a thin layer of frosting over the bottom layer; top with the second half. Spread frosting over the sides and top of the cake. You can decorate the sides of the cake by pressing on the ground pecans; and finish the top with the pecan halves. Chill until ready to serve.

CARAMELIZED APPLE CHEESECAKE

Make this cake the day before; the work is easy and does not take long, but there is a bit of baking time – you can easily be doing something else. The creamy cheesecake is an excellent contrast with the sweet and crunchy apples.

Serves 10 or more.

FOR THE CRUST

1 cup	**all-purpose flour**
3 Tbs	**granulated sugar**
1 tsp	**Grated Lemon Zest** (see page 237)
½ cup	**unsalted butter**, cold (see page 23)
2 large	**egg yolks**

THE DAY BEFORE SERVING

1. Preheat the oven to 350° F. You will need a 8½" or 9" springform pan.

2. Prepare the crust: Combine the flour, sugar, and lemon zest in the work bowl of a food processor. Pulse once or twice to aerate. Cut the cold butter into cubes and distribute them over the flour. Process just enough to make the mixture look like coarse meal.

FOR THE FILLING

1½ lbs	**cream cheese**
⅔ cup	**granulated sugar**
3	**eggs**
½ tsp	**vanilla extract**
1 tsp	**grated lemon rind**

FOR THE TOPPING

7 medium	**tart apples**, peeled and cored
2 Tbs	**unsalted butter**
⅔ cup	**granulated sugar**
½ cup	**all-purpose flour**
¼ cup	**granulated sugar**
1½ tsp	**ground cinnamon**
⅓ cup	**unsalted butter**, melted

3. With the motor running, drop the yolks through the feed tube; process only until the dough starts to come together. Turn out into the springform pan and press the crust evenly over the bottom. Refrigerate for 20 minutes.

4. Bake in the preheated oven for 20 minutes. Remove and cool.

5. Cream the cream cheese until light, then add the sugar. Add the eggs, one at a time, beating well after each addition; mix in the vanilla and lemon zest. Pour onto the cooled crust and return to the oven. Bake for 45 to 50 minutes, until just set.

6. While the cream cheese is baking, prepare the topping. Cut the apples into ¼″ to ⅓″ slices. Melt the butter over medium heat in a heavy-bottom frying pan or skillet. Add the sugar and cook until the sugar browns, then put in the apple slices and reduce the heat to low. Cover the pan and cook for 15 minutes. Remove the cover, raise the heat to medium high, and cook until the pan juices are quite thick and syrupy. Set aside.

7. In a small bowl, combine the flour, sugar, and cinnamon. Pour the melted butter over and stir until well mixed and crumbly. Set aside.

8. When the cheesecake has cooled, gently spread the apple mixture over the top. Sprinkle with the crumble topping.

9. Heat the broiler for 5 minutes; then broil the cheesecake for 3 to 5 minutes until it bubbles – be careful it does not burn.

10. Allow to cool, then *refrigerate overnight* so that it sets completely.

11. Leave at room temperature for 1 hour before serving.

CHOCOLATE SOUR CREAM CAKE WITH CHOCOLATE BUTTERCREAM

An excellent chocolate birthday cake.

Serves 10 or more.

FOR THE CAKE

4 oz	**unsweetened chocolate**
4 oz	**unsalted butter** (see page 23)
1 cup	**hot water**
1 tsp	**instant coffee powder**
2 cups	**granulated sugar**
1½ cups	**all-purpose flour**
1½ tsp	**baking soda**
½ tsp	**baking powder**
¼ tsp	**salt**
2 large	**eggs**
½ cup	**sour cream**

FOR THE BUTTERCREAM

4 oz	**unsweetened chocolate**, in pieces
6 oz	**semi-sweet chocolate**, in pieces
4 large	**egg whites**
1 cup	**granulated sugar**
14 oz	**unsalted butter**, softened

1. Preheat the oven to 325° F. Lightly butter and flour two 8½" or 9" springform pans. Line the bottoms with a circle of parchment paper.

2. Place the chocolate, butter, water, and coffee powder in a bowl that can go over hot water (or in the top of a double boiler). Set over simmering but not boiling water. Heat, stirring occasionally, until the mixture is smooth.

3. Remove from the heat and stir in the sugar; whisk until completely dissolved. Set aside to cool slightly.

4. Sift together the flour, soda, baking powder, and salt. Set aside.

5. Combine the eggs and the sour cream in a bowl and mix well.

6. Whisk ⅓ of the sour cream mix into the chocolate, then ⅓ of the flour; repeat until all the sour cream and flour are incorporated and the batter is smooth.

7. Pour ½ the batter into each of the two prepared springform pans. Bake in preheated oven for 30 to 40 minutes until a tester comes out clean. Remove from the oven and allow to cool in the pans for 10 minutes. Then remove from the pans and cool completely.

8. Combine the two chocolates in a bowl over simmering water and cook until completely melted and smooth. Remove from the heat and cool completely.

9. Combine egg whites and sugar in a medium bowl set over simmering water. Heat, whisking constantly, until the mixture is hot (so hot that you can't keep your finger in for more than an instant). Remove from the heat and (the easy way) transfer to the bowl of an electric mixer fitted with the whip attachment; beat at high speed until the mixture is cold and very thick. (You can do it all by hand if you are very energetic.)

10. When the meringue is cold, add the softened butter in 4 parts, beating very well between each. Now add the cooled chocolate, and beat again until completely blended in.

11. To assemble: Set one cake round on a cake turn-table (or platter). Spread about ¾ cup of the butter-cream evenly over the top, then place the second layer over the first and ice, first, the sides and, finally, the top of the cake with the buttercream, making sure that all the edges are smooth and no cake is peeking through. You may decorate the cake with rosettes of buttercream piped through a pastry bag fitted with a star tip, if you wish.

12. Remove the cake from the refrigerator *30 minutes before serving* to allow the buttercream to soften and its flavour to develop.

AUNT DOROTHY'S CHEESECAKE

Out of pity for a new and struggling business, Aunt Dorothy (not mine, but I wish she was) divulged the secret of her cheesecake. We still use her recipe.

Serves 10 or more.

FOR THE CRUST
¼ cup   **melted unsalted butter** (see page 23)
1 cup   **graham cracker crumbs**

FOR THE FILLING
2 lbs   **cream cheese**
1 cup   **granulated sugar**
4 large   **eggs**
1 cup   **table cream (18%)**
2 tsp   **vanilla extract**

FOR DECORATION
   strawberries OR **raspberries** OR **blueberries**

Optional
   Glaze (see page 170)

1. Preheat the oven to 325° F. Select an 8½" spring-form pan.

2. Make the crust: Combine the melted butter and graham-cracker crumbs in a small bowl and stir to combine. Pat this into the bottom of the springform pan. Bake in the preheated oven for 8 minutes. Remove and set aside to cool.

3. With an electric mixer fitted with the paddle, beat the cream cheese until fluffy. Gradually add the sugar and beat until smooth. Set the mixer speed to medium; add the eggs one at a time, beating well after each. Scrape down the sides of the bowl occasionally.

4. In a steady stream, add the cream and vanilla and beat until thoroughly mixed; pour onto the graham-cracker bottom. Bake for 35 to 40 minutes in the pre-heated oven, until set. It may appear a bit wobbly in the middle, but will continue to cook after it comes out. (If it is still really soft, give it a bit longer.) Remove from the oven and allow to cool to room temperature. Then refrigerate overnight before taking it out of the pan.

5. The next day carefully remove from the pan; decorate the top with fresh fruit – strawberries, rasp-berries, and blueberries (and combinations thereof) are the most popular. If using strawberries, they will be better glazed.

CHOCOLATE MARQUISE

Serves 8 to 10.

10 oz	**semi-sweet chocolate**, chopped
4 oz	**unsalted butter**, cut into pieces (see page 23)
4 large	**egg yolks**
2 tsp	**instant coffee powder**
1 tsp	**hot water**, to dissolve the coffee
4 large	**egg whites**
2 Tbs	**granulated sugar**

1. Have ready a 4-cup mould; it does not need to be greased.

2. In the top of a double boiler (or in a bowl set over simmering but not boiling water) melt the chocolate and the butter, stirring occasionally.

3. Add the egg yolks to the chocolate, one at a time, beating well after each. Add the dissolved coffee. Set aside to cool to room temperature.

4. Beat the egg whites to soft peaks; add the 2 Tbs sugar and continue to beat until stiff and glossy. Stir ⅓ of the whites into the chocolate to lighten it. Gently fold in the rest. Pour in the 4-cup mould; chill for at least 3 hours.

5. To unmould: Dip the pan into a bowl of hot water. Run a sharp knife around the edge of the mould, then invert onto a serving platter. Serve thin slices (it is rich) with whipped cream and fresh fruit or with a coffee Crème Anglaise (see page 237).

HAZELNUT MERINGUE TORTE

Start the cake the day before; the meringues must dry out overnight.

Serves 8 to 12.

FOR THE MERINGUES

6 large	**egg whites**, at room temperature
½ tsp	**cream of tartar** (see page 233)
⅛ tsp	**salt**
2 cups	**granulated sugar**
2 cups	**toasted almonds** (see page 185), chopped

FOR THE PASTRY CREAM

1 recipe	**Pastry Cream** (see pages 152-53)
6 oz	**semi-sweet chocolate**

1. Preheat the oven to 250° F. Cover one large or two smaller baking sheets with parchment (there is really no good alternative for meringues). Draw three 8" circles on the parchment; turn the paper over so that you can still see the circles but the meringue won't pick them up.

2. Beat the egg whites until frothy; add the cream of tartar, salt, and 4 Tbs sugar. Beat to stiff peaks (see page 156), then fold in the rest of the sugar, all at once. Fold in the toasted hazelnuts.

3. Divide the meringue evenly between the three circles; with a palate knife, gently spread the meringue out to the edge of the circles (don't worry if it is not exact). Bake in the preheated oven for 1 hour, or until the meringues feel firm. Then turn off the oven and let the meringues dry out with the door closed for at least 3 hours (preferably overnight).

FOR THE BUTTERCREAM

3 large   **egg whites**
⅔ cup   **granulated sugar**
10 oz   **unsalted butter**,
           at room temperature
           (see page 23)
2 Tbs   **instant coffee powder**

FOR THE GANACHE TOPPING

4 oz   **unsalted butter**
6 oz   **semi-sweet chocolate**
1 Tbs   **corn syrup**

FOR DECORATION

           **whole toasted
           hazelnuts**
           (see page 182)

4. Make the pastry cream following the recipe on pages 152-53). As soon as it is made, melt the chocolate in a bowl set over simmering water. Fold the melted chocolate into the pastry cream and allow to cool completely.

5. Make the buttercream: Combine the egg whites and sugar in a bowl set over hot water. Whisk until the whites are very thick and too hot to keep your finger in for more than an instant. Transfer to the bowl of an electric mixer fitted with the whisk; beat until very thick and completely cool. (You can do it by hand, but it is a lot of work.)

6. When cool, add the soft butter, ⅓ at a time (it is *important* that the egg whites be completely cool before you add the butter). Set aside.

7. Make the ganache topping: Combine the chocolate, butter, and corn syrup in a bowl set over simmering water. Stir occasionally until melted and completely smooth. Remove from the heat and set aside at room temperature.

8. To assemble: Make the meringue circles reasonably round; carefully trim any large bumps from the edges, using a serrated knife. (If you break a meringue, don't panic – make it the middle layer; if you break two, the bottom and middle; you can probably guess what to do if you break all three.) Set one meringue layer on a large cake plate. With a palette knife, spread the chocolate pastry cream over the meringue.

9. Place the second meringue on top; spread it with a ½″ layer of coffee buttercream. Put the last meringue on top. By this time the ganache should be about spreading consistency (if it is too firm, simply replace over hot water). Pour the ganache over the cake, letting it run down the sides. With your palette knife, smooth the top and sides, so that the cake is completely enclosed in smooth dark chocolate.

10. Decorate the top with rosettes of buttercream or with whole toasted hazelnuts.

LEMON ROULADE

Make the lemon curd a day ahead. It is delicious, so make some extra to spread on bread or to spoon into small completely baked tart shells for tea.

Serves 10.

FOR THE LEMON CURD

4 oz	**unsalted butter** (see page 23)
⅔ cup	**lemon juice**
¼ tsp	**salt**
1¼ cup	**granulated sugar**
3 large	**eggs**
3	**eggs yolks**

FOR THE CAKE

4 large	**eggs**
½ cup	**granulated sugar**
¾ cup	**cake flour**, sifted (see page 233)
½ tsp	**baking powder**
pinch of	**salt**
1 tsp	**Grated Lemon Zest** (see page 237)
1 tsp	**vanilla extract**

FOR THE BUTTERCREAM

3 large	**egg whites**
⅔ cup	**granulated sugar**
1¼ cups	**unsalted butter**, at room temperature
1 Tbs	**orange flavouring** OR **orange liqueur**

FOR DECORATION

¼ cup	**whipping cream** **blueberries**

1. Combine the butter, lemon juice, salt, and sugar in a bowl set over simmering water. Heat, stirring occasionally, until the butter is completely melted and the sugar dissolved.

2. Whisk together the eggs and yolks in a separate bowl; slowly pour in ¼ of the hot lemon-juice mixture, whisking all the time; then pour in the rest in a thin stream. Place over the hot water and cook, stirring constantly, until thickened. Remove from the heat, cover tightly, and refrigerate for at least 12 hours.

3. Preheat the oven to 400° F. Lightly butter and flour, or line with parchment, a 11" by 16" by 1" jelly-roll pan.

4. In a bowl that can go over hot water, whisk together the eggs and sugar until well blended. Set over hot (not boiling) water and heat, stirring constantly, until warm to the touch (it should not be hot).

5. Transfer to an electric mixer and whip until doubled in volume and very pale yellow. (May be done with a hand mixer, or with a whisk.) Fold the sifted cake flour, baking powder, and salt into the batter; add the lemon rind and vanilla. Pour into the prepared jelly-roll pan and bake for 13 to 15 minutes, until springy to the touch.

6. Dampen two tea towels. When the cake is done, run a small sharp knife around the edges, turn the pan upside down onto the towels, and ease the cake out. Roll up, starting with a short edge: do *not* roll up the towel as well. Cool completely.

7. Make the buttercream as the cake is cooling. Combine the egg whites and sugar in a bowl set over simmering water. Heat, whisking constantly, until very hot (too hot for your finger to withstand for more than an instant). Pour into the bowl of an electric mixer (or whisk by hand) and mix until very thick and quite cool. It must be completely cool before the butter is added or it will simply melt rather than emulsify.

8. Add the softened butter, ⅓ at a time, beating very well after each addition. Beat in the orange flavouring. Your buttercream should be smooth and fluffy.

9. To assemble: Unroll the cake; spread a thin layer of orange buttercream over it; cover with a layer of lemon curd (use it all). Roll up the cake again. Ice the outside with a layer of buttercream.

10. Whip the cream to quite firm peaks; pipe rosettes down the centre of the roulade, and around the edges. Top each rosette with a fresh blueberry. Serve at room temperature.

SUNRISE COFFEE CAKE

Serves 8 or more.

FOR THE TOPPING

½ cup	**granulated sugar**
1 tsp	**ground cinnamon**
¾ cup	**chopped pecans**

FOR THE CAKE

2 cups	**all-purpose flour**
1 tsp	**baking powder**
½ tsp	**baking soda**
¼ tsp	**salt**
½ cup	**unsalted butter**, softened (see page 23)
1 cup	**granulated sugar**
1 tsp	**vanilla extract**
1 Tbs	**grated orange zest** (see page 237)
2 large	**eggs**
½ cup	**orange juice**, strained of pulp
¾ cup	**sour cream**

1. Preheat the oven to 375° F. Lightly butter and flour an 8″ square baking pan.

2. Combine all the topping ingredients in a small bowl and mix well.

3. Sift together the flour, baking powder, baking soda, and salt and set aside.

4. In the bowl of an electric mixer fitted with the paddle attachment, cream together the butter and sugar. (This may also be done by hand or with a hand mixer.) Beat in the vanilla and orange zest. Add the eggs one at a time, beating well after each addition. By hand, or with the mixer on low, beat in the flour alternately with the orange juice and sour cream.

5. Transfer half of the batter to the prepared baking pan and smooth it out. Sprinkle half of the topping mix over it. Spread on the rest of the batter, and top with the rest of the nut mixture.

6. Bake in the preheated oven for 40 minutes, until a tester comes out clean. Serve warm.

VARIATIONS
Use any combination of the following in the topping; use the amount of sugar you think is needed to give the right amount of sweetness: chopped dried apricots, poppy seeds, chocolate pieces, raisins, currants, dates, walnut pieces.

OPERA CAKE

Serves 6 to 8.

FOR THE CAKE

3 oz	**walnuts**
3 Tbs	**granulated sugar**
2 Tbs	**cornstarch**
5 large	**egg yolks**
4 large	**egg whites**
¼ cup	**all-purpose flour**
4 Tbs	**unsalted butter**, melted (see page 23)

FOR THE COFFEE BUTTERCREAM

3 large	**egg whites**
⅔ cup	**granulated sugar**
1¼ cups	**unsalted butter,** at room temperature
2 Tbs	**instant coffee powder**

FOR THE CHOCOLATE GLAZE

3 oz	**semi-sweet chocolate**, in pieces
1½ oz	**unsalted butter**
2 Tbs	**water**

1. Preheat the oven to 375° F. Line a baking pan approximately 10″ by 15″ by 1½″ with parchment paper.

2. Combine the walnuts, sugar, and cornstarch in the work bowl of a food processor or blender. Process until finely ground.

3. Beat the egg yolks and 3 Tbs sugar until they become pale yellow and thick; set aside.

4. Whip the egg whites until frothy; continue to beat to stiff peaks, gradually adding 3 Tbs sugar (see on page 156).

5. Gently fold the nut mixture into the egg yolks; then fold in the beaten egg whites. Fold in the flour, and lastly the melted butter (it should be warm) – the best way is to pour the butter slowly onto the spatula with which you are folding, so that it is directly incorporated. If it sinks to the bottom of the bowl, it is hard to fold it into the batter without knocking all the air out of the whites.

6. Spread the batter on the prepared baking sheet. Bake in the preheated oven for 10 minutes, until the cake feels firm. Remove from the oven and cool completely.

7. Make the buttercream: Combine the whites and the sugar in a bowl that can go over hot water. Place over simmering but not rapidly boiling water and heat, whisking constantly, until the mixture is very thick and very hot (you should not be able to keep your finger in for more than an instant). Now is a good time to have an electric mixer: transfer the egg whites to the bowl of the mixer and beat with the whisk attachment until they are completely cool. You can, of course, do it by hand (or with a hand mixer) but it is a bit more tiring.

8. Add the softened butter, ⅓ at a time, beating after each addition. It is important that the whites are completely cool or they will melt the butter and spoil your buttercream. Finally beat in the instant coffee powder.

9. Make the chocolate glaze: Melt the chocolate and butter in the top of a double boiler. When it is smooth stir in the water; keep warm.

10. To assemble: Cut the cake into 4 equal rectangles (use a ruler or a template to make it easier). Set one layer on a platter; spread a thin layer of buttercream over it; lay the second layer on top, spread with butter-cream, repeat until all four layers are on. Spread the top and sides with buttercream, making it as smooth as you can.

11. With a palette knife, spread the melted chocolate over the top only – a professional Opera cake would have a perfect rectangle of chocolate on the top, and completely smooth buttercream sides. The authentic decoration for the top is the word "Opera" written in an Art Nouveau style with the same melted chocolate you used for the glaze. However, no one will mind if you pipe buttercream rosettes, or stick on walnut halves, or simply do nothing at all.

RASPBERRY NIGHT AND DAY CAKES

These cakes have a white chocolate mousse filling enclosed by a circle of dark chocolate – hence the name. There are three steps involved, but two of them can be done the day before. The final result is well worth the trouble.

FOR THE CAKE

2 cups	**all-purpose flour**
½ tsp	**salt**
1 cup	**unsalted butter**, at room temperature (see page 23)
1⅔ cups	**granulated sugar**
5 large	**eggs**
½ tsp	**vanilla extract**

FOR THE WHITE CHOCOLATE MOUSSE

4½ oz	**white chocolate**
1 Tbs	**water**
1 Tbs	**Kirsch** (optional)
¾ cup	**whipping cream**
8 oz	**semi-sweet chocolate**, in chunks
	parchment OR **waxed paper**
	fresh raspberries OR **fresh strawberries**

1. Make the pound cake first: Preheat the oven to 325° F. Butter and flour a large loaf pan – about 9" by 5" by 3" deep.

2. Sift together the flour and salt; set aside.

3. Cream the butter with an electric mixer; gradually add the sugar until the mixture is light and fluffy. Add the eggs, one at a time, beating well after each one is added. Add the vanilla, then turn the mixer speed to low and add ⅓ of the flour; mix, add another ⅓, mix again, then add the final ⅓. Beat until smooth and well blended.

4. Pour into the prepared loaf pan and smooth the top. Bake in the preheated oven for 1 hour, until a toothpick or skewer comes out clean. Remove from oven and cool in the cake pan for 5 minutes; turn out onto a rack to finish cooling. When cool, wrap in plastic or store in an airtight container.

5. Make the white chocolate mousse: Combine the chocolate, water, and Kirsch in a bowl that can go over hot water; set it over simmering but not boiling water.

Heat until melted, stirring occasionally to remove the lumps. Remove from heat and allow to cool completely.

6. When the chocolate is cool, whip the cream to soft peaks; fold into the chocolate. Cover with plastic wrap and refrigerate.

7. Cut the pound cake into slices about ¾" to 1" thick (you will need 1 slice per person). With a round 2" to 2½" cookie cutter (use a thin-rimmed glass in a pinch) cut a round from each slice of cake. (Freeze the rest for trifle.)

8. Spoon the white chocolate mousse into a pastry bag and pipe it carefully onto each round. Try to make the top of the mousse flat (the berries need a flat surface to sit on). Put all the cakes in the refrigerator.

9. Melt the dark chocolate over hot but not boiling water; stir to smooth it out. Remove the pan from the heat, but leave the chocolate over the water to keep warm.

10. Cut the parchment paper into strips about 9" long by 3" wide.

11. Work with one cake at a time. Remove it from the fridge. Lay a strip of paper on a clean work surface; spoon 3 to 4 Tbs of melted chocolate onto the paper (spread it over the paper as evenly as you can, right to the edges). Peel the paper off the surface and wrap it around the cake, chocolate side to the cake, one long edge as close to the bottom of the cake as you can. The strip may overlap itself, but it doesn't matter. Return this cake to the fridge. Repeat until all the cakes are wrapped in chocolate. If the chocolate gets too sticky to work with, return the pan to the heat and melt it again. Chill all the cakes for 2 hours or more. *(May be prepared up to 1 day ahead at this point.)*

12. Remove the cakes from the fridge a few at a time. Very gently peel the paper away from the chocolate (slowly does it!).

13. Arrange the raspberries or sliced strawberries on top of the chocolate mousse, inside the dark chocolate ring.

14. Serve as they are, or with raspberry, strawberry, or blackcurrant purée.

SOUFFLÉS

Frozen Lemon Tangerine Soufflé

This is a frozen dessert presented to look like a soufflé, but with none of the last-minute timing problems associated with one.

Serves 6 to 8.

2½ cups	**crushed amaretto cookies**
4 large	**egg yolks**
4 Tbs	**granulated sugar**
⅓ cup	**lemon juice**
⅓ cup	**tangerine juice**
1 Tbs	**Grated Lemon Zest** (see page 237)
1 Tbs	**grated tangerine zest**
1½ tsp	**gelatin**
3 Tbs	**water**
4 large	**egg whites**
½ cup	**granulated sugar**
¾ cup	**whipping cream**

1. Lightly brush a 4-cup soufflé mould with flavourless oil. Cut a strip of parchment paper or aluminum foil to go round the dish, and tie it as a collar, rising above the edge of the dish.

2. Crush the amaretto cookies in a food processor or with a rolling pin. Sprinkle the inside of the soufflé dish with the crumbs, reserving ⅔ of them for use later.

3. Place egg yolks, 4 Tbs sugar, lemon and tangerine juice, and the grated rind in a bowl that can go over hot water. Set over hot but not boiling water, and whisk until very thick, light and hot (it should reach 160°F to be properly cooked). Remove from heat and set in a larger bowl filled with cold water. Allow to cool, stirring occasionally.

4. Pour the 3 Tbs water into a small bowl and sprinkle gelatin over top. Allow to dissolve; then set bowl in a pan of hot water and allow to liquefy. Set aside.

5. Beat egg whites to soft peaks; add the ½ cup of sugar, 2 Tbs at a time, beating well between each addition. Beat until the sugar is completely dissolved and the egg whites are very glossy (see page 156).

6. Whip the cream until lightly thickened; trickle in the melted gelatin, then beat again to soft peaks. Fold the whipped cream and the egg whites into the lemon mixture.

7. Spoon ¼ of the soufflé into the prepared mould; smooth the top. Sprinkle over ¼ of the remaining amaretto crumbs; then another ¼ of the soufflé, and so on, ending with the crumbs.

8. Freeze until solid. Peel off the collar and serve.

HONEY RUM SOUFFLÉ

This is simple, but has a wonderful flavour.

Serves 4.

4 large	**egg yolks**
½ cup	**icing sugar**
1 Tbs	**flour**
¼ tsp	**salt**
pinch of	**ground cloves**
¼ cup	**honey**
4 oz	**unsalted butter**, melted and cooled (see page 23)
2 Tbs	**dark rum**
4	**egg whites**
1 Tbs	**granulated sugar**

1. Preheat oven to 400° F. Butter a 4-cup soufflé dish; coat the butter with a light layer of granulated sugar.

2. Place the egg yolks in a medium-sized bowl that can go over simmering water.

3. Sift the icing sugar, flour, salt, and cloves onto the eggs.

4. Set the bowl over simmering but not boiling water. Whisk the egg yolks vigorously until they become pale yellow and very thick.

5. Whisk in the melted butter, honey, and rum, and beat several more seconds over the heat to thicken again.

6. Beat the egg whites until frothy; add the tablespoon of sugar and beat to stiff peaks (see page 156).

7. Fold the beaten whites gently into the base; pour and spoon it into the prepared mould.

8. Bake in preheated oven for 15 to 20 minutes, until golden brown on top. Resist the temptation to open the oven door before 15 minutes are up. Serve immediately.

SOUFFLÉ AU GRAND MARNIER

Serves 5 or 6.

3 Tbs	**unsalted butter** (see page 23)
2 Tbs	**all-purpose flour**
½ cup	**milk**
5 large	**egg yolks**
2 Tbs	**granulated sugar**
7 Tbs	**Grand Marnier** OR **orange liqueur**
5	**egg whites**
pinch of	**salt**
3 Tbs	**granulated sugar**

1. Preheat oven to 375° F. Butter a 6-cup soufflé dish and coat the inside with a thin layer of granulated sugar. Cut a strip of parchment or waxed paper long enough to go round the dish; tie it to make a collar that rises above the edge of the dish.

2. In a heavy-bottom saucepan, melt the butter. Add the flour and cook for 2 to 3 minutes, stirring constantly.

3. Add the milk. Bring to a boil stirring constantly; remove from the heat.

4. Beat the egg yolks and 2 Tbs sugar until pale yellow.

5. Scoop the milk sauce into the egg yolks and stir. Add the Grand Marnier and stir gently until thoroughly incorporated.

6. Beat the egg whites until frothy; add 3 Tbs sugar and whisk to stiff peaks (see page 156).

7. Stir ¼ of the egg whites into the sauce; then gently fold in the rest.

8. Scoop into the prepared dish; smooth off the top with your finger. Now make a ½″ depression in the top, leaving a 1″ border around the edge.

9. Bake in preheated oven for 30 to 40 minutes, until golden brown on top; but it should still be soft in the centre. Serve immediately.

APRICOT SOUFFLÉ WITH SABAYON

Serves 6.

½ lb	**dried apricots**
¾ cup	**granulated sugar**
¼ cup	**water**
1 oz	**cognac** OR **rum**
5 large	**egg whites**
2 Tbs	**granulated sugar**

FOR THE SABAYON

3 large	**egg yolks**
⅓ cup	**granulated sugar**
½ cup	**dry white wine**
1 oz	**cognac** OR **rum**

1. Simmer dried apricots in water until soft. Drain, and purée in food processor.

2. Preheat oven to 400° F. Butter a 6-cup soufflé dish; cover the inside with a thin coating of granulated sugar.

3. Combine ¾ cup sugar and water in a heavy saucepan. Bring to boil, and cook to 264° F on a candy thermometer (hard-ball stage). Remove from heat and add to apricot purée. Add the liqueur.

4. Beat egg whites until frothy. Add 2 Tbs sugar and whisk to stiff peaks (see page 156). Stir ⅓ of the whites into the apricots; gently fold in the rest.

5. Scoop into the prepared mould and bake in preheated oven for 20 to 25 minutes, until golden brown on top. Resist the temptation to open the oven for the first 20 minutes.

6. Make the sabayon: Place egg yolks, white wine, sugar, and liqueur in a bowl that can go over hot water. Set over a pan of simmering but not boiling water. Whisk until very thick and foamy, and tripled in volume.

7. Serve the soufflé as soon as it is done; serve the sabayon with it as a sauce.

Capuccino Soufflé

Serves 5 or 6.

4 large	**egg yolks**
1 Tbs	**instant espresso powder**
1 tsp	**Grated Lemon Zest** (see page 237)
1 Tbs	**granulated sugar**
5 large	**egg whites**
2 Tbs	**granulated sugar**
½ cup	**whipping cream**
1 tsp	**cocoa powder**
1 Tbs	**icing sugar**

1. Preheat oven to 400° F. Butter and lightly sugar a 6-cup soufflé mould.

2. Combine egg yolks, espresso powder, lemon rind, and 1 Tbs of sugar in a bowl that can go over hot water. Set the bowl over simmering but not boiling water and whisk until the mixture is thick and doubled in volume.

3. Beat egg whites until frothy. Add 2 Tbs sugar and beat to stiff peaks (see page 156). Stir ⅓ of the whites into the egg-yolk base; gently fold in the rest. Turn into the prepared soufflé dish.

4. Bake in preheated oven for 12 to 14 minutes. Do not peek until 12 minutes are up.

5. While the soufflé is baking, whip the cream to soft peaks.

6. Sift together the cocoa and sugar, and fold into the whipped cream. Serve as a sauce with the soufflé.

SWEET BREADS, MUFFINS & COOKIES

Most of the recipes in this section are for sweet breads – coffee cakes, muffins, and fruit breads. Almost all of them are very easy (few things could be simpler than a muffin), but there are a few recipes for yeast-leavened doughs that I am sure some people will find intimidating. Please don't write them off completely, because there is a great deal of pleasure in working with yeast doughs. It is one of the most basic activities in cooking; if you enjoy the feel of food, you will almost certainly find real satisfaction in this work.

Choose a day when there is no pressure of time or other activities, find a recipe that you like the sound of, and give it a go. It is very unlikely that you will get it absolutely right the first time, because doughs more than anything depend on feel, something that really only comes with experience. But the ingredients are inexpensive and, if you throw in your time for free, it will not cost you a lot to experiment. A word of caution: The first time I worked with yeast, I made a wholewheat loaf. The actual making of it was quite a success – it rose at the right time, by what seemed to be the right amount; it even looked pretty good when it was baked – but when I sat down with the butter and laid into it, it turned out to be the most boring loaf of bread I had ever eaten. I had chosen a boring recipe, where the ingredients were so ordinary that there was very little opportunity for the end product to taste like very much. Most of the yeast recipes in this chapter are much more interesting – but when you make pizza you might feel somewhat the same way; given what goes into it, it is hard for pizza crust to taste of very much; texture is the thing and that only comes with experience.

SWEET BREADS

CRANBERRY ORANGE WALNUT LOAF

2 cups	**all-purpose flour**
1 cup	**granulated sugar**
1½ tsp	**baking soda**
¼ tsp	**salt**
½ tsp	**baking powder**
1 large	**orange**, zested and juiced
2 Tbs	**melted butter**, cooled **boiling water**
1 large	**egg**
1 cup	**chopped walnuts**
1 cup	**firm cranberries**, halved

1. Preheat the oven to 325° F. Lightly butter and flour a loaf pan.

2. Sift together the flour, sugar, baking powder, salt, and baking soda into a large bowl.

3. Put the zest, orange juice, and melted butter in a measuring cup; add enough boiling water to make up ¾ cup of liquid.

4. Beat the egg well; add it and the orange juice mixture to the flour. Mix well until thoroughly moistened and combined (there should be no streaks of flour left in the batter). Mix in the chopped walnuts and the halved cranberries.

5. Turn the batter into the prepared loaf pan. Bake in the preheated oven for about 1 hour, until the top is golden and a tester comes out clean.

CINNAMON BUNS

Most of the work can be done the day before; total time the day of serving is about 1½ hours.

Makes 16 buns.

FOR THE DOUGH

1 cup plus 2 Tbs	**milk** slightly warmed
6 Tbs	**granulated sugar**
1⅔ Tbs	**active dry yeast** (1⅔ envelopes) OR **instant dry yeast**
2 large	**eggs**
5 cups	**all-purpose flour**
¾ cup	**melted unsalted butter** (see page 23)
1 Tbs	**oil**

FOR THE FILLING

¼ cup	**melted unsalted butter**
1 cup	**brown sugar**, firmly packed
1 Tbs	**ground cinnamon**
1 cup	**raisins**
1 cup	**walnut pieces**
1 large	**egg**, beaten

FOR THE ICING

1 cup	**icing sugar**, sifted
2 Tbs	**whipping cream**

1. Make the dough first: Pour the warmed milk (should be just above body temperature) into a large bowl. Stir in the sugar. Sprinkle the yeast over the top and allow to dissolve and bubble up (about 8 minutes). (If using instant dry yeast, sift it with the flour, pour the milk into the bowl, and proceed to Step 2.)

2. Mix the eggs into the milk, then pour in the melted butter (which should be just warm), and stir.

3. Add the flour to the liquid, ¾ cup at a time, stirring well. Add only enough flour to make a workable dough (it should be soft and not dry). Use the rest of the flour to prevent the dough from sticking on your work surface.

4. Scrape the dough out onto your work surface; knead for 8 to 10 minutes, until elastic and smooth. Add flour as necessary to stop it sticking.

5. Wash out the large bowl and dry it. Pour in 1 Tbs oil, then put in the dough and roll it around until it is well coated. Cover the bowl with plastic wrap or a damp cloth and set aside in a warm place to rise until doubled in bulk (about 1½ hours).

6. Turn the dough out onto a lightly floured surface; punch it down and knead once or twice. If not planning to bake the buns straightaway, return the dough to the bowl, cover it, and put it in the refrigerator overnight (it will rise slowly during the night). *(May be prepared the day before to this point.)*

7. Lightly butter, or line with parchment, 2 cookie sheets.

8. Knead the dough once or twice; then roll it out on a floured surface to a rectangle about 16″ by 14″. Brush the melted butter for the filling over the dough; sprinkle on the brown sugar, then the raisins, walnuts, and cinnamon, leaving a 1″ strip on one of the long sides uncovered. Brush this 1″ strip with the beaten egg.

9. Starting with the opposite long side, roll up the dough jelly-roll fashion (it should be quite tight). Press the strip with the beaten egg against the roll to seal it up.

10. With a sharp knife, cut the roll into 16 rounds. Lay them on the prepared baking sheet so that you can see the pinwheel – i.e. flat, not standing up. Brush with the egg glaze. Let sit in a warm place for about ½ hour.

11. Preheat the oven to 375° F.

12. Bake in the preheated oven for 25 to 30 minutes, until the buns are golden brown and the filling is bubbly. Allow to cool.

13. Sift the icing sugar into a bowl, mix in the whipping cream, and stir until it forms a thin paste. Drizzle the icing over the buns.

BANANA BREAD

FOR THE TOPPING

1 Tbs	**all-purpose flour**
1 cup	**shredded coconut**
½ cup	**brown sugar**
1 tsp	**nutmeg**
2 Tbs	**melted unsalted butter** (see page 23)

FOR THE BATTER

2 cups	**all-purpose flour**
1 tsp	**baking soda**
1 tsp	**baking powder**
½ cup	**unsalted butter**, softened
1 cup	**brown sugar**
3 large	**eggs**
1 tsp	**vanilla extract**
1 cup	**mashed banana**
1 cup	**raisins** (optional)

1. Preheat the oven to 325° F. Lightly butter and flour a regular-sized loaf pan.

2. Combine flour, coconut, sugar, and nutmeg in a bowl; pour on the melted butter and mix well together until crumbly. Set aside.

3. Sift together flour, baking soda, and baking powder; set aside.

4. Cream together the butter and sugar until smooth (may be done in an electric mixer or by hand). Add the eggs one at a time, beating well after each addition. Mix in the vanilla.

5. Fold ⅓ of the flour into the eggs and butter; then ⅓ of the banana; repeat until all the flour and banana are folded in. Fold in the raisins if you are using them.

6. Turn the batter into the prepared loaf pan and sprinkle the topping on top. Bake in preheated oven for about 1 hour, until the tester comes out clean.

BLUEBERRY LEMON LOAF

FOR THE STREUSEL TOPPING

¼ cup	**granulated sugar**
¼ cup	**light brown sugar**, firmly packed
½ cup	**all-purpose flour**
¼ cup	**unsalted butter** (see page 23)

FOR THE BATTER

1 cup	**all-purpose flour**
1 tsp	**baking powder**
¼ tsp	**salt**
¼ cup	**unsalted butter**, at room temperature
½ cup	**granulated sugar**
1 large	**egg**
1 tsp	**vanilla extract**
⅓ cup	**milk**
1 Tbs	**Lemon Zest**, grated or chopped (see page 237)
¾ cup	**blueberries**, fresh or frozen

1. Preheat the oven to 350° F. Lightly butter and flour a small loaf pan (about 6″ by 3″ by 2″ deep).

2. Put the two sugars and the flour in the work bowl of a food processor (or other bowl if working by hand). Pulse once or twice to combine.

3. Cut the cold butter into pieces and distribute them on top of the flour. Process only until the mixture resembles fine crumbs (do *not* let it form large clumps). (If working by hand, cut in the butter using a pastry cutter.) Set the topping aside.

NOTE: This recipe makes enough topping for two loaves. A smaller quantity will not work in a food processor (less doesn't fill the work bowl adequately and would be difficult to work by hand). The best solution is to make two loaves and freeze one. Or you can keep the topping in the fridge for 5 days.

4. Sift together the flour, baking powder, and salt; set aside.

5. Cream the butter and sugar together in bowl until light and fluffy. Add the egg and vanilla and beat well. This may all be done with an electric mixer, a hand mixer, or a wooden spoon if you wish to develop your forehand smash.

6. With the mixer on low speed add half the flour, then half the milk; add the rest of the flour, and the other half of the milk. Mix in the lemon zest.

7. Gently fold ¼ cup of blueberries into the batter; scoop it into the prepared pan. Sprinkle the rest of the blueberries over the top of the batter.

8. Sprinkle the streusel topping (remember: only half the amount per loaf). Bake in the preheated oven for 40 to 50 minutes, until the top is pale golden brown and a toothpick comes out clean.

CREAM CHEESE DANISH

We may as well be straight with you: This is not the easiest recipe in the book. Actually, it is more time-consuming than difficult. However, working with yeast dough is very satisfying, and it can almost all be done the day before. A couple of hints: Allow enough time for the final assembly on the morning of your party and be modest in your acceptance of the compliments of your friends.

Makes 20 to 24.

1 recipe	**Basic Danish Dough** (see pages 234-35)
12 oz	**cream cheese**
4 oz	**granulated sugar**
1	**egg yolk**
¼ cup	**flour**
½ tsp	**lemon zest**, (see page 237)
¼ tsp	**vanilla extract**

1. Prepare the danish dough – you should start *the day before serving.*

2. *THE DAY OF SERVING*, combine the cream cheese, sugar, egg yolk, flour, lemon zest, and vanilla in a large bowl and mix until smooth.

3. Line a baking sheet with parchment paper or lightly butter it.

4. Roll out the dough to a rectangle about ⅛" thick, and 12" on one side (the other dimension is not important). Cut the dough into strips 1½" wide and 12" long. One at a time, take a strip and set it on the surface, the long edge facing you. Twist it into a spiral (the quick way is to place the fingers of one hand lightly on one end of the dough, and the fingers of your other hand on the other end, then push one hand away from you while you pull the other towards you. You may also just hold one end and twist the other until you have a spiral).

5. Now make the pinwheel with the spiral: Anchor one end on the surface and twist the other around it. Tuck the end under and press it against the dough so that it stays put. Repeat with the rest of the strips. Place the finished ones on the baking sheet.

6. Make a depression in the middle of each danish, and divide the filling between them. Beat the egg with 1 Tbs water, and brush the danish. Set aside in a warm place to rise for 30 minutes,

7. Preheat your oven to 400° F.

8. Bake for 20 to 30 minutes, until golden brown. Allow to cool for 20 minutes before serving.

Poppy Seed Yoghurt Bread

Makes 1 loaf or 12 rolls.

1 envelope	**active dry yeast**
½ cup	**warm water**
½ cup	**plain yoghurt**
1 Tbs	**granulated sugar**
¼ cup	**dry milk powder**
1 tsp	**salt**
4 Tbs	**unsalted butter**, melted (see page 23)
3 to 3½ cups	**all-purpose flour**
1 tsp	**oil**
1	**egg**
1 tsp	**water**
2 Tbs	**poppy seeds**

1. Pour the warm water into a small bowl and sprinkle the yeast over the surface; allow to stand until dissolved and bubbly (about 10 minutes). (If using instant dry yeast, follow the package directions: it is not necessary to first dissolve this yeast; it is mixed directly with the flour.)

2. In a large bowl combine the yoghurt, sugar, milk powder, and melted butter. Whisk in the yeast mixture. Now add 3 cups of flour, ½ cup at a time, stirring to incorporate. Turn the dough out onto a lightly floured work surface.

3. Knead the dough until it becomes soft and very smooth, adding more flour as needed to prevent it sticking (do *not* add so much that it becomes dry). Kneading time will be about 5 minutes. Form the dough into a ball.

4. Wash out the bowl and dry it. Pour in 1 tsp of oil, then roll the dough around in it until coated with a thin film of oil. Cover the bowl with plastic wrap or a damp towel and let the dough rise in a warm place until doubled in bulk, about 45 minutes to 1 hour.

5. Preheat the oven to 375° F. Lightly grease a standard loaf pan.

6. Punch down the dough and remove it from the bowl. Knead it on the work surface for 1 to 2 minutes; then form into a loaf shape and place in the preheated pan. Cover with a towel and let rise for 20 minutes.

7. Beat the egg with 1 tsp water; brush the top of the loaf with the glaze, then sprinkle with the poppy seeds. Bake in the preheated oven for 25 to 30 minutes, until golden brown. Serve warm or cold. (This dough is also excellent formed into rolls; one recipe will make about a dozen.)

SWEET WALNUT RING

Serves 6 to 8.

2 tsp	**active dry yeast** (⅔ of a package) OR **instant dry yeast**
¼ cup	**warm milk**
½ cup	**buttermilk**
2 Tbs	**butter** (see page 23)
2 Tbs	**granulated sugar**
½ tsp	**salt**
¼ cup	**rolled oats**
2 cups	**all-purpose flour**
1 Tbs	**oil**
¾ cup	**chopped walnuts**
3 Tbs	**brown sugar**
1 tsp	**ground cinnamon**
3 Tbs	**melted butter**
1	**egg**, beaten
¼ cup	**sliced almonds**

1. Pour the warm milk (it should be just a little above body temperature) into a bowl; sprinkle the yeast over it and allow it to bubble up. (If using instant yeast, mix it directly with the flour in Step 3.)

2. In a small saucepan, melt the butter; add the buttermilk and heat until it is just warm. Mix in the sugar, salt, and oats, then add to the yeast mixture.

3. Add the flour, ⅓ of a cup at a time, whisking the mixture in between. Keep adding flour until a smooth, soft dough has formed. Turn it out onto a lightly floured surface, and knead for 5 to 8 minutes. Sprinkle with flour as necessary to prevent the dough from sticking.

4. Lightly grease a large bowl with oil; roll the dough around it until it is coated. Cover with plastic wrap or a damp towel and allow to rise in a warm place until doubled in bulk (about 1 to 1½ hours).

5. Preheat the oven to 375°F. Lightly butter a cookie sheet, or line it with parchment.

6. Combine the walnuts, brown sugar, and cinnamon in a small bowl.

7. Turn out the dough onto a lightly floured work surface. Roll out to a 10″ by 14″ rectangle (it should be about ½″ thick). Brush the surface with the melted butter; sprinkle the walnut mixture over the top. Roll up the dough into a log (the longer edge should be the length of your log). Pinch the seams to seal.

8. Form the dough into a ring, pressing the ends together. Cover loosely with plastic wrap and allow to rise in a warm place for 40 minutes.

9. With a sharp knife, score the top of the ring at regular intervals (these will be the divisions between servings). Brush with the beaten egg, and sprinkle with the almonds.

10. Bake in the preheated oven until golden brown (about 30 to 40 minutes). Allow to cool for 20 minutes before cutting.

MUFFINS

Muffins have come a long way since the days of the lead-weight bran and molasses variety. We still do get asked for bran muffins in the store, but generally not by people who have experienced the new wave of muffin. Shape is about the only thing these muffins have in common with their forefathers; their ingredients are certainly good quality, but not necessarily good for you. However, the taste and texture are very good. The rule of thumb is that anything that looks like a muffin can be eaten in the morning with a clear conscience.

Muffins are also very simple to make – there are just three secrets to success: (1) keep the wet ingredients separate from the dry until the last moment; (2) mix the dry ingredients thoroughly to distribute the baking soda and powder evenly; and (3) mix the muffins as little, as lightly, and as quickly as possible once you have combined the wet with the dry. Muffins are leavened by the carbon-dioxide gas produced when the baking soda comes in contact with an acid – fruit juice, buttermilk, sour cream, etc. (Baking powder contains both the acid and alkaline components: it starts to work first when the liquid is added, and a second time when exposed to heat – that's why it's called double-action.) If the muffin batter is mixed too long, or there is a delay in putting them in the oven, the gas will escape before they are baked and the muffins will be heavy.

Having said all this, some of the recipes use a technique borrowed from cake-making – creaming the butter and sugar together first, adding the eggs and then the flour. No wonder muffins aren't like they used to be.

APPLE PIE MUFFINS

Mary McGrath was kind enough to write about these muffins in the Toronto Star; *since then they have soared to the top of the muffin charts, and stayed there. It couldn't have happened to a nicer muffin.*

Makes 15 muffins.

FOR THE TOPPING

½ cup	**brown sugar**, firmly packed
6 Tbs	**all-purpose flour**
¼ cup	**unsalted butter**, melted (see page 23)
1 tsp	**ground cinnamon**

FOR THE BATTER

1½ cups	**brown sugar**, firmly packed
⅔ cup	**vegetable oil**
1 large	**egg**
1 tsp	**vanilla**
2½ cups	**all-purpose flour**
1 tsp	**baking soda**
½ tsp	**salt**
1 cup	**buttermilk**
2 cups	**diced apple**

1.   Preheat the oven to 325° F. Grease and flour a 15-cup muffin tin; line them with paper cups if you wish.

2.   Make the topping: Combine the brown sugar, flour, melted butter, and cinnamon in a small bowl and mix until crumbly. Set aside.

3.   Combine the brown sugar, oil, egg, and vanilla in a large bowl. Mix and set aside.

4.   Sift together the flour, soda, and salt. Blend the flour into the mixture, alternately with the buttermilk. Add the diced apple. Mix until just combined. Spoon into the prepared muffin tins. Sprinkle generously with the topping.

5.   Bake in the preheated oven for 30 minutes, until golden brown and the top springs back when touched.

BANANA PECAN RAISIN MUFFINS

The other end of the two early muffin favourites in the store, with some raisins added.

Makes 12 muffins.

1 large	**egg**
½ cup	**granulated sugar**
6 Tbs	**vegetable oil**
1 cup	**mashed bananas**
1 tsp	**vanilla extract**
1½ cups	**wholewheat flour**
1 tsp	**baking powder**
1 tsp	**baking soda**
½ tsp	**salt**
½ cup	**raisins**
¼ cup	**pecan pieces**

1. Preheat the oven to 350° F. Grease and flour a 12-cup muffin tin; line with paper cups if you wish.

2. In a large bowl, beat the egg, then add the sugar, oil, banana, and vanilla; mix well together.

3. Sift together the flour, baking powder, soda, and salt. Pour all this into the wet ingredients, then fold in the raisins and pecans.

4. Spoon the batter into the prepared muffin cups. Bake in the preheated oven for 25 to 30 minutes, until the top is golden brown and springy.

COFFEE CAKE MUFFINS

These muffins are more like an afternoon cake than a muffin; but they pass the acid test (they look like a muffin) so enjoy them.

Makes 16 muffins.

FOR THE FILLING

¾ cup	**brown sugar**, firmly packed
½ cup	**dried apricots**, finely chopped
½ cup	**chopped walnuts**
⅓ cup	**semi-sweet chocolate chips**
2 Tbs	**cocoa powder**
1 Tbs	**instant coffee powder**
2 tsp	**ground cinnamon**
1 cup	**unsalted butter**, (see page 23)
2 cups	**granulated sugar**
4 large	**eggs**
2 tsp	**vanilla extract**
1 cup	**all-purpose flour**
2 cups	**cake flour**, sifted (see page 233)
2 tsp	**baking soda**
3 tsp	**baking powder**
½ tsp	**salt**
2 cups	**sour cream**

1. Preheat the oven to 350° F. Grease a 16-cup muffin tin; line with paper cups if you wish.

2. Combine brown sugar, apricots, walnuts, chocolate chips, cocoa, coffee, and cinnamon in a bowl and mix well together.

3. Cream the butter with the sugar in an electric mixer until light and fluffy (may be done with a hand mixer, or even by hand). Add the eggs one at a time, beating well after each addition. Add the vanilla.

4. Sift together the flour, soda, baking powder, and salt.

5. With the mixer speed set on low, add half the flour, then half the sour cream, the other half of the flour and the rest of the sour cream. Make sure that there are no pockets of unincorporated flour.

6. Spoon the mixture into the muffin cups, adding the filling in the middle: fill the cups ⅓ full, distribute all the filling, then fill up with the rest of the batter.

7. Bake in preheated oven 20 to 30 minutes, until muffins are golden brown and springy to the touch.

BLUEBERRY MUFFINS

This was one of the favourite muffins in the early days of the store (the other was banana pecan); it has a very nice light texture. I still consider that my blueberry muffins came close to the peak of the muffin maker's art: I am sorry to say that not everyone agrees with me.

Makes 8 muffins.

1 large	**egg**
¼ cup	**melted butter**
¾ tsp	**vanilla extract**
⅓ cup	**milk**
1 cup	**all-purpose flour**
½ cup	**sugar**
1 tsp	**baking powder**
¼ tsp	**salt**
1–1½ cups	**blueberries**, fresh or frozen

1.   Preheat the oven to 350° F. Grease and flour a 8-cup muffin tin; line with paper cups if you wish.

2.   In a large bowl cream together the butter and sugar, then beat in the egg and vanilla.

3.   Sift together the flour, baking powder, and salt. Add to the butter mixture, together with the milk. Don't worry if it's a bit lumpy. Add the blueberries and fold them in gently (if you mix too hard their juice will run and you will have a purple batter).

4.   Spoon into the muffin tins; bake in the preheated oven for 25 to 30 minutes, until pale golden brown, and the top springs back when touched.

PERSIMMON MUFFINS

Makes 12 muffins.

1½ cups	**all-purpose flour**
½ tsp	**baking soda**
½ cup	**granulated sugar**
2 tsp	**baking powder**
¼ tsp	**salt**
½ tsp	**ground cinnamon**
½ tsp	**ground nutmeg**
¼ tsp	**ground cloves**
½ cup	**persimmon pulp**, fresh or frozen
¾ tsp	**lemon juice**, if using fresh pulp
1 large	**egg**
½ cup	**milk**
¼ cup	**unsalted butter**, melted (see page 23)
1 tsp	**Grated Lemon Zest** (see page 237)
½ cup	**raisins** OR **currants**

1.   Preheat the oven to 375° F. Grease a muffin pan; line with muffin cups if you wish.

2.   Sift together the flour, sugar, soda, baking powder, salt, and spices.

3.   In a separate bowl, combine the persimmon pulp, egg, milk, melted butter, and lemon zest; mix them well together.

4.   Pour the dry ingredients into the wet. Stir to mix, but only the flour is evenly moistened (there will still be lumps). Fold in the raisins. Spoon into the prepared muffin pan, not quite filling each cup. Bake for 15 to 25 minutes until golden brown. Remove from the oven and allow to cool.

ORANGE POPPY SEED MUFFINS

Makes 16 medium muffins.

1 cup	**granulated sugar**
½ cup	**unsalted butter**, at room temperature (see page 23)
2 large	**eggs**
1 tsp	**baking soda**
1 cup	**buttermilk**
2 cups	**all-purpose flour**, sifted
¼ tsp	**salt**
zest of 2	**oranges**
2 Tbs	**orange juice**
½ cup	**poppy seeds** OR **raisins**

1.   Preheat the oven to 375° F. Grease and flour a 16-cup muffin tin: line with paper cups if you wish.

2.   Cream together the butter and sugar until light and smooth. Add the eggs, one at a time, beating well after each addition.

3.   Mix the baking soda with the buttermilk; then by hand mix in the sifted flour and salt to the butter and eggs, alternately with the buttermilk.

4.   Mix in the orange zest, orange juice, and poppy seeds (or raisins). Scoop into prepared muffin cups and bake in the preheated oven 25 to 30 minutes, until springy to the touch.

RHUBARB STREUSEL MUFFINS

Makes 12 muffins.

FOR THE STREUSEL TOPPING

¼ cup	**granulated sugar**
¼ cup	**finely ground pecans**
½ Tbs	**unsalted butter**, melted (see page 23)
½ tsp	**ground cinnamon**

FOR THE BATTER

1 large	**egg**
1 cup	**brown sugar**, firmly packed
¼ cup	**unsalted butter**, melted
¾ cup	**sour cream**
2 cups	**all-purpose flour**
1 tsp	**baking soda**
¼ tsp	**salt**
¼ tsp	**ground cinnamon**
1⅓ cups	**diced rhubarb**, fresh or frozen

1.   Preheat the oven to 350° F. Grease and flour a 12-cup muffin tin; line with paper cups if you wish.

2.   Make the topping: Combine sugar, ground pecans, melted butter, and cinnamon. Set aside.

3.   Assemble the wet ingredients: Beat the egg in a large bowl, then add the brown sugar, melted butter, and sour cream.

4.   Sift the flour, soda, salt, and ground cinnamon into another bowl. Mix well to distribute the soda. Pour it all into the wet ingredients and mix just to combine. Fold in the diced rhubarb gently.

5.   Spoon into the prepared muffin tins and sprinkle generously with topping. Bake in the preheated oven for 20 to 25 minutes, until lightly browned and firm to the touch.

Hot Cross Buns

Makes about 15.

1²⁄₃ Tbs	**active dry yeast** (1²⁄₃ **envelopes**) OR **instant dry yeast**
¾ cup	**warm milk**
1 large	**egg**
1 large	**egg yolk**
¼ cup	**melted unsalted butter** (see page 23)
½ cup	**granulated sugar**
2 cups	**all-purpose flour**
1 tsp	**ground cinnamon**
½ tsp	**ground cloves**
¼ tsp	**ground nutmeg**
2 more cups	**all-purpose flour**
½ cup	**currants** OR **raisins**
1 Tbs	**oil**
1 large	**egg white**
1 Tbs	**water**

1.   Pour the warm milk into a bowl; sprinkle the yeast over the top and allow it to dissolve and bubble up. Then stir in the egg, egg yolk, melted butter (which should be just warm), and sugar. (If using instant yeast, sift it directly with the flour in Step 2. For now, just mix together the milk, egg, egg yolk, and butter.)

2.   Blend 2 cups flour with the cinnamon, cloves, and nutmeg (and instant yeast if using it); ½ cup at a time, mix it into the liquid; add just enough flour to make a smooth, soft dough (you may not need all 4 cups). Add the raisins or currants.

3.   Turn the dough onto a lightly floured work surface and knead for 8 to 10 minutes.

4.   Pour 1 Tbs oil into a (preferably straight-sided) bowl; put in the dough and roll it around until well coated. Cover the bowl with plastic wrap or a damp towel and let rise in a warm place for 1½ to 2 hours, until doubled in bulk.

5.   Preheat the oven to 400° F.

6.   Punch down the dough, turn out onto the work surface, and knead once or twice, with a knife, cut off bun-size pieces of dough, knead them once or twice and then set on baking sheets (if you don't cut off enough, just add another piece and knead together). Set aside to rise again for 25 minutes.

7.   Beat together the egg white and water; brush all the buns with it. Cut a cross in the top of each bun with a sharp knife. Bake in the preheated oven for 15 to 20 minutes, until nicely browned.

COOKIES

BISCOTTI DI PRATO

Biscotti are crisp and very hard cookies that in Italy are dipped into capuccino, and especially into "vin santo" – Holy wine, a sweet white wine from Tuscany, which is often served after dinner. Please tell your guests not to try to eat them without first dipping them to soften them up.

Makes about 48 biscotti.

2 cups	**all-purpose flour**
2½ cups	**granulated sugar**
1 tsp	**baking powder**
pinch of	**salt**
4 large	**eggs**
1	**egg yolk**
1 tsp	**vanilla extract**
1⅔ cups	**raw almonds**

1. Preheat the oven to 350° F. Lightly butter 2 cookie sheets or line them with parchment.

2. On a clean work surface, make a mound with the flour, sugar, baking powder, and salt. Mix them together, then make a well in the centre.

3. Put the whole eggs, yolk, and vanilla into the well; whisk lightly with a fork to break them up. Now stir more slowly and in gradually wider circles so that you draw more and more flour into the centre and mix it with the eggs. Continue until a rough dough is formed. Then start working with your hands, and knead to a smooth dough.

4. Adding a handful at a time, knead in the almonds. (Total kneading time should be about 5 minutes.) Add flour to the work surface as necessary, to prevent the dough from sticking.

5. Divide the dough into 4. With your hands, roll each piece into a log shape, about 2" to 2½" in diameter. Lay the logs on the cookie sheets, about 3" apart, as they will spread during baking. Bake in the preheated oven for 30 to 35 minutes; then remove from oven.

6. Turn down the oven temperature to 325° F. Cut the logs (which will have flattened considerably) on the diagonal into slices about ½" to ¾" thick. Stand these slices upright on the baking sheets, and return to the oven for 15 to 20 minutes longer, until golden brown. Remove from the oven and cool on racks.

7. Biscotti will keep for 2 to 3 weeks in a tightly covered container.

CHOCOLATE CHUNK COOKIES

These cookies are one of the stars of the store. The secret to success is to mix the batter as little as possible after the flour is added, and to underbake them just a bit.

Yields 18 large cookies, or 36 small.

2 cups	**all-purpose flour**
1 cup	**granulated sugar**
¼ tsp	**salt**
¼ tsp	**baking soda**
1 cup	**unsalted butter**, at room temperature (see page 23)
1 cup	**light brown sugar**, firmly packed
2 large	**eggs**
1½ cups	**semi-sweet chocolate**, chopped in chunks

1. Sift together the flour, sugar, salt, and soda. Set aside.

2. Cream the butter and brown sugar together until light and fluffy. This may be done in an electric mixer, or with a hand mixer. Scrape down the sides with a spatula once or twice to ensure that all the butter is being thoroughly creamed.

3. Turn the mixer to slow speed, and add the eggs one at a time, beating well after each. Now add the flour all at once, immediately followed by the chocolate chunks. Mix only until just incorporated. (If some of the flour is not incorporated, mix it in by hand.) Cover dough with plastic wrap and chill for 6 hours, or overnight.

4. Preheat the oven to 350° F. Lightly butter a cookie sheet; or line it with parchment paper.

5. Scoop out balls of dough: 1 oz (a heaped table-spoon) for small cookies; 2 oz (a regular ice-cream scoop) for large. Place the balls 3″ apart on the prepared cookie sheet, as they spread during baking. Bake for 10 to 12 minutes, until lightly browned around the edges, but still slightly underdone in the centre. Cool on a rack.

6. Unbaked dough will keep for 3 days in the refrigerator.

LEMON SQUARES

Makes 20 to 24 squares.

FOR THE CRUST

2 cups	**all-purpose flour**
⅔ cup	**powdered sugar**, sifted
1 cup	**unsalted butter**, at room temperature, cut into pieces (see page 23)

1. Place flour and sugar in the work bowl of a food processor fitted with the steel blade. Pulse 1 to 2 times to aerate.

2. Distribute the butter pieces over the top of the flour; process until the mixture resembles fine meal. Remove from the processor and let rest at room temperature for 20 to 30 minutes.

3. Preheat oven to 375° F.

FOR THE TOPPING
6 large	**eggs**
3 cups	**granulated sugar**
½ cup	**all-purpose flour**
1 cup	**lemon juice**
5 cups	**shredded coconut**

4.   Work the dough in your hands and press into the bottom of a 12″ by 18″ cookie sheet. Chill for 5 minutes.

5.   Bake in preheated oven for 15 to 20 minutes, until pale golden brown.

6.   While the base is baking, prepare the topping. In a large bowl whisk the eggs until well mixed. Gradually add the sugar and continue whisking until all the sugar has dissolved. Whisk in the flour and the lemon juice; add the coconut.

7.   When the base is ready, whisk the filling again to stir up the coconut (it tends to sink to the bottom). Pour it over the crust and spread it evenly.

8.   Bake in 375°F oven for 25 to 30 minutes until lightly browned around the edges and the centre is no longer wobbly. Remove from oven and cool completely.

9.   Cut into bars (you should get 20 to 24 from the recipe).

OATMEAL RAISIN COOKIES

For a boring-sounding cookie, these are really quite good; they certainly sell well in the store.

Makes 25 large or 50 small cookies.

⅔ cup	**all-purpose flour**
½ tsp	**baking soda**
¼ tsp	**salt**
¼ tsp	**cinnamon**
¾ cup	**unsalted butter**, at room temperature (see page 23)
½ cup	**granulated sugar**
1 cup	**light brown sugar**, firmly packed
1 large	**egg**
2 Tbs	**water**
1½ tsp	**vanilla extract**
3 cups	**quick-cooking rolled oats**
1 cup	**raisins**

1.   Preheat the oven to 350°F. Lightly grease 2 cookie sheets, or line them with parchment paper.

2.   Sift together the flour, baking soda, salt, and cinnamon; set aside.

3.   Cream the butter with both sugars in an electric mixer (or with a hand mixer) until light and fluffy. Add the egg and beat well, then the water and vanilla, and beat again. Turn the mixer speed to low and add the sifted flour. Finally, mix in the oats and raisins by hand. The batter will be quite sticky, but don't worry.

4.   For large cookies, roll the batter into 2-oz balls; or scoop with a large ice-cream scoop. Roll 1-oz balls for small cookies. Set on the prepared cookie sheet, and press flat with palm of your hand. (The cookies should be spaced at least 1″ apart as they will spread during baking.)

5.   Bake in the preheated oven for about 15 minutes, until the edges are golden brown but the centres are still soft. Cool on a rack.

6.   Unused batter may be refrigerated and used the next day.

Nanaimo Bars

Makes 16.

FOR THE BASE

¼ cup	**granulated sugar**
2 Tbs	**cocoa powder**
½ cup	**unsalted butter** (see page 23)
1 large	**egg**
1 cup	**graham cracker crumbs**
1 cup	**shredded coconut**
½ cup	**pecan pieces**

FOR THE FILLING

3 Tbs	**unsalted butter**, at room temperature
2½ cups	**icing sugar**, sifted
5 Tbs	**instant vanilla pudding mix**
¼ cup	**milk**

FOR THE TOPPING

6 oz	**semi-sweet chocolate**, in pieces
2 tsp	**unsalted butter**

1. Line the bottom of an 8″ square baking pan with parchment or plastic wrap.

2. In a large bowl, combine the sugar and cocoa. Melt the butter and pour it into the bowl; whisk to combine. Whisk in the egg. Add the graham crumbs, coconut, and pecan pieces and mix well until thoroughly combined. Do not worry if it seems a bit greasy; it will come together when it is refrigerated. Pat this mixture into the prepared baking pan (smooth it over with the back of a spoon to ensure that the thickness is uniform). Refrigerate while you make the filling and topping.

3. Cream the butter in an electric mixer (or with a hand mixer). Reduce the speed to low and add the sifted sugar in 4 installments, beating well after each. Scrape down the sides with a spatula.

4. Add the pudding mix and beat well; pour in the milk and beat until no lumps remain. Spread the filling over the base, making sure that it is even again. Put it back in the fridge.

5. Combine the chocolate pieces and butter in a bowl set over hot water, or in the top of a double boiler. Stir occasionally, and make sure that it is completely smooth. Pour the melted chocolate over the filling, and spread it out with a palette knife. With a clean knife, score the surface of the chocolate into 16 bars. Return to the refrigerator.

6. To serve: While it is still in the pan, cut along the score lines down to the bottom of the pan. Carefully ease the bars out.

PEANUT BUTTER COOKIES

An easy recipe with a great result.

Makes about 48 cookies.

1½ cups	**all-purpose flour**
¾ tsp	**baking soda**
5 oz	**butter** (see page 23)
½ tsp	**vanilla extract**
½ cup	**granulated sugar**
½ cup	**light brown sugar**, firmly packed
1	**egg**
½ cup	**smooth peanut butter**
¾ cup	**salted peanuts**

1. Preheat the oven to 375° F.

2. Sift together the flour and soda; set aside.

3. Cream the butter in an electric mixer (or with a hand mixer). Add both the sugars and the vanilla and cream until light and fluffy (1 to 2 minutes).

4. Beat in the egg; then reduce the mixer speed to low and add half the sifted flour. Stop the mixer and scrape down the sides of the bowl.

5. Add the peanut butter; beat until smooth. Scrape down the sides again. Add the rest of the flour and the peanuts and mix again. The dough may be quite stiff. Don't worry – knead it a little by hand to bring it together if necessary.

6. Scoop out the dough into roughly 1½-oz balls (you can use an ice-cream scoop). Set them on an ungreased cookie sheet, and press down with the palm of your hand to flatten them to about ½" thick.

7. With the back of a fork, make a criss-cross pattern on top. Bake in the preheated oven for about 12 minutes, until they are very lightly browned. Watch them carefully: they burn quite easily.

CHOCOLATE CHUNK PEANUT BUTTER COOKIES

Make the cookies as directed in the recipe above; at Step 7, just before putting them in the oven, press 2 or 3 chunks of chocolate into the top of each cookie. Bake as directed.

BASICS

A number of sauces, dressings, and pastries are used more than once in this book. The recipes for these are collected together here; they are the foundations on which much of your cooking is based. Cooking is like working with computers – what you get out can only be as good as what you put in. If your basic ingredients are not first class, you cannot expect the finished product to be of the quality that your time and efforts deserve.

BASIC TOMATO SAUCE

½ cup	**fine chopped onion**	**1.** In a heavy, non-corrodable saucepan, sauté the onions in the oil over medium heat until soft and translucent. Add the drained tomatoes, breaking them up with a spoon. Bring to a boil, turn the heat down, and cook at a gentle simmer for 20 to 30 minutes, until slightly thickened.
¼ cup	**extra virgin olive oil,** (see page 133)	
1 28-oz can	**Italian plum tomatoes** drained	
¼ tsp	**salt**	
¼ tsp	**black pepper**	**2.** Pass the sauce through a food mill fitted with the fine disk, or through a sieve. Season with salt and pepper.

TOMATO, BASIL, AND GARLIC SAUCE

Serve as a sauce on chicken or fish. To make a tomato dressing for cold pasta, add ½ cup of extra virgin olive oil to the tomato, basil, and garlic sauce – it yields enough for 1 lb of cooked pasta.

1 recipe	**Basic Tomato Sauce,** (see above)	**1.** Stir the basil and garlic into the finished basic tomato sauce.
2 Tbs	**coarsely chopped basil leaves**	
½ tsp	**finely chopped garlic**	

TOMATO, ROSEMARY, CAPER, AND BALSAMIC VINEGAR SAUCE

Serve with pasta, roast pork, grilled chicken or fish.

1 recipe	**Basic Tomato Sauce,** (see above)	**1.** Add the chopped rosemary, the capers, and the vinegar to the finished basic tomato sauce.
2 tsp	**coarsely chopped fresh rosemary**	
1 Tbs	**capers**, drained and rinsed	
1 Tbs	**balsamic vinegar,** (see page 138)	

SPICY TOMATO AND CORIANDER SAUCE

Use as a dip for shrimp, tortilla chips, or deep-fried squid; or as a sauce with enchiladas, refried beans, and tostadas.

1 recipe	**Basic Tomato Sauce,** (see above)	**1.** Add the coriander leaves, red pepper flakes, and green onions to the finished basic tomato sauce.
½ cup	**coarsely chopped coriander leaves**	
½ tsp	**dried red pepper flakes**	
¼ cup	**finely sliced green onions**	

BEURRE BLANC (WHITE BUTTER SAUCE)

This is a classic sauce of French cooking; it is easy to make if your butter is very cold so put it in the freezer for a while after it is cut into cubes.

Yields about 1 cup.

8 – 10 oz	**cold butter** (see page 23)
1 Tbs	**white wine**
1 Tbs	**lemon juice**
1 Tbs	**white wine vinegar**
1 Tbs	**chopped fresh tarragon** (optional)

1. Cut the butter into ½" cubes and put it in the fridge or freezer until ready to use it.

2. In a small (non-aluminum) pan bring the wine, lemon juice, and vinegar to a boil over medium-high heat. Add the tarragon, if using it. Reduce the heat to a bare simmer; one at a time, whisk in the cold butter cubes. Don't add the next until the first is absorbed. Regulate the heat by taking the pan off the burner from time to time—the sauce should not get too hot. The sauce will gradually thicken to the consistency of whipping cream (before it has been whipped).

3. This sauce is best served immediately; it may be kept warm for 20 minutes in the pan in which it was made on top of the stove, but *not* on the element.

BÉCHAMEL SAUCE

2 cups	**milk**
1 small	**onion**, peeled
1	**bay leaf**
8	**black peppercorns**
3 Tbs	**butter**
3 Tbs	**flour**
¼ cup	**whipping cream** (optional)
	salt and **pepper**

1. Rinse out a small saucepan with water. Pour in the milk, onion, bay leaf, and peppercorns; heat to almost boiling, over medium heat. Set aside for at least 10 minutes for the flavours to infuse.

2. In a medium-sized saucepan, melt the butter over medium heat; add the flour and cook, stirring, for 2 or 3 minutes without browning. Remove the pan from the heat and strain in the hot milk. Return to the heat and bring to a boil, stirring and whisking to smooth it out. Allow to boil for 1 minute.

3. Remove from the heat and stir in the cream, if you are using it. Season to taste with salt and pepper.

PEANUT SAUCE

A spicy sauce; excellent with grilled meat or chicken, satays, and spring rolls. Also good as a dip for shrimp chips or fresh vegetables. A few tablespoons are a good addition to a stir-fry.

1 Tbs	**finely chopped garlic**
2 Tbs	**Thai red curry paste**
2 Tbs	**vegetable oil**
4 cups	**coconut milk**, from a can
2 stalks	**lemon grass**, (see page 114)
1 cup	**roasted, unsalted peanuts**, ground
4 Tbs	**lemon juice**
1 Tbs	**sugar**
2 Tbs	**fish sauce** (see page 114)

1.   Sauté the garlic in the vegetable oil until it starts to turn pale gold. Add the red paste and stir over low heat until the paste starts to look dry.

2.   Remove the dry, fibrous parts from the lemon grass stalks. Cut the stalks into 1″ lengths. Add the coconut milk and the lemon grass to the garlic, and bring to a boil.

3.   Stir in the ground peanuts; turn down the heat to low and cook, stirring frequently for 20 minutes, until the sauce thickens. Remove from the heat and allow to cool. Remove the lemon grass and discard.

4.   Stir in the lemon juice, sugar, and fish sauce.

VEAL DEMI-GLACE

Veal demi-glace is made by cooking veal stock down until it becomes thick and syrupy. When it cools, it becomes a firm jelly. It freezes well; if you need some but not all of the frozen demi-glace, melt it all in a covered saucepan over medium-low heat, bring it to a boil, use what you need, and then refreeze the rest.

5 lbs	**veal bones**
2 large	**onions**, peeled and halved
2 large	**carrots**, peeled
2 stalks	**celery**
1 cup	**white wine**
1	**bouquet garni**
10 cups	**cold water**

1.   Preheat the oven to 400°F.

2.   Place the veal bones, onions, carrots, and celery in a roasting pan; roast uncovered for 45 minutes, until well browned, turning from time to time. Remove the pan from the oven and transfer the bones to a large stock pot. Pour in the white wine and scrape up all the brown bits. Pour the wine and scrapings into the stock pot.

3.   Fill the pot with cold water; set over medium-high heat and bring to a boil. Turn the heat down to low, skim the scum from the surface, and put in the bouquet garni. Simmer, with the water barely bubbling, for 8 hours.

4.   Strain the stock into a clean bowl and allow to cool. When cold, remove the fat from the surface and return to the clean pot. Set over medium-high heat, bring to a boil, and continue to cook until the stock is reduced to about 1 cup. Allow to cool, then transfer to a small container and refrigerate or freeze.

CHICKEN STOCK

If you want a clear chicken stock, do not let it boil for more than a minute or two at the beginning. For its long cooking time, it must barely simmer.

Yields about 6 cups.

5 lbs	**chicken bones**
2	**onions**
2	**carrots**
2	**celery stalks**
1	**bouquet garni**
1 gallon	**water**

1.   Put the chicken bones in a large stock pot, cover with cold water, and bring to a boil over high heat. Drain the bones into a large colander, discarding the water. Return the bones to the pot; cover with fresh cold water; add the onions, carrots, celery, and bouquet garni, and bring to a boil.

2.   As soon as it boils, reduce the heat to a bare simmer, and skim as much of the scum from the surface as you can. Simmer for 6 to 8 hours (*not* longer or you will get a bone taste to the stock). Do not cover during the cooking. From time to time, skim fat and scum from the surface.

3.   Strain through cheesecloth into a bowl. Refrigerate until ready to use. Chicken stock will keep for 2 days in the fridge; if you need to keep it longer, either freeze it or boil it up every second day.

CRÈME FRAÎCHE

You must start to make crème fraîche at least one day before you plan to use it. Once made, crème fraîche will keep in the fridge for a month.

2 cups	**whipping cream**
½ cup	**sour cream**

1.   Mix together whipping cream and sour cream; cover with plastic wrap and *let sit out at room temperature for at least 1 day, preferably 2 days*. It will become very thick. Transfer to smaller containers (if you wish) and refrigerate.

CREAMY SHALLOT DRESSING

2 Tbs	**finely chopped shallots**
¼ tsp	**salt**
2 tsp	**red wine vinegar**
2 tsp	**Dijon mustard**
4 Tbs	**extra virgin olive oil** (see page 133)
2 Tbs	**Crème Fraîche** (see above) OR **whipping cream**

1.   Stir shallots, salt, and vinegar together until the salt dissolves.

2.   Stir in the mustard. Slowly beat in the oil: it should form an emulsion (i.e., get thick).

3.   Stir in the crème fraîche or whipping cream.

MAYONNAISE

Yields 3 cups.

3 large	**egg yolks**
1 Tbs	**Dijon mustard**
1 tsp	**salt**
1 cup	**vegetable oil**
1½ cups	**olive oil**
2 Tbs	**lemon juice**

1. Whisk yolks, mustard, and salt together or combine in work bowl of a food processor and blend.

2. Mix olive oil with vegetable oil; slowly drizzle oil into bowl, whisking (or processing) constantly.

3. Beat in the lemon juice. Correct seasoning if necessary.

4. Store covered in the refrigerator.

> **WHAT TO DO IF MAYONNAISE SEPARATES**
> Mayonnaise will separate if you add oil too fast – but it's hard to make this mistake in a food processor. If it does separate, get a clean bowl and put in a teaspoon of Dijon mustard, then add a few drops of the split mayonnaise and whisk like mad. Add a few more drops, whisk again, and *very gradually* add the rest.

DILL MAYONNAISE

1 cup	**Mayonnaise** (see above)
1½ Tbs	**chopped fresh dill**
1 tsp	**Dijon mustard**
1 Tbs	**lemon juice**
few drops of	**Worcestershire Sauce**
	salt and **pepper**

1. Stir mayonnaise, dill, mustard, lemon juice, and Worcestershire Sauce together. Add salt and pepper to taste.

JALAPEÑO TARTARE SAUCE

Good with crab cakes, fish, and seafood.

1 cup	**Mayonnaise** (see above)
1 Tbs	**chopped green onions**
2 tsp	**chopped cornichons**
2 tsp	**capers**
1 Tbs	**chopped jalapeño pepper**
1 Tbs	**lemon juice**
2 tsp	**chopped parsely**

1. Combine all ingredients in the work bowl of a food processor; process until the vegetables are finely chopped – but *not* so fine that they are reduced to a purée. (You can chop all the vegetables by hand and just mix them into the mayo.)

BEARNAISE MAYONNAISE

A tarragon-flavoured mayonnaise that does great things for roast beef sandwiches or cold beef tenderloin.

¾ cup	**Mayonnaise** (see page 227)	**1.** Combine all ingredients and mix well. Chill for several hours to allow flavours to blend.
1 Tbs	**grainy mustard**	
1 Tbs	**Dijon mustard**	
1 clove	**very finely chopped garlic**	
1 Tbs	**finely choped shallot**	
1 Tbs	**lemon juice**	
3 Tbs	**chopped fresh tarragon**	
1 Tbs	**red wine** OR **tarragon vinegar**	
½ tsp	**black pepper**	

CORIANDER MAYONNAISE

The flavour of the Southwest – great with almost everything.

1 cup	**Mayonnaise** (see page 227)	**1.** Mix mayonnaise and coriander together well. Let sit for 30 minutes or more to develop the flavour.
4 Tbs	**chopped fresh coriander**	

TOMATO CONCASSÉ

A concentration of raw tomatoes.

4 medium **firm tomatoes**

1. Peel the tomatoes – Karen's way is to peel them with a very sharp vegetable peeler, just like an apple (as you can imagine, it is important that the tomatoes are firm). Or you can choose riper tomatoes, pour boiling water over them, nick the skins in a few places and let them sit for 20 seconds (longer if necessary). Remove and slip the skins off. (It is only fair to tell you that Karen does not agree with this second method.)

2. Cut the tomatoes in quarters and remove the seeds. Then cut the centre away from the outside, just as you would cut a wedge of melon away from the skin. Cut the outer parts into thin strips, then cut them across into small dice. Chop the centre parts as well.

3. Place all the diced flesh in a sieve to drain for at least ½ hour. It is now ready for use.

HOLLANDAISE SAUCE

An easy method for making a sauce that has a reputation for being difficult.

8 oz	**unsalted butter**, chilled (see page 23)
3	**egg yolks**
2 Tbs	**lemon juice**

1.   Cut a 1-oz chunk from the butter; place the rest in a small saucepan and melt it over medium heat. Set aside in a warm place.

2.   Place the egg yolks and lemon juice in a small, non-corrodable saucepan. Beat them with a whisk until very well mixed. Put in the chunk of cold butter and place the pan over medium-low heat. Heat, stirring all the time, until the butter melts and the yolks get hot and start to thicken. Remove from the heat from time to time and beat well to stop it cooking on the bottom. It is heated enough when the lines left by the whisk in the eggs do not immediately fill in – the yolks should just be starting to thicken. Immediately remove from the heat and beat well.

3.   Pour a small amount (less than a teaspoon) of melted butter into the yolks and beat until incorporated. Add another small amount and beat again. Keep doing this, gradually increasing the amount of butter that you add. The process is just like making mayonnaise, using melted butter instead of oil. Use up all clear part of the melted butter, but do not use the milky solids, as they will thin your sauce.

4.   Set aside in a warm place until ready to use. *Hollandaise should not be kept for more than 2 hours, because of the danger of bacteria forming in the yolks when they are held at this temperature.*

SPRINGROLL SAUCE

Springroll sauce will keep for 2 months in the refrigerator.

2 cups	**granulated sugar**
1 cup	**water**
4 cloves	**garlic**, peeled
½	**red pepper**, seeds in; green stem only removed
3 Tbs	**Thai fish sauce** ("Squid Brand") (see page 114)
5 Tbs	**lemon juice**
1 tsp	**salt**
1 Tbs	**hot sauce**, preferably Vietnamese but Harissa or even Tabasco will do

1.   Combine the sugar and water in a saucepan. Bring to a boil over high heat, stirring until the sugar is dissolved. Boil rapidly for 10 minutes; remove from the heat and allow to cool completely (don't worry if the sugar crystallizes around the edge).

2.   Place the garlic, red pepper, and half a cup of sugar syrup from Step 1 in the work bowl of your food processor or blender. Process until reduced to a smooth purée.

3.   Add the fish sauce, lemon juice, salt, hot sauce, and the rest of the syrup. Process again until well blended.

Olio Santo
"Holy Oil" – Spicy Olive Oil

Drizzle this oil onto vegetable soups, tomato-based pasta sauces, vegetables, pizza, salad dressings, grilled bread, and goat cheese. It is a specialty of Tuscany.

½ litre	**extra virgin olive oil** (see page 133)
3 cloves	**garlic**, peeled and cut in half
6 perfect	**basil leaves**, washed and well dried
2	**dried chili peppers**

1.   Drop the garlic cloves, basil leaves, and hot peppers into the bottle of oil, pushing them in with a skewer or chopstick. Put the cap back on the bottle and store in a cool dark place for a month. Give it a shake whenever you remember.

Basic Vinaigrette

2 Tbs	**wine vinegar**
½ tsp	**salt**
1 Tbs	**Dijon mustard**
¼ tsp	**ground black pepper**
¾ cup	**olive oil**

1.   Mix the vinegar with the salt until it is almost dissolved; stir in the mustard and pepper. Slowly beat in the oil.

Walnut Vinaigrette

1 Tbs	**wine vinegar**
¼ tsp	**salt**
pinch of	**ground black pepper**
2 Tbs	**walnut oil**
2 Tbs	**vegetable oil** (or mild olive oil)

1.   Mix the vinegar with the salt until it is almost dissolved; stir in the pepper. Slowly beat in the two oils.

Basil Balsamic Vinaigrette

1 Tbs	**chopped fresh basil**
1½ tsp	**grainy mustard**
½ tsp	**black pepper**
½ tsp	**salt**
2 cloves	**garlic**, crushed
¼ cup	**balsamic vinegar** (see page 138)
¾ cup	**olive oil**

1.   Combine basil, mustard, pepper, salt, garlic, and vinegar in a blender (this quantity will not work in a food processor). Blend until smooth.

2.   With the motor running, pour in the oil; it will make quite a thick dressing.

PUFF PASTRY

This is the easiest recipe in the book: you go to a store and buy it. This piece of advice really goes against the grain, and I do not mean to discourage anyone who wants to make their own; it is not difficult and it will be far better than almost anything you can buy. As with all pastry recipes, practice and motivation are the keys to success; after you have made it a couple of times you will, if you want to do it, be making first-rate puff pastry.

The other reason we are not giving a recipe is that we don't have one that is better than those already available; either Julia Child's or Jacques Pépin's classic recipes are excellent; and Julia's quick puff pastry is very rich and really works well.

Almost all commercially available puff pastry is frozen; let it defrost in the fridge if you have time. Keep it as cold as you can (refrigerate it after rolling it out and before baking). You are unlikely to be able to find puff pastry made with all butter; most use a mixture of butter (for taste) and shortening (for lightness). Commercial puff rises well; but the taste leaves a lot to be desired. However, in most recipes this is not disastrous because the lion's share of flavour will be coming from whatever it is that the puff pastry is enclosing.

CHOUX PASTRY

This is a cooked pastry that is very simple to make and is the base for such wonderful things as éclairs and gougère puffs.

1 cup	**water**
½ cup	**unsalted butter** (see page 23)
¼ tsp	**salt**
1 Tbs	**sugar** (optional, for dessert use only)
1 cup	**all-purpose flour**
4 plus 1	**eggs**

1. Combine water, butter, and salt in a saucepan; bring to a boil over medium-high heat. Remove from heat and add the flour all at once. Stir to incorporate it.

2. Return the pan to the heat; cook it, stirring constantly until the dough comes away from the side of the pan and forms a ball. Continue to cook for 1 minute or so more, scraping the dough off the bottom of the pan. It is done when you can see the melted butter just starting to bead on the surface of the dough. Remove from heat.

3. Add 4 eggs, one at a time, beating very well between each one (they have to be thoroughly incorporated). The dough should be smooth and glossy and firm enough to hold its shape on the spoon. Add the last egg only if it is still very firm.

4. Choux pastry is best used immediately; but it may be stored for 2 to 3 days in the refrigerator.

SWEET PASTRY

I hear a lot of people say they cannot make pastry to save their lives. If you feel this way, try this recipe before you say it again. The pastry tastes very good, has a remarkable texture, and is very easy to make and to work with when forming it into the pan – it will take all kinds of abuse.

Makes two 9" tart shells.

2¼ cups	**all-purpose flour**
¾ cup	**granulated sugar**
7 oz	**unsalted butter** (see page 23)
2 tsp	**Grated Lemon Zest** (see page 237)
1 large	**egg**
1	**egg yolk**
1 tsp	**vanilla extract**

1.   Place sugar and flour in the work bowl of your food processor. Pulse once or twice to aerate.

2.   Cut the cold butter into ½" cubes and distribute over the flour. Add the lemon zest and process using the pulse action until the mixture resembles coarse meal.

3.   Whisk the egg, egg yolk, and vanilla together; with the motor running, add the eggs through the feed tube. Process only until the pastry starts to come together (no more or the pastry will be tough).

4.   Turn the pastry out onto your work surface (don't worry if it is crumbly). Knead gently until it comes together – if it is too dry, drizzle 1 to 2 tsp lemon juice over it and work it in. Bring the pastry together into a ball, wrap it in plastic, and refrigerate until required. It will keep for up to 3 days in the fridge, or 1 month if frozen.

SHORTCRUST PASTRY

A general-purpose short pastry; it will keep for about 5 days in the fridge or up to 3 months frozen. If you do freeze it, remember to thaw it overnight in the fridge before using.

3⅓ cups	**all-purpose flour**
½ tsp	**salt**
9 oz.	**unsalted butter**, cold (see page 23)
2	**egg yolks**
6 – 8 Tbs	**cold water**

1.   Combine the flour and salt in the work bowl of your food processor; pulse once or twice to aerate.

2.   Cut the cold butter into cubes (about ½") and distribute them over the flour. Process just until the mixture resembles coarse meal – not too much or your pastry will be tough.

3.   Add the yolks and 6 Tbs cold water through the feed tube and process just until the dough starts to come together (again, don't process too much).

4.   Turn the pastry out onto the work surface and gently knead until it comes together into a ball; if it is a bit dry, add the other 2 Tbs cold water. Wrap in plastic and refrigerate for at least 30 minutes.

LADY FINGERS

Lady fingers are best made with an electric mixer since they take a lot of whisking. The trick is to get both the yolk mixture and the whites thick enough that they hold their shape when you pipe them out; if the mixture is at all runny, they will spread when you pipe them and you will get very thin lady fingers – and an F in Baking 101.

4	**egg yolks**
4 Tbs	**granulated sugar**
1 tsp	**vanilla extract**
4	**egg whites**
⅛ tsp	**cream of tartar** (see below)
½ cup	**granulated sugar**
1 cup less 2 Tbs	**cake flour**, sifted (see below)
1 cup	**icing sugar**, sifted

CREAM OF TARTAR
A fine white powder that helps to increase the volume of beaten egg whites and to stabilize them. The acid reacts with the protein in egg whites and makes them less likely to collapse.

CAKE FLOUR
Cake flour is made from soft wheat, which has a lower gluten content than all-purpose flour (medium) or bread flour (hard wheat). Gluten is what makes a dough springy and elastic as you knead it; it allows the dough to stretch and retain the gas produced by the fermentation of the yeast. For bread and pizza it is just what you want. But with pastry, working a dough too much will make it tough. Cakes will have a shorter and finer texture if made with soft flour. However, unless you do a lot of baking, it's probably not worth keeping a separate container of cake flour; just use the same amount of all-purpose flour.

1. Preheat the oven to 400° F. Lightly butter and flour two cookie sheets; or line them with parchment paper.

2. Whisk the yolks with the sugar until pale yellow and very thick (5 to 8 minutes).

3. Whisk the whites with the cream of tartar to the soft-peak stage. Keep the machine running and gradually add the sugar in a thin stream. Continue beating until very stiff.

4. Fold together the yolks, the whites, and the sifted cake flour: add ⅓ of the whites to the yolks, sift ⅓ of the flour over the top and gently fold together. When almost incorporated, add another ⅓ of the whites, sift more flour over the top, and fold again. Repeat with the remaining whites and flour.

5. Gently scoop the mixture into a pastry bag fitted with a ¾" plain nozzle. Pipe 2" to 3" long strips onto the prepared baking sheets, leaving about 1½" between. Sift the icing sugar over the top. Bake in the preheated oven for 12 to 15 minutes. (They must be cooked enough that they don't collapse as they cool – but not so cooked that they become dry and boring.) They should look light to medium brown at the edges, while still quite pale on the tops.

BASIC DANISH DOUGH

Yields enough for 20 to 24 danish.

⅓ cup	**warm water**
1 oz	**sugar**
1 Tbs	**active dry yeast** (a package) OR **instant dry yeast**
1¼ cups	**milk**
2 Tbs	**vegetable oil**
2 large	**eggs**
5 cups	**all-purpose flour**
14 oz	**unsalted butter**, cold (see page 23)

1. Pour the warm water (should be body temperature or a little warmer) into a large bowl. Add the sugar and stir. Sprinkle the yeast on top and allow it to bubble up. (If using instant yeast, follow package directions.)

2. Beat the milk, oil, and eggs together, and add to the yeast mixture. Gradually add the flour, mixing it in with a rubber spatula. Add the flour only until all the liquid has been absorbed.

3. Turn the dough out onto a lightly floured work surface; knead it lightly until smooth. Add more flour as necessary to prevent it from sticking. Return the dough to a clean bowl, cover with plastic wrap, and chill for 1 hour.

4. Flour the work surface, set the cold butter on it and use your rolling pin to work it into a rectangle about ⅓″ thick.

5. Remove the dough from the fridge and lay it on the work surface; roll it out to a rectangle almost twice as long and about 1½ times the width of the butter.

6. Set the butter on the dough; it should cover about ⅔ of the dough. At one end there should be a 1″ border on three sides of the butter; on the fourth side of the butter, there should be a much larger area of uncovered dough.

7. Fold the dough into three, as you would a letter: first fold the uncovered dough over the butter (it should come about half way over it). The fold the other end over the flap that you have just folded (this will involve folding the butter). Seal the edges as well as you can.

8. Turn the dough on the work surface so that the opening of the last flap that you folded is on the right. Roll it out into a large rectangle, and fold it again; fold the bottom third up, than the top third down over it. Seal the edges again. (This operation is call a "turn".) Cover with plastic wrap and refrigerate for 1 hour, or more.

9.   Repeat Step 8 twice more, refrigerating the dough in between. The dough should now be refrigerated for at least 6 hours, or overnight. It will rise in the refrigerator; (do *not* be alarmed – it will deflate when you roll it out).

SWEET SHORTCRUST PASTRY

Makes enough for one 9" to 11" tart.

1½ cups	**all-purpose flour**
¼ cup	**granulated sugar**
6 oz	**unsalted butter**,
	chilled (see page 23)
1½ tsp	**vinegar**

1.   Place flour and sugar in the work bowl of a food processor fitted with the steel blade; pulse 2 to 3 times to aerate.

2.   Cut the butter into small pieces and distribute over the flour. Process until the mixture resembles very fine meal.

3.   With the machine running, pour the vinegar through the feed tube and process for 5 seconds. Do not overprocess – the dough should still be very mealy, and should not gather into a ball.

4.   Remove dough from the work bowl and let rest at room temperature for 30 minutes before using.

SWEET FLAKY PASTRY

3⅓ cups	**all-purpose flour**
4 Tbs	**granulated sugar**
9 oz	**unsalted butter**,
	chilled (see page 23)
2	**egg yolks**
6 to 8 Tbs	**cold water**

1.   Combine flour and sugar in the work bowl of a food processor fitted with the steel blade. Pulse twice to aerate. Cut the cold butter into pieces and distribute over the flour. Process until the mixture resembles very coarse meal – don't overdo it.

2.   Have the egg yolks and 6 Tbs of water ready. Turn the motor on and pour the yolks and water down the feed tube. Process *just until the dough starts to come together*. Do *not* let it form a ball, or the pastry will be tough. Turn it out onto a clean work surface; knead gently to bring it together. If the dough seems too dry, add the last 2 Tbs of water. Wrap in plastic and chill for 30 minutes. Roll out as required.

YORKSHIRE PUDDING

Yorkshire pudding served the same purpose in Yorkshire that pasta served in Italy – to fill up hungry people before the meat and make it go farther. In some places, it was served with the meat juices before the roast, and with syrup afterwards.

For many people Yorkshire pud is still the best thing about roast beef. You can bake it in muffin cups to make individual ones (called popovers in New England). But in England it is usually baked in the pan in which the meat has been roasted. You get a large pudding with different textures – light and crispy around the edges, and soft and soggy in the middle; not everyone's cup of tea but my personal favourite.

The trick to successful Yorkshire pudding is in the mixing – just enough to get a smooth batter; if you mix too much the pudding will be tough. It also helps to let it stand for an hour before you bake it (to relax the glutens that have developed in the mixing). The method described here sounds awkward but is really quite easy.

Makes 12 popovers; serves 6 or 8.

1½ cups	**flour, all-purpose**
¾ tsp	**salt**
¼ tsp	**pepper**
pinch of	**ground nutmeg**
3 large	**eggs**
1¼ cups	**milk**
1¼ cups	**water**
¼ cup	**beef fat** or **oil**

1.   Sift the flour, salt, pepper, and nutmeg into a large bowl. Make a well in the centre with your hands. Break the eggs in the well and mix them up with a fork.

2.   Mix the water and milk together; pour about ¼ of the mixture on top of the eggs, and beat them together with a fork; gradually widen your mixing stroke to draw more flour into the liquid; when it starts to get thick, add more liquid. Continue mixing, drawing more flour in, and adding more liquid until all the liquid has been added and the batter is quite smooth. If it is still a bit lumpy, strain it through a sieve into another bowl. Set aside to sit for 1 hour (if you have the time – if not just go ahead an bake it).

3.   Turn the oven up to 450° F.

4.   Pour a ¼ tsp of fat or oil into each muffin cup (or about 2 Tbs into a large pan). Put the pans into the oven and let them get really hot (about 8 minutes). Remove from the oven and pour in the batter – the cups should be about ½ full – the large dish will have about ⅓″ on the bottom. Return to the oven and bake at high heat for 15 minutes. Then turn down the heat to 350° F and bake another 5 to 10 minutes for small, and 20 to 30 minutes for the large.

CRÈME ANGLAISE (CUSTARD)

This is a foolproof method of making crème anglaise; it works well, particularly if you can make it the day before.

Yields about 5 cups.

9 large	**egg yolks**
2 cups	**whipping cream**
2 cups	**milk**
⅔ cup	**granulated sugar**

1.   Beat the egg yolks thoroughly in a bowl large enough to hold all the milk.

2.   Rinse out a saucepan with water; pour in the cream, milk, and sugar; and bring to a boil over medium heat. Stir to ensure that the sugar does not stick to the bottom and burn.

3.   As soon as the mixture boils, pour into the egg yolks in a slow stream, stirring constantly.

4.   Strain the custard into a clean bowl and cover with plastic wrap. Refrigerate overnight.

RASPBERRY PURÉE

3½ pints	**fresh raspberries** OR
1 package	**unsweetened frozen raspberries** (12 oz)
	icing sugar

1.   Put the raspberries in the work bowl of your food processor fitted with the steel blade. Pulse a few times until the raspberries are liquified (*don't* overdo it or you will grind the seeds up).

2.   A cup at a time, press the purée through a fine sieve into a bowl; discard the seeds.

3.   Sweeten to taste with icing sugar.

GRATED LEMON ZEST

This method is easier on your fingers than using a cheese grater.

lemons, as many as you need

1.   Using a lemon zester, remove the zest from the lemons.

2.   Put the zest on your chopping board; with a cook's knife (or mezzaluna – an Italian chopping knife) chop the zest as finely as you can. It is easiest to hold the knife in both hands – your dominant hand on the handle, and the other holding the blade – and use a short and quick up-and-down chopping action. Scrape down the zest off the blade once or twice.

APPENDIX

METRIC CONVERSION CHART

WEIGHT CONVERSIONS

1 pound = 454 grams	1 kilo = 2.24 lbs
8 ounces = 227 grams	500 grams = 1.12 lbs
4 ounces = 113 grams	250 grams = 0.56 lbs
1 ounce = 28 grams	100 grams = 3.5 oz

LIQUID MEASURES

1 cup = 240 ml	1 litre = 4½ cups
½ cup = 120 ml	500 ml = 2¼ cups
1 Tbs = 15 ml	100 ml = 6½ Tbs

TEMPERATURE CONVERSIONS

200°F = 95°C	375°F = 190°C
225°F = 110°C	400°F = 200°C
250°F = 120°C	425°F = 220°C
275°F = 135°C	450°F = 230°C
300°F = 150°C	475°F = 250°C
325°F = 160°C	500°F = 260°C
350°F = 175°C	

COMMON INGREDIENTS – Approximate Equivalents

All-purpose flour	1 cup = 150 grams	100 grams = ⅔ cup
Granulated sugar	1 cup = 210 grams	100 grams = ½ cup
Icing sugar	1 cup = 135 grams	100 grams = ¾ cup
Light brown sugar	1 cup = 200 grams	100 grams = ½ cup
Rolled oats	1 cup = 95 grams	100 grams = 1 cup
Graham cracker crumbs	1 cup = 120 grams	100 grams = ⅘ cup
Cocoa powder	1 cup = 125 grams	100 grams = ⅘ cup
Chocolate chips	1 cup = 175 grams	100 grams = generous ½ cup
Sultanas, raisins	1 cup = 165 grams	100 grams = generous ½ cup
Almonds – sliced	1 cup = 75 grams	100 grams = 1⅓ cups
Almonds – ground	1 cup = 120 grams	100 grams = ⅘ cup
Hazelnuts – whole	1 cup = 140 grams	100 grams = ¾ cup
Hazelnuts – ground	1 cup = 105 grams	100 grams = 1 cup
Walnut halves	1 cup = 110 grams	100 grams = 1 cup
Walnut pieces	1 cup = 120 grams	100 grams = ⅘ cup
Pecans (whole)	1 cup = 110 grams	100 grams = 1 cup
Peanut butter	1 cup = 225 grams	100 grams = scant ½ cup

INDEX